THE ROAD TO OLYMPIA

origins of the Olympic Games

Published by Periplus Publishing London Ltd
Publisher: Danièle Juncqua Naveau
Managing editor: Nick Easterbrook
Assistant editors: Chris More, Jenny Finch
Production manager: Sophie Chéry
Production assistants: Arvind Shah, Ludovic Pellé
Picture research: Jane Lowry

© 2003, Periplus Publishing London Ltd, 98 Church Rd, London SW13 0DQ, UK
English translation: John Flower, Rima Devereaux
Reprographics: Periplus Publishing London Ltd
Printed and bound in Italy by Graphicom
ISBN: 1-902699-46-7

THE ROAD TO OLYMPIA

origins of the Olympic Games

ANDRÉ BERNAND

Periplus

London

In memory of Kostas Papagiannakis, an Athenian lawyer from Crete who died prematurely and suddenly on 7 July, 1998. He was my young pupil, my friend, my host and my guide in his beautiful country. His happiness, his high spirits, his unceasing attention towards me and those of my family increased the pleasure of my stays in Greece; in Athens, Crete, Achaiea, Corinth, Messenia, and Laconia, the main stages in the course of our friendship.

Contents

Editor's note: the quotations in italics are taken from verse texts and those in roman from prose texts

2. PLAYING THE GAME

3. LIGHT AND SHADE

The Parthenon in Athens: the ancient finishing point
for the Panathenean torch race, the ancestor of the
modern Olympic torch relay that takes place prior
to the Games.
© Charles O'Rear / CORBIS

Preface

Of all that Ancient Greece has bequeathed to us, nothing gives more pleasure than the Games. I use the capital letter, which is common when the Olympic Games are discussed and which I will use to emphasise the joyful aspect of the competitions which took place in the Ancient Greek world.

Both Pierre de Coubertin, who re-established the Olympic competition in 1894, after a gap of 1,500 years, and Juan-Antonio Samaranch, one of the presidents of the first modern Olympic Committee, insisted on the feelings that this competition should inspire. In 1900 when the Games took place, Pierre de Coubertin could not foresee that the world was entering one of the cruellest centuries in history, and those who came after him nobly maintained their faith in the possibility of improving human nature thanks to the Olympic ideal.

Juan-Antonio Samaranch stated this conviction with some force:

> The Olympic ideal is a philosophy of life that exalts and brings together
> in perfect balance the qualities of the body, of the will, and of the mind. By
> linking sport with culture and education, this ideal strives to create a way of
> life based on happiness through effort, the educational value of good example,
> and respect for fundamental, universal ethical principles.[1]

We should no longer allow to pass in silence the divide between these fine words and their realisation, for there have been too many breaches of ethics and too great a hurry to draw material profit from the event – all of which has tarnished the underlying principles. But let us pay tribute to those who have defined this noble ideal, since the history of the past 100 years is too sad not to welcome a call to joy. Pierre de Coubertin knew from ancient times that some of those who took part or organised the events betrayed the spirit of the Games. Be that as it may, no event could or can bring together so many competitors, spectators and admirers.[2]

The idea for this book stems from a contradiction that I noticed in the opening remarks at the Eighth International Congress of Greek and Latin Epigraphy which took place in Athens between 3-9 October 1982.

The opening speech stated:[3]

> We should say straight away that it is absurd to maintain the old and vague
> tradition of the Olympic Games or Pythic Games. For the Greeks, games
> were tops, hoops, bones, dice and everything that Becq de Fouquière
> compiled more than a century ago as games for children. The deadly struggles
> (agônes) of Olympia and elsewhere were a serious and testing matter. People

---

1   *Esprit olympique*, P. de Coubertin and J. A. Samaranch, L'Esprit du Temps, Bordeaux, 1992, p. 68.

2   *Ibid.*, p. 12.

3   *Acts of the Eighth International Congress of Greek and Latin Epigraphy, Athens, 3-9 October 1982*, Athens, 1984, p. 36.

did not take part for amusement; they fought to win and to be declared the winner and, in most cases, no one came second. The same word *agón* means "confrontation in battle where life is at stake" or "a court trial that can cause the loss of life and fortune". Such deadly struggles are the complete opposite of playful activities. The *agón*, struggle, is radically different from *epideixis* – a non-competitive recital or representation. When the Greek competitions spread into the Latin world, a distinction was made between play and combat.

After these strong words and a discussion of the Greek competitions during the Hellenistic period and during the Empire, the same speaker remarks: "We can see from inscriptions and coins the pleasure and joy in the festivities in and beyond Greece".

Nothing makes sense anymore. Is it a question of a struggle to the death or of happy and joyous pastimes? This book attempts to get to the heart of the question.

We can ask ourselves whether it is reasonable today to write about the Greek Games when we know from copious historical documents everything about the way they took place. Not only texts, but to a greater extent, engraved monuments teach us in the most detailed way about these events. Sculptures, paintings, mosaics, coins, and scenes painted on vases also provide us with precise information, and sometimes the most intimate detail of the competitions.

For example, we know the details of the boxing gloves used in antiquity – mittens that left the fingers uncovered, their joints strengthened with strips of hard leather and held in place by laces. There is nothing we do not know about boxing at that time; no ring, no rounds, blows aimed above all at the head which made the boxer keep his guard up and his arms stretched out.

The demands of these sporting activities and the way they were carried out are also known. We know how the runners in a race set off; that they were upright, leaning slightly forward with their feet close together. Hurdles did not exist, nor relays; only running on a flat and rectangular track was practised. The movements of ancient athletes were very different, depending on the event, from those of their modern counterparts. Ancient statues teach us that to throw the discus demanded of the thrower a very special style. The area from which the discus was thrown, the *balbis* – as H.I. Marrou[4] and others have told us – was not a circle but an area enclosed in front and at the sides:

> The thrower held the discus in both hands, lifted it to the level of his head and then, pressing it tightly against his right forearm with his hand, he brought his arm down violently behind him, his head and body turning and following the movement. All the weight of the body rested on the right foot, which acted as a pivot; the left foot and the left arm were simply used to keep the balance. Then came the fling: the force of it did not come from the arm but from the sudden straightening of the thigh and the bent body. The discus had previously been rubbed with sand to prevent it from slipping.

It is doubtful that modern sports coaches would approve of this style of ancient discus throwing.

4 H. I. Marrou, *A History of Education in Antiquity* (trans. George Lamb), The University of Wisconsin Press, Madison, WI, 1982, p. 121.

To describe the practices and rituals of these games is not enough. While it is useful to describe the technical vocabulary of these competitions, the way in which they were organised, and the fraudulent behaviour that could occur, it is more important to understand their deeper sense, the underlying philosophy, if we are to situate them properly in the history of civilisation and to appreciate what we have inherited from Ancient Greece. Knowing the colour of the buttons on the gaiters of Napoleon's soldiers does not mean we understand the success of his military campaigns. Certainly, it is well to know some details, but it is better to analyse the deep meaning of these competitions and the kind of civilisation which they entail.

That is why I do not claim to challenge the scholarship on the manner in which these ancient games took place. I think it is time to reject the idea that the Games were confrontations in which the competitors aimed to crush their opponents. Interpretations based on feelings rather than on facts have given rise to mistaken theories that have acquired the status of truths. I want to rectify this impression by suggesting that the competitions were Games celebrated with joy and not with hatred and aggression.

In truth, the debate about the nature of the ancient Games is not new and Lucian of Samosata (circa 120–180 AD) has the Scythian Anacharsis, who is wearing a large pointed hat made of felt or skin, discuss the matter with Solon. The scene is supposed to have taken place at the beginning of the 6th century BC. Anacharsis only sees brutality in the exercises practised by the Greeks:[5]

And why are your young men doing all this, Solon? Some of them, locked

---

5   Lucian, *Anacharsis or Athletics* (trans. A. M. Harmon), Loeb Classical Library, Harvard University Press, Cambridge, MA, 1925, 1-3; 11.

Six athletes playing a game resembling hockey, using sticks. Marble relief, kept in the National Archaeological Museum of Athens.
© National Archaeological Museum of Athens

in each other's arms are tripping one another up, while others are choking and twisting each other and grovelling together in the mud, wallowing like swine. Yet, in the beginning, as soon as they had taken their clothes off, they put oil on themselves and took turns at rubbing each other down very peacefully – I saw it. Since then, I do not know what has got into them that they push one another with lowered heads and butt their foreheads together like rams. And see there! That man picked the other one up by the legs and threw him to the ground, then fell down upon him and will not let him get up, shoving him all down into the mud; and now, after winding his legs about his middle and putting his forearm underneath his throat, he is choking the poor fellow, who is slapping him sidewise on the shoulder, by way of begging off, I take it, so that he may not be strangled completely. Even out of consideration for the oil, they do not avoid getting dirty; they rub off the ointment, plaster themselves with mud, mixed with streams of sweat, and make themselves a laughing-stock, to me at least, by slipping through each other's hands like eels.

Another set is doing the same in the uncovered part of the court, though not in mud. They have a layer of deep sand under them in the pit, as you see, and not only besprinkle one another but of their own accord heap the dust on themselves like so many cockerels, in order that it may be harder to break away in the clinches, I suppose, because the sand takes off the slipperiness and affords a firmer grip on a dry surface.

Others, standing upright, themselves covered with dust, are attacking each other with blows and kicks. This one here looks as if he were going to spew out his teeth, unlucky man, his mouth is so full of blood and sand; he has had a blow on the jaw, as you see. But even the official there does not separate them and break up the fight – I assume from his purple cloak that he is one of the officials; on the contrary, he urges them on and praises the one who struck the blow.

The Scythian, for his part, only sees useless violence in the scenes of wrestling, pancratium (a violent combination of boxing and wrestling) and boxing that take place in the arena. It is ironic that the barbarian Scythian in a supposedly more refined Greece questions why, as Solon puts it, "a huge public comes to witness these Games, how the amphitheatres are filled with thousands of spectators, the athletes applauded, and winners deemed to be the equals of the gods". Anacharsis responds indignantly:

It is exactly that, Solon, which is pitiful. It is not that they are putting up with this treatment in front of the eyes of a handful of people but in front of thousands of spectators who witness these brutalities and no doubt consider the combatants to be happy as they see them running with blood or being stifled by their opponents. That is the real happiness that they attach to their victory. In Scythia, Solon, if somebody hits one of our citizens either he is attacked and thrown down or people tear his clothes. The elderly citizens severely punish him even if he has only committed his act of violence in front of a small number of witnesses and not as though he were in one of these great amphitheatres such as you describe them at Isthmus and Olympia. However it is, I cannot stop myself from feeling sorry for the wrestlers and

Panathenaic amphora showing a discus thrower.

what they suffer. As for the spectators who are, so you tell me, the elite of the country and who come to these festivities from all parts of Greece, I cannot withhold my astonishment at the fact that they give up their business and waste their time at these spectacles. I cannot understand what pleasure they take in seeing men beaten, thrown to the ground, and battered.

Let us reflect on what the orator Lysias says:

> Of all the fine deeds that we celebrate, Heracles deserves to be remembered because he was the first out of love for the Greeks to bring them together for these festivities. Before that the regions were divided up. But after having put an end to tyranny and having done away with violence, he introduced a festivity involving competitions of strength, wealth, and intelligence in the most beautiful part of Greece. In this way Greeks came together to see and to understand these marvellous things and he thought that bringing people together like this would give rise to mutual affection between them.

I have made an effort to understand the values that the Games defended, the lessons for civilisation[6] that emerged from these gatherings where the Greeks made an example of courage and healthy and joyful competition. What were the feelings of the competitors, the spectators, and the organisers? Through a full analysis and the use of historical psychology (though these terms may seem pretentious) I have sought to define the philosophy and the political lessons to be drawn from the culture of the Games. Greece has given us cause for hope in human nature, in the wisdom of a nation. I recently denounced the wars and violence that Greece witnessed,[7] now, having examined the dark side, I wish to look at the light.

---

6   A. Bernand, *Leçon de civilisation*, Fayard, Paris, 1994.

7   A. Bernand, *Guerre et violence dans la Grèce antique*, Hachette Littératures, Paris, 1999.

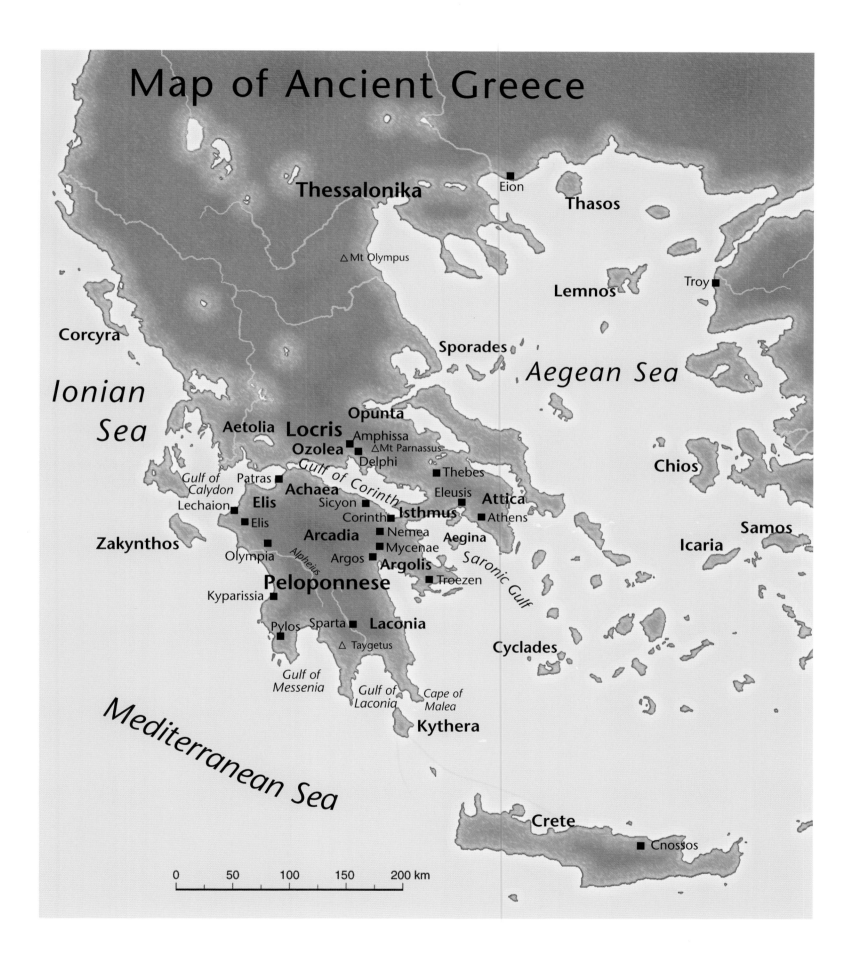

Map of Ancient Greece

Eion

Thasos

Thessalonika

Lemnos

Troy

△ Mt Olympus

Corcyra

Ionian

Sea

Sporades

Aegean Sea

Opunta

Aetolia **Locris**

Amphissa

Ozolea △Mt Parnassus

Delphi

Chios

Gulf of Calydon Patras

Thebes

Achaea

Eleusis

Attica

Gulf of Corinth

Lechaion **Elis**

Sicyon

Isthmus

Athens

Corinth

Elis

Arcadia

Nemea

Aegina

Samos

Zakynthos

Mycenae

Icaria

Olympia *Alpheius*

Argos

Argolis

Saronic Gulf

Peloponnese

Troezen

Kyparissia

Pylos Sparta **Laconia**

Cyclades

△ Taygetus

Gulf of Messenia

Gulf of Laconia

Cape of Malea

Kythera

Mediterranean Sea

Crete

Cnossos

| 0 | 50 | 100 | 150 | 200 km |

1
THE PHILOSOPHY

Image on previous page:
Bronze statue of a veteran boxer, showing the
ravages of his trade. In the Museo Nazionale
Romano, Rome.

Chapter I
Triumph over death

The Greeks emulated Helen in their ambition to "live in the memory of men". This wish was not easily fulfilled and in order to understand it, we have to follow in Homer's writing how an attitude was conceived that would later give rise to the Games.

There is a sense of the word *agôn* that does not figure in the list of accepted meanings. If we believe dictionaries, *agôn* designates the result of an *agein*, and simply means "gathering" or "assembly", a sense in which Homer[1] uses it, applying it to a gathering of the gods or of ships. We can follow this first sense from the *Odyssey*[2] to the *Iliad*. In the pre-Classical period, the *agôn* is very different from what it becomes in the Classical period, but it already anticipates certain of its features.

In the *Odyssey*[3] the Games are part of the festivities which Alcinous, the king of the Phaeacians, gives in honour of Ulysses. It is a joyous gathering that took place in public (*agora*) rather than a religious ceremony. It is a secular occasion that includes not only physical games but also dancing and singing, where the singer Demodocus distinguished himself by evoking the love of Ares and Aphrodite. The herald took Demodocus by the hand and

> led him out of the cloister, and set him on the same way as that along
> which all the chief men of the Phaeacians were going to see the sports; a
> crowd of several thousands of people followed them, and there were many
> excellent competitors for all the prizes. [4]

These young people come together to challenge each other in a series of different tests: running, wrestling, jumping, discus throwing, boxing.[5] Invited to demonstrate his own talents, Ulysses distinguishes himself at discus throwing[6] and talks about his skills with the bow and javelin.[7]

The gathering continues with singing and dancing just as, at a later date in the Classical period, musical games followed physical contests.

Laodamas, the son of Alcinous, got the better of Ulysses' moroseness when he said to him:[8]

> I hope, Sir, that you will enter yourself for some one or other of our
> competitions if you are skilled in any of them – and you must have gone in
> for many a one before now. There is nothing that does anyone so much credit

---

1   Homer, *Iliad* (trans. S. Butler), Barnes & Noble Books, New York, 1995, VII, 298.

2   *Agôn* was sometimes personified. See F. Canciani *Lexicon Iconographicum Mythologiae Classicae*, I, 1, pp. 303-5.

3   Homer, *Odyssey* (trans. S. Butler), Jonathan Cape, London, (2nd edition) 1922, VIII, 107-384.

4   *Ibid.*, VIII, 107-9.

5   *Ibid.*, VIII, 120-30.

6   *Ibid.*, VIII, 186-98.

7   *Ibid.*, VIII, 214-29.

8   *Ibid.*, VIII, 145-9.

Two teams of youths playing ball. Marble relief discovered in Athens, reused in the city wall built by Themistocles.
© National Archaeological Museum of Athens

all his life long as the showing himself a proper man with his hands and feet. Have a try therefore at something, and banish all sorrow from your mind.

This *agôn* is a joyful gathering made more pleasurable by ball games and dancing:[9]

> Then Alcinous told Laodamas and Halius to dance alone, for there was no one to compete with them. So they took a red ball which Polybus had made for them, and one of them bent himself backwards and threw it up towards the clouds, while the other jumped from off the ground and caught it with ease before it came down again. When they had done throwing the ball straight up into the air they began to dance, and at the same time kept on throwing it backwards and forwards to one another, while all the young men in the ring applauded and made a great stamping with their feet.

When the singer sings of the Trojan War,[10] Ulysses is moved and people offer him presents to comfort him. Not all of these festive occasions result in competition and we do not see people at one another's throats. No winner is designated even if nine referees have been chosen among the people. Their job is to organise the games,[11] flatten out the ground, and prepare a superb arena.

In the *Iliad*, the Games have a completely different significance. People do not compete for glory but to honour the dead Patroclus. What we have here are funeral games that bear witness to the love people had for the person who has died and at the same time for the victory of life over death. The initiative comes from Achilles. No ritual ceremony, no traditional timetable of events, no priests, nor any altars give these celebrations a religious character. It is not a question of a struggle between

9   Homer, *Odyssey, op. cit.*, VIII, 370-80.
10 *Ibid.*, VIII, 499-520.
11 *Ibid.*, VIII, 258-60.

Black-figure vase on a yellow background, showing a race in honour of Patroclus between a black and a white horse. The Achaean spectators look on, seated in stalls. Signed by the Sophilos Painter.
© National Archaeological Museum of Athens

violent opponents but the need to follow the example of one who is no longer there and whose memory must not perish. The site chosen by Achilles for these Games was not determined by any tradition. The burial place of Patroclus is the subject of Book 16 and in Book 17 the exploits of Menelaus are celebrated when he arranges for the body of Patroclus to be taken away and buried with dignity. The respect for valour, friendship, and the celebration of an exemplary death are what animate those who take part in these funerary games, which take place in an atmosphere of general mourning in which even Achilles' horses, who were witnesses of this sad event, participate:[12]

> The horses of the descendant of Aeacus stood out of the fight and wept
> when they heard that their driver had been laid low by the hand of
> murderous Hector. Automedon, valiant son of Diores, lashed them again and
> again; many a time did he speak kindly to them, and many a time did he
> upbraid them, but they would neither go back to the ships by the waters of
> the broad Hellespont, nor yet into battle among the Achaeans; they stood
> with their chariot stock still, as a pillar set over the tomb of some dead man
> or woman, and bowed their heads to the ground. Hot tears fell from their
> eyes as they mourned the loss of their charioteer, and their noble manes
> drooped all wet from under the yokestraps on either side the yoke.

In the *Iliad* the funeral games do not take place in front of enthusiastic spectators who have come to applaud athletes. Those taking part have not queued for tickets but are inspired by the passion for glory and the desire to forget the horrors of war and death. Achilles' horses have not come to see the kinds of cruelty they have too often witnessed in war, but to deplore the fact of a life cut short too quickly and to delight in a competition that is the exact opposite of the brutality of warfare.

The description of the funerary games is also the subject of Book 18. The poet

---

12 Homer, *Iliad, op. cit.,* XVII, 425-40.

first evokes the honours paid to Patroclus by the Myrmidons[13] and then describes the funeral feast.[14] Lying "on the beach of the sonorous sea", Achilles sees the spirit of Patroclus[15] come forth and then goes on to make the funeral preparations:[16] the building of a fire, the funeral cortege to accompany Patroclus' body, the burning of the corpse, the gathering of his ashes, and the building of a burial mound.

Only then, and once Achilles had decided on prizes for the winners, did the athletics take place. The same procedure will be adopted in the Classical period when every winner must receive a reward. In the *Iliad*, these rewards are linked to the reality of war and to the needs of the soldiers engaged in military campaigns:[17]

> [...] but Achilles stayed the people and made them sit in assembly. He brought prizes from the ships: cauldrons, tripods, horses and mules, noble oxen, women with fair girdles, and swart iron. The first prize he offered was for the chariot races – a woman skilled in all useful arts, and a three-legged cauldron that had ears for handles, and would hold twenty-two measures.

These were the prizes offered to the winners of the most prestigious competition – the chariot race. Achilles refuses to take part in the chariot race on the grounds that his horses are too sad, a constant theme reminding us that these were funeral games.[18]

> At any other time I should carry off the first prize and take it to my own tent; you know how far my steeds excel all others for they are immortal; Neptune gave them to my father Peleus, who in his turn gave them to myself; but I shall hold aloof, I and my steeds that have lost their brave and kind driver, who many a time has washed them in clear water and anointed their manes with oil. See how they stand weeping here, with their manes trailing on the ground in the extremity of their sorrow. But do you others set yourselves in order throughout the host, whosoever has confidence in his horses and in the strength of his chariot.

It is worth emphasising that only a single winner is honoured, although according to when and where the Games took place procedures sometimes varied.

The lesson that Nestor gives to his son Antilochus allows us to understand the risks and tricks of the chariot race:[19] it is skill and not strength that guarantees victory. You should not take the corner too widely but cling as closely as possible to the kerb and know how to leave the reins of the horse on the right slack, and hold tightly those of the horse on the left without having the chariot run into the marker at the end of the track:[20]

---

13 Homer, *Iliad, op. cit.*, XXIII, 1-23.
14 *Ibid.*, XXIII, 24-58.
15 *Ibid.*, XXIII, 65-107.
16 *Ibid.*, XXIII, 109-257.
17 *Ibid.*, XXIII, 257-70.
18 *Ibid.*, XXIII, 273-86.
19 *Ibid.*, XXIII, 306-48.
20 *Ibid.*, XXIII, 334-45.

Proto-Attic *loutrophoros*: sphinxes, dancers, and chariot processions. By the Analatos Painter, 700-680 BC.

© Photo RMN – Hervé Lewandowski, Louvre (inv. CA 2985)

hug it as close as you can, but as you stand in your chariot lean over a little to the left; urge on your right-hand horse with voice and lash, and give him a loose rein, but let the left-hand horse keep so close in, that the nave of your wheel shall almost graze the post; but mind the stone, or you will wound your horses and break your chariot in pieces, which would be sport for others but confusion for yourself. Therefore, my dear son, mind well what you are about, for if you can be first to round the post there is no chance of anyone giving you the go-by later.

The unforeseen events of the chariot race justify Nestor's advice and Homer describes the race that Antilochus wins, as well as the distribution of the prizes.[21] When the moment for the prize giving comes, there is a competition between Menelaus and Antilochus to see who can be the most courteous, the latter awarding the former the prize, a mare, saying, "Now everyone will know/that my heart bears no arrogance or cruelty".[22]

---

21 Homer, *Iliad, op. cit.,* XXIII, 350-650.

22 *Ibid.,* XXIII, 611.

Neither animosity nor brutality casts a shadow over these games. After the chariot race, Homer describes the boxing, *pugmachia*,[23] and wrestling.[24] These competitions are aggressive but fought according to the rules. The first pits Epeius against Euryalus and the second, Ajax against Ulysses. Epeius – who wins the first – helps Euryalus, and Ajax and Ulysses are declared equal. And yet the opponents do not give presents to one another!

Homer describes how the boxers are kitted out. Euryalus, who faces Epeius, is prepared by his friend Diomedes, who gives him his athlete's belt and his leather gloves. The fight between the two boxers is furious: [25]

> [...] the two men being now girt went into the middle of the ring, and immediately fell to; heavily indeed did they punish one another and lay about them with their brawny fists. One could hear the horrid crashing of their jaws, and they sweated from every pore of their skin.

Knocked out by Epeius, Euryalus, spitting blood, is carried off by "the worthy Epeius" and his "good friends". Homer does not overstate the scene: he underlines the fact that the prize is a two-handled cup and that the combat finishes in smiles.

The fight between Ajax and Ulysses is not an easy one:[26]

> The two girded themselves and went into the middle of the ring.[27] They gripped each other in their strong hands like the rafters which some master builder frames for the roof of a high house to keep the wind out. Their backbones cracked as they tugged at one another with their mighty arms – and sweat rained from them in torrents. Many a bloody weal sprang up on their sides and shoulders, but they kept on striving with might and main for victory and to win the tripod.

Homer says quite explicitly that the purpose of this fight is glory and not the destruction of the opponent. In fact, it finishes without a victor, neither combatant managing to throw down the other. Achilles therefore declares a draw.[28]

The foot race, the supreme contest in the stadium of the Classical period takes place on a track that has not been prepared and which is covered in dust and cattle dung.[29] The value of the prizes proposed by Achilles underlines the importance of this race. To the winner he offers a huge Sidonian silver vase. To the second he gives an enormous bull; to the last a gold half-talent.

The rivalry between Ulysses and Ajax, who have left Antilochus ("the winner of the young people's foot race") well behind, is related with humour. The fact that these are funeral games does not mean that humour is absent, as for example after Ulysses has addressed a prayer to Athena, Ajax slips on the innards of the bulls that Achilles

---

23 Homer, *Iliad, op. cit.,* XXIII, 653-99.
24 *Ibid.,* XXIII, 700-39.
25 *Ibid.,* XXIII, 685-9.
26 *Ibid.,* XXIII, 710-8.
27 The text has the words *es meson agóna,* which shows that *agôn* here means "a gathering".
28 Homer, *Iliad, op. cit.,* XXIII, 721-37.
29 *Ibid.,* XXIII, 740-97.

has just killed in honour of Patroclus. In this way the dead man somehow colludes in the events that are related in such a colourful way.[30]

> Ajax, through Minerva's spite slipped upon some offal that was lying there from the cattle which Achilles had slaughtered in honour of Patroclus, and his mouth and nostrils were all filled with cow dung. Ulysses therefore carried off the mixing-bowl, for he got before Ajax and came in first. But Ajax took the ox and stood with his hand on one of its horns, spitting the dung out of his mouth. Then he said to the Argives, "Alas, the goddess has spoiled my running; she watches over Ulysses and stands by him as though she were his own mother." Thus did he speak and they all of them laughed heartily.

The next contest is armed combat between Ajax and Diomedes,[31] the stakes being the arms – javelin, shield, and helmet – that Patroclus had seized from Sarpedon. The fight is dangerous: the two adversaries in armour each have to pierce the other with a lance. To the first one who draws blood, Achilles will give the Thracian dagger which he had won from Asteropaeus. Blood has to flow but the wound must not be mortal. That is why when Diomedes aims to strike Ajax in the neck, the Achaeans bring the fight to a close. The Game must not lead to death.

The discus throwing also gives rise to mirth when Epeius drops the discus and all the Achaeans burst out laughing.[32] There is rivalry but there is also amusement and Polypoetes is admired when he throws the iron block further than Leonteus and Ajax.

After contests relying on strength comes one that tests skill with a bow and arrow.[33] The participants do not fight but use their skill to try to hit a dove tied to a ship's mast driven into the ground. If the dove is hit the prize is 10 double axes. If it is only the string that is hit the prize is 10 axes. But something unforeseen happens: Teucer cuts through the string and the dove flies away. Meriones takes Teucer's bow and with Apollo's help (having promised to slaughter newborn lambs for him) strikes the bird which settles on the mast and dies, "drooping his head and wings" before falling to the earth. There is no desperate struggle involved in this game of skill.

Javelin throwing[34] is not a brutal competition. The prize is a spear and "a vase decorated with flowers equal to the value of a bull". Agamemnon and Meriones present themselves for the competition but Achilles gives the vase to Agamemnon, recognised by everybody as the best javelin thrower, and the spear to Meriones. There is no contest.

We look then in vain in Homer's writing for evidence of the alleged bitterness and violence in these competitions, which would have diminished the Games' stature. We see scenes of convivial gatherings that are often humorous and from which happiness is never absent even when the Games are in honour of someone who has died. The important lesson that emerges from these texts is the intense love of life, of achievement and of glory – feelings that allow people to overcome death. This image

---

30 Homer, *Iliad, op. cit.*, XXIII, 777-84.
31 *Ibid.*, XXIII, 798-825.
32 *Ibid.*, XXIII, 826-49.
33 *Ibid.*, XXIII, 850-83.
34 *Ibid.*, XXIII, 884-97.

A bearded herald proclaims the victory of a young horseman. Behind the horse a young man bears the victor's trophy – a tripod. Black-figure vase, in the British Museum.
© The British Museum

given by Homer, the great educator of the Greeks, would make its mark on the Games of the Classical period.

The funeral games are not then sad affairs and that is why, no doubt, other Games attributed by ancient authors to this period are intended to honour the dead. Pausanias[35] recalls that Acastus, king of Iolcus, held Games in honour of his father Pelias. Plutarch tells that Minos, king of Crete, held a gymnastics competition in honour of his son Androgeos who had been killed by the people of Attica. The prizes given to the winners were the children kept in the Labyrinth. According to the legend about this king:[36]

> The first that overcame in those games was one of the greatest power and command among them, named Taurus, a man of no merciful or gentle disposition, who treated the Athenians that were made his prize in a proud and cruel manner.

35 Pausanias, *Description of Greece* (trans. W. H. S. Jones and H. A. Ormerod), Loeb Classical Library, Harvard University Press, Cambridge, MA, 1988, III, 16; V, 10; VI, 19.

36 Plutarch, "Theseus", in *Lives* (trans. J. Dryden), Modern Library Classics, New York, 1992, XVI.

We owe this Cretan tale to Philochorus, historian from the 4ᵗʰ century BC, but even if he talks about the cruelty to these children who were given as prizes to the winner, he does not tell us that the games themselves ended in blood.

The *Iliad* mentions other funeral Games. For example, the elderly Nestor evokes his victories in the country of the Epeans when they organised the Games at the funeral of their king, Amarynceus.[37]

> Would that I were still young and strong as when the Epeans were
> burying King Amarynceus in Buprasium, and his sons offered prizes in his
> honour.

The *Iliad* also tells of the festivities that took place at Thebes "after the fall of Oedipus, to celebrate his funeral".[38] Pausanias[39] tells how athletic Games took place in Arcadia in honour of Azan, the son of Arcas, the eponymous hero of the Arcadians. Here for the first time there were horse-races. On the island of Lemnos,[40] Games were introduced in memory of Thoas, the legendary king of the island, by his daughter Hypsipyle. All of these examples, provided by Daremberg and Saglio's *Dictionary of Antiquities*, could be added to but they are enough to illustrate that in all of these Games we have perhaps the origin of the great Games of Greece. In any case, to celebrate vigour and skill was to challenge death and was a way of showing the dead man that his example was being followed and that life would continue with energy and happiness.

Occasionally things did go wrong in one of the Games. But those taking part did not cause accidents intentionally. The spirit of the Games was opposed to any trap that would cause death. A good example of loyalty in competition is given to us by Sophocles[41] when he describes the death of Orestes in the chariot race at Delphi. The poet remembers the lessons that Nestor in the *Iliad* gave to his son Antilochus.[42]

We know that the race took place on the Crisean plain at the foot of the mountain where the sanctuary of Delphi was to be found. The port of Itea on the Gulf of Corinth was close and made it easy for participants and spectators to travel there. The valley of Pleistos – rising up from the port to the sanctuary and planted, as it still is today, with green olive trees – flattened out near the sea and was ideal for chariot races.

In Sophocles' story we learn that the day before this chariot race Orestes had won the track events as well as all the other competitions. Such wide-ranging talent was rare. Sophocles gives us a list of those taking part: one competitor came from Achaea, another from Sparta, two from Libya, one from Aetolia. The seventh was a Magnesian, the eighth an Aenian, the ninth an Athenian, and the tenth a Boeotian.

There is a case for thinking that these rival regions could fix things in order to try to win the prize but in this case the facts tell us otherwise. It was not forbidden

37 Homer, *Iliad, op. cit.,* XXIII, 628-31.

38 *Ibid.,* XXIII, 680.

39 Pausanias, *op. cit.,* VIII, 1-6.

40 As Pindar observed, *Olympian Odes,* in *Odes* (trans. D. Svarlien), Perseus Project, Yale, 1991, IV, 32.

41 Sophocles, *Electra* (trans. H. Lloyd-Jones), Loeb Classical Library, Harvard University Press, Cambridge, MA, 1994, 698-711.

42 Homer, *Iliad, op. cit.,* XXIII, 334-45.

to have horses of a better breed than the others in the race. Orestes, for example, the fifth in the group, had Thessalian horses that were particularly valued, while the Aetolian had young chestnut horses. The start was signalled by a blast on a brass trumpet and the chariots, lined up in their starting positions, decided in a draw by the judges, gallop off not into the stadium, as Paul Mazon calls it, but into the *dromos* – in other words the hippodrome.

Then the accident occurs, as Sophocles describes:[43] "This is how things happened, but when a god wishes evil on a man however strong he may be he cannot escape."

The circumstances show well enough that it was an accident and not sabotage.[44] Going round in the usual way, Orestes takes his corners tight up against the kerb, but going into the seventh lap the Aenian's horses get the bit between their teeth, and bump into the Cyrenean chariot, causing a general collision in which the chariots break up and collapse, one upon the other. Having stayed back, Orestes avoids this disaster and finds himself confronted by a single opponent. But as he slips to the left at the moment of taking the corner, he bumps into the kerb, breaks his axle and wheel hub and is thrown over the bar of his chariot. The accident is fatal:[45]

> And when the crowd saw his fall from the chariot, they cried out with
> pity for the young man, seeing what misfortunes followed upon such deeds, as
> at one moment he was borne earthwards, at another with legs skywards, until
> the charioteers with difficulty checked the horses' career and released him, all
> bloody, so that none of his friends that saw him could have recognised his
> wretched shape.

The other athletes cremate his corpse and collect his ashes in an urn that the Phocians carry to Mycenae, the country of Orestes' forebears.

None of the participants utters cries of joy and none celebrates the elimination of an opponent but as the reporter of the event says: "These are painful facts to hear and for those who have seen it with their own eyes, this spectacle will remain the most painful of all the Games at which they have been present."

Far from witnessing a deliberate killing we can see that there was a surge of compassion and solidarity, an illustration of the friendship and loyalty that existed.

This accident recalls those suffered by Hippolytus who was a victim in the region of Troezen when his horses bolted, and he was attacked by the monster bull that came out of the sea:[46]

> [...] then was dire confusion, axle-boxes and linchpins springing into the
> air. While he, poor youth, entangled in the reins was dragged along, bound by
> a stubborn knot, his poor head dashed against the rocks, his flesh all torn, the
> while he cried out piteously.

There is no need to claim that human mischief could lie behind such accidents.

---

43 Sophocles, *Electra, op. cit.*, 696-7.

44 *Ibid.*, 720-63.

45 *Ibid.*, 749-63.

46 Euripides, *Hippolytus* (trans. E. P. Coleridge), Players Press, London, 1998, 1234-40.

Detail from a black-figure stamnos, showing a four-horse chariot race.
© Photo RMN – Hervé Lewandowski, Louvre (inv. F 314)

In both cases, the goodwill of the friends of Orestes and Hippolytus is clear and extremely touching.

Homer's lessons were not lost on Pindar who made a moral out of them in his *Olympian, Pythian, Isthmian* and *Nemean Odes*. This aristocratic, traditional man preaches moderation. When he allies the praise given to the winners with homage to the gods, Pindar advocates good behaviour and is totally opposed to insults and extravagance. He admires the victors in the Games and praises them, but he warns against going too far.

The historic period of the Olympiads begins in 776 BC, the year when Koroibos won a competition in the public arena. The year was named in his honour, a tradition that lasted until 393 AD when the edict of Theodosius put an end to the pagan games. The Games survived under the Roman and Byzantine empires but in a different form.

The praise that Pindar gives to the winners at the Games is a mixture of wisdom and a way of attaining happiness and glory through effort and generosity. He is against all forms of violence and he rejects as blasphemous any stories that suggest the gods or heroes could be guilty of barbaric acts. For example, in the fifth Nemean ode[47] he draws back from describing the murder of Phocus, whose half-brothers Telamon and Peleus, the sons of Aeacus, killed him with a blow from a discus.

> I hesitate to relate how at last they left the famous island, and what was
> the doom that drove the bold heroes from Oenone. I will halt: it is not every

---

47 Pindar, *Nemean Odes*, in *Odes, op. cit.*, V, 25-33.

truth that is the better for showing its face undisguised; and full oft is silence
the wisest thing for a man to heed.

According to Pindar, the role of the poet is not to celebrate brute and bloody strength, but valour when it is merited.

That is why he devotes his art to praising men like Hieron of Syracuse whose goodness he celebrates:[48]

> [...] the rich and happy hearth of Hieron; Hieron, who wieldeth the
> sceptre of law in fruitful Sicily, culling the prime of all virtues, while he
> rejoiceth in the full bloom of song, even in such merry strains as we men full
> often raise around the friendly board.

We can be surprised by this praise of Hieron, who reigned in Syracuse from 478 to 466 BC; Diodorus[49] does not recognise his gentleness any more than the goodness of his older brother, Gelon. But Pindar is grateful to him for his love of literature and for his role as interpreter. He dedicates no less than four triumphal odes to his victories, the first Olympian ode and the first, second, and third of his Pythian odes. For Pindar, Hieron, who founded the town of Aetna, was "a king who ruled over Syracuse, full of gentleness for his citizens, bearing no jealousy against those who were good, and admired as a father even by foreigners".[50]

How could such a sovereign have allowed the Games to get out of control and not recognise the virtues of gentleness and humanity? If the winners at the Games had been mad brutes would they have been allowed to raise a statue of themselves in the Altis at Olympia, a sanctuary reserved for the gods, and to have had their achievements celebrated by poets? All of Pindar's work is a plea for the Games to be a happy and passionate event. In the fourth Isthmian ode[51] he warns against "noisy excesses" and finishes his ode by evoking, in a graceful way, Melissus of Thebes, who won the gymnastics competition, appearing "with his head adorned with white myrtle". His name, based on the word for a bee (*melissa*), invokes the image of "the dew of praise" celebrating the young athlete.

In Pindar's work the Games are not characterised by *hybris*, the excess which brings with it violence, but by the word *charis*, often used by the poet and full of different meanings. It suggests "what shines, what gives pleasure", and relates to the "delights of beauty and grace" and also means "joy and pleasure". A second sense of the word is "grace" in the sense of "favour, kindness, delight in victory". Aimé Puech[52] gives a reading of "delight of victory", but in line 48 at the beginning of the second stanza, he translates *charis* as "the genius to which all mortals owe everything that delights them, honours them, and often makes credible what was not dreamed of!" The translator recognises the difficulty of finding a word bringing all of these meanings together. The *Dictionnaire étymologique de la langue grecque* (Etymological Dictionary of the Greek Language) begun by Pierre Chantraine and finished by his

---

Red-figure *oinochoe* depicting a young *acontist,* (javelin thrower). Attributed to the Painter of the Brussels, circa 450 BC.

© Photo RMN – Hervé Lewandowski, Louvre

48 Pindar, *Olympian Odes*, in *Odes, op. cit.*, I, 27-35.
49 Diodorus, *Library of History* (trans. C. H. Oldfather), Loeb Classical Library, Heinemann, London, 1935, II, 67.
50 Pindar, *Nemean Odes*, in *Odes, op. cit.*, III, 124-6.
51 Pindar, *Isthmian Odes*, in *Odes, op. cit.*, IV, 14-5.
52 Pindar, *Olympian Odes*, in *Odes, op. cit.*, IV, I, 29.

Black-figure amphora showing a victor carrying his tripod trophy on his shoulder, which is decorated with a long red ribbon. Two naked men behind him each carry a garland. Two naked men stand in front of him, perhaps other competitors. The vase is housed in the department of Classical and Near Eastern Antiquities in the National Museum of Denmark (Chr VIII 322).

© National Museum of Denmark

successors suggests that the abstract noun must be a derivative of *chairô* (to enjoy or to take pleasure), which shows that the Games were a matter for enjoyment and not confrontation.

The fact that these funeral ceremonies were the occasion for the Games is a fine illustration of the fundamentally optimistic character of Greek culture as Homer describes it.

Pindar also describes the joyful atmosphere surrounding these Games, showing that the competition was not a confrontation based on brutality, but one of peace. The reward for the winners was in the form of the prizes distributed to them and the inscriptions carved in stone which recalled the nature of these festivities, the names of the winners, the families and towns that were honoured, the list of events, the different categories of those taking part, and gave an indication of the generosity of those funding the Games. All of these texts constitute a mine of information complementing the descriptions found in literary texts and on figurative monuments – statues, vases, mosaics, paintings, or coins. From all of this archaeological material, we know in detail what the Games were like.

We should note here in passing that it would be an illusion if we believed that the Ancient Greeks read these texts carved in stone since they were often very long, sometimes difficult to decipher, and put in places where it was difficult to see them.

Some of the stones, we are told, were put "in the most obvious place" but the majority were piled up in squares and along the sides of streets.

Paradoxically, we can say that to read an inscription in Ancient Greek at the time was more difficult than it is today. Words were not separated and a phonetic reading was necessary, spelling out each syllable. Moreover, the ancient reader did not have the means of taking an imprint by using unsized paper soaked in water and pressed on with a soft brush, nor did he have equipment to photograph either the stone or the impression once it had been taken off the wall. Given these conditions it is reasonable to think that the texts had been carved in stone to remain as monuments forever and to resist the ravages of time. Here we have another example of the Greek dream of a victory over death and disappearance.

By leaving to us numerous steles with long texts on them, Egypt helped us understand the difficulties of this "writing in stone", the title that I gave to my collection of 77 prose texts preserved from the Hellenistic and Roman period of Egyptian history. These inscriptions included decrees, royal or imperial commands, decisions taken by priests, protests by citizens who thought themselves overtaxed, recommendations by the prefect of Egypt, proclamations of victorious sovereigns, funerary texts, commercial tariffs, letters and lists. Who could read in its totality, the so-called Rosetta stone, written in Greek, Demotic and Hieroglyphics?

As far as the Games are concerned, the inscriptions come to us from all over the Greek world and grow in number throughout antiquity: they are a fundamental feature of the *paideia*, or Greek culture, destined first and foremost to be in the service of the gods but also as a means for man to triumph over death.

This victory over death that the Games celebrated explains how, many years after Homer, the Ten Thousand were saved from death by forcing back the sea at Trapezous-Pontus and celebrated their escape with Games: [53]

> After this they made ready the sacrifice which they had vowed; and a sufficient number of oxen had come to them so that they could pay their thank-offerings to Zeus for deliverance, to Heracles for guidance, and to the other gods according as they had vowed. They instituted also athletic games on the mountain side, just where they were encamped; and they chose Dracontius, a Spartan, who had been exiled from home as a boy because he had accidentally killed another boy with the stroke of a dagger, to look out for a race-course and to act as manager of the games. When, accordingly, the sacrifice had been completed, they turned over the hides to Dracontius and bade him lead the way to the place he had fixed upon for his race-course. He pointed out the precise spot where they chanced to be standing, and said, "This hill is superb for running, wherever you please." "How, then," they said, "can men wrestle on ground so hard and overgrown as this is?" And he replied, "The one that is thrown will get hurt a bit more." The events were, a stadium race for boys, most of them belonging to the captives, a long race, in which more than sixty Cretans took part, wrestling, boxing, and the pancratium; and it made a fine spectacle; for there were a great many entries

53 Xenophon, *Anabasis*, in *Xenophon in Seven Volumes*, Vol. III (trans. C. L. Brownson), Loeb Classical Library, Harvard University Press, Cambridge, MA, 1980 IV, 25-8.

and, inasmuch as the comrades of the contestants were looking on, there was a great deal of rivalry. There were horse races also, and the riders had to drive their horses down the steep slope, turn them around on the shore, and bring them back again to the altar. And on the way down most of the horses rolled over and over, while on the way up, against the exceedingly steep incline, they found it hard to keep on at a walk; so there was much shouting and laughter and cheering.

This expression of collective joy proves that the object of the Games was to bring Greeks together to defend values in which they all believed.

Chapter II
Pathway to the gods

The Games were imbued with a spirit of happiness and fervour. They were first and foremost intended as a tribute to the gods. Participants, spectators and organisers made a kind of pilgrimage in order to reach these competitions and sometimes travelled long distances. From as far back as we can go, the areas which served as the settings for these religious gatherings were sacred places. In the 7th century BC, the *Hymn to Apollo* lists the sites where Apollo chose to be honoured in this way: [1]

> And you, O lord Apollo, god of the silver bow, shooting afar, now walked on craggy Cynthus, and now kept wandering about the islands and the people in them. Many are your temples and wooded groves, and all peaks and towering bluffs of lofty mountains and rivers flowing to the sea are dear to you, Phoebus, yet in Delos do you most delight your heart; for there the long robed Ionians gather in your honor with their children and shy wives: with boxing and dancing and song, mindful, they delight you so often as they hold their gathering.

Thucydides explains that after Delos had been purified – in other words, the dead, the dying, and pregnant women had been carried off to the nearby island of Rhenea, the Athenians celebrated for the first time the *pentaetéris* festivity of the *Delia*. It was on this occasion that athletics and the competitions for poetry recited to music took place. After quoting the *Hymn to Apollo* he concludes:

> This is the evidence Homer has given that in antiquity also there was a great assemblage and festival on Delos. Later the islanders and the Athenians continued to send choruses and offerings, but most things including the competitions were abandoned, naturally enough, as a result of misfortune, that is until the Athenians held the competition on this occasion. They added a horse race, which had not been held before.[2]

The four major festivals celebrated by Pindar that took place at Olympia, Delphi, Isthmia, and Nemea, were organised in the sanctuaries of the gods: Zeus at Olympia and Nemea, Apollo at Delphi, Poseidon at Isthmia. Taken together the Games made a "season" and the winner at all four was known as the *periodoníkés*. As we shall see, he had a right to special honours and to the same kind of consideration given to today's winners of the grand slam at tennis.

The Olympic Games were a *pentaetéris* festival: celebrated every four years. As Aimé Puech tells us, the date was changeable. "It was controlled by a cycle of 99

1   *Homeric Hymns and Homerica* (trans. H. G. Evelyn-White), Loeb Classical Library, Harvard University Press, Cambridge, MA, 1914, verses 140-2, 179-81, 143-5, 145-50.

2   Thucydides, *History of the Peloponnesian War*, Books 1-8 (trans. C. F. Smith), Loeb Classical Library, Harvard University Press, Cambridge, MA, 1930, III, 104.

Poseidon sits on his throne while the young Theseus holds out his left hand. Attic red-figure krater, by the Syriskos Painter, 480 BC.
© Bibliothèque Nationale de France, Paris

months (50 plus 49) and fell alternately at the beginning or in the middle of the cycle, to coincide with the full moon in the month of *Parthenios* or of the month of *Apollonios,* which caused it to vary between the end of our month of July and the beginning of September."[3] To set the date of this festival in relation to astrological factors gave it an increased religious significance.

The Greeks of the Hellenistic period understood how important it was to refer to the stars to legitimise the date of important festivals. Thus the decree in three languages (hieroglyphics, Demotic and Greek) issued by the priests gathered at Canopus in honour of Ptolemy III Evergetes I, of his wife Berenice II, and of his daughter Berenice, dated 7 March 238 BC and carved on the stele found at Momemphis,[4] places side by side a eulogy of the kings, a reform of the calendar, and an indication of the ceremonies linked to this panegyry.

The Rosetta stone, dated 27 March 196 BC,[5] links the Macedonian and Egyptian calendars with the prescribed eulogies. The passing of the seasons – marked by the flooding of the Nile, the rising of Sothis, Sirius or the Dog (20 July), the sowing time and harvests – marked the dates of the major festivals. For example, those linked to the rebirth of Osiris took place in the fourth month of the Egyptian year or in the month of Khoiak (27 November – 26 December).

The date of the Olympic Games was thus fixed with reference to the natural world and the cosmos. This date then conditioned that of the Pythian Games, which began in the third year of the Olympiad 49 (582 BC). The mythical origins of these Games went back to Apollo's victory over the serpent. The Nemean Games occurred every two years during the second and fourth year of each Olympiad and, according to A. Puech, took place on the 12th day of the month of Panemos, which corresponds more or less to our month of July. The Isthmian Games were celebrated every two years in the second and fourth year of the Olympiad. In the Classical period they would have taken place in the spring (April or the beginning of May). It is in this way that the cycle of Games developed.

We cannot understand the spirit in which the ancient Games took place without trying to experience the feelings that animated the participants when they set out to journey to the places where the competitions took place. Even if we are not able to relive all the Games that were organised we can at least imagine the attitude of mind of those who went to meet with their gods in the four great sanctuaries where the Games took place: Olympia, Delphi, Isthmia, and Nemea.

The way to Olympia

The most celebrated Games were those of Olympia. But how did people reach the scene where these famous competitions took place and what was it that encouraged them to set out on their pilgrimage?

The pilgrim had to have a certain courage and a deep faith if he was to leave his family, his town, his region in order to go to a place that was sometimes very far from his home. A journey in ancient times was not undertaken lightly. We could compare these journeys towards the gods with the tiring stages of the journey pilgrims made

3   Aimé Puech's introduction to Pindar, *Olympiques,* Les Belles Lettres, Paris, 1970, p. 4.

4   A. Bernand, *Les Confins libyques,* t. 3, 1970, pp. 989-1036 and *La prose sur pierre dans l'Égypte hellénistique et romaine,* 1992, 8.

5   A. Bernand, *La prose sur pierre,* Fayard, 1994, 16.

Metope from Temple E at Selinunte, showing the divine marriage of Zeus and Hera on Mount Ida.
© 1990, Photo Scala, Florence – courtesy of the Ministero Beni e Att. Culturali. Palermo, Museo Archeologico

when they went to Compostela or the risky ones that the Crusaders undertook on their way to the sacred places in Jerusalem. In ancient times no journey was safe whether it was by land or sea. Robbers and pirates lay in wait and it was unsafe to travel alone. Conditions were harsh with very basic lodgings and rudimentary modes of transport, the most common being on foot.

To reach Olympia, it was possible to go by land or by sea. To arrive by sea was not as easy as one might imagine, for "the hollow Elis", as Strabo tells us, offered no port worthy of the name. Three capes – Araxos, at the mouth of the Gulf of Corinth, Chelonatas, to the southwest of the Gulf of Calydon and the most western point of the Peloponnese, and finally Ichthys (Katapolo) further to the south – offered no real protection and in addition were not easy to pass in heavy seas.

The western coast of the Peloponnese is sheltered from the northeast winds, which are to be feared in summer, but is narrow, flat and crossed with little rivers sometimes difficult to negotiate, not to mention the mouth of the Alpheius, which could be treacherous, especially when the snows were melting.

The entire coast as far as Kyparissia is sandy, formerly made up of dunes and marshes. Only Pylos further to the south and sheltered by Cape Koryphasion and the island of Sphacteria offers a port (Navarin), though in fact it is not very deep between Sphacteria and the coast.

To go via Elis the ancient pilgrims had the choice of two moorings. To the north of Cape Chelonatas, the harbour of Kyllene the maritime base for the Eleans 20km from the town of Elis on the left bank of the Pennius[6] at the foot of the first range of hills. The geographer Strabo[7] informs us that Kyllene, to which Homer refers, was a township (*kome*) and a mooring (*epineion*) separate from the town it served. When the French occupied Morée, the town was called Clarenza. Fifteen kilometres or so separate it from the island of Zanta (Zakynthos). In reality it was only a trading post (*emporion*) but, as Pausanias[8] tells us, it was a place of transit for the traders coming from Aegina who disembarked there to take their goods on into Arcadia. From Kyllene the sanctuary of Olympia was reached by Elis, Oenoe and Salmone or by the valleys of the Ladon, the Enipeus, and the Alpheius. After the monotonous plain of Elis came the undulating and friendly countryside of Olympia.

The most practical harbour for reaching the sanctuary was the one at Pheia at the base of Cape Ichthys, Katapolo. Strabo describes it as a small town and a harbour. It was a sacred harbour, *hieros limén*, as any harbour serving a sanctuary was called in ancient texts and inscriptions. Strabo describes the countryside:[9]

> After Chelonatas comes the long seashore of the Pisatans; and then Cape Pheia. And there was also a small town called Pheia: "beside the walls of Pheia, about the streams of Iardanus," for there is also a small river nearby.

---

6   It may be that Strabo was mistaken in his description of the race at Penea, according to an article by Jean-Jacques Dufaure and Eric Fouache "Le cours antique du Pénée : une erreur de Strabon ? Pour une solution géomorphologique du problème", which appeared in *Achaie und Elis in der Antike*, t. 13, pp. 293-303.

7   Strabo, *Geography* (trans. C. F. Smith, Horace L. Jones), Loeb Classical Library, Harvard University Press, Cambridge, MA, 1918, VII, 3-4.

8   Pausanias, *Description of Greece* (trans. W. H. S. Jones and H. A. Ormerod), Loeb Classical Library, Harvard University Press, VIII, 5, 8.

9   Strabo, *op. cit.*, VIII, 3, 12.

According to some, Pheia is the beginning of Pisatis. Off Pheia lie a little
island and a harbor, from which the nearest distance from the sea to Olympia
is one hundred and twenty stadia. Then comes another cape, Ichthys, which,
like Chelonatas, projects for a considerable distance towards the west; and
from it the distance to Cephallenia is again one hundred and twenty stadia.

Having followed the Mouria lagoon the pilgrim then entered the wooded,
peaceful valleys of Olympia and could look forward to the happiness he would feel
in the welcoming domain of Zeus.

If he came by land, having crossed the Achaea, the pilgrim would feel the peace
and gentleness of the Olympian countryside even more. Crossing the mountains of
Achaea was no small matter. This mountainous region backs onto three high ranges
that separate it from Arcadia and whose summits rise to more than 2,000m. These are
from east to west, the Kyllene (today called Ziria), Chelmos (Aroania), and Olonos
(Erymanthus). Over the Gulf of Corinth the slopes are steep, cut by ravines and
narrow gorges that plunge into the arid mountain. One of the ways of getting to
Olympia was from Diakopton, a resort situated 47km to the east of Patras and 85km
west of Corinth. Going along the Bouraikos river, named after the town of Boura
(destroyed in 373 BC, along with the neighbouring town of Helike, by an earthquake)
a narrow, twisting gorge opens up in the mountain and reaches the ancient Kynaitha
(today Kalavryta) about 50km to the south. This town, at an altitude of 725m is called
the "town of the fine springs", which in itself tells us something about Arcadia and
Elis.

After another 100km or so, the pilgrim going down the valley first of Aroanios
and then of the Ladon arrived at Heraia and then Olympia by way of the valley of
the Alpheius. Or from Kynaitha, he could reach first the valley of the Erymanthus and
then join that of the Alpheius. Today from Diakopton a narrow gauge railway, in part
a rack rail, allows you to go from the Gulf of Corinth to Kalavryta. From Patras it
used to be necessary to cross a mountain called Panachaikon Oros to reach the town
of Leontion by the elevated valley of Peiros at the source of the Selinous and then the
town of Psophis near the source of the Erymanthus, the valley of which led to that
of the Alpheius. This magnificent but austere countryside, quite the opposite of the
valley of Olympia, made for a demanding journey during which people would long
for the peace of the sanctuary.

The attraction of the site of Olympia certainly played a major part in the choice
of it for the Games. However, in the 5th century BC, Hippocrates of Cos (born 460,
died between 375 and 351 BC)[10] warned of the dangers to the character of its
inhabitants of a land that was too fertile with too gentle a climate. Talking of central
Asia, he praises its moderate climate but expresses reservations about the character of
its people.[11]

This region, both in character and in the mildness of its seasons might
fairly be said to bear a close resemblance to spring [...] Courage, endurance,
industry and high spirit could not arise in such conditions either among the

---

10   J. Jouanna, *Hippocrate*, Fayard, Paris, 1992, pp. 22 and 58-9.

11   Hippocrates, *Airs, Waters, Places* in *Works* (trans. W. H. S. Jones), Loeb Classical Library, Heinemann, London, 1923,
     XII, 6 and XIII, 1-5.

natives or among immigrants, but pleasure must be supreme [...] The land is affected by them exactly as human beings in general are affected. For where the seasons experience the most violent and the most frequent changes, the land too is very wild and very uneven; you will find there many wooded mountains, plains and meadows. But where the seasons do not alter much, the land is very even. So it is too with the inhabitants, if you will examine the matter. Some physiques resemble wooded, well-watered mountains, others light, dry land, others marshy meadows, others a plain of bare, parched earth. For the seasons which modify a physical frame differ.

Herodotus[12] has Cyrus say: "Normally soft countries beget soft men; and it is not going to be the case that the same soil produces admirable fruit and courageous warriors."

If these words are applied to the countryside of Olympia it is easy to understand how this place chosen for the Games was one of relaxation and pleasure and not of struggles in which the aim was to destroy the opponents. What pilgrims would seek at Olympia was moments of happiness, allowing them to forget the harsh realities of daily life. Strabo, in a few lines, has evoked the advantages offered by the site of Olympia:[13]

The temple is in Pisatis, less than three hundred stadia distant from Elis. In front of the temple is situated a grove of wild olive trees, and the stadium is in this grove. Past the temple flows the Alpheius, which, rising in Arcadia, flows between the west and the south into the Triphylian Sea. At the outset the temple got fame on account of the oracle of the Olympian Zeus; and yet, after the oracle failed to respond, the glory of the temple persisted none the less, and it received all that increase of fame of which we know, on account both of the festal assembly and of the Olympian Games, in which the prize was a crown and which were regarded as sacred, the greatest games in the world. The temple was adorned by its numerous offerings, which were dedicated there from all parts of Greece. Among these was the Zeus of beaten gold dedicated by Cypselus the tyrant of Corinth. But the greatest of these was the image of Zeus made by Pheidias of Athens, son of Charmides; it was made of ivory, and it was so large that, although the temple was very large, the artist is thought to have missed the proper symmetry, for he showed Zeus seated but almost touching the roof with his head, thus making the impression that if Zeus arose and stood erect he would unroof the temple.

The charm of the site, the presence of the river, the prestige of the Olympic Games, the presence of Zeus, and the generosity of the sponsors – nothing was lacking at Olympia to ensure that it would prosper. That was the reason for the place

12 Herodotus, *Histories* (Trans. A. D. Godley), Loeb Classical Library, Harvard University Press, Cambridge, MA, 1920, IX, 122, 3.

13 Strabo, *op. cit.*, VIII, 3, 30. Raoul Baladié refers to several literary sources in his evocation of this charming countryside, in his article "L'apport des sources littéraires à la connaissance topographique de l'Elide et de l'Achaïe antiques", published in *Archaie und Elis in der Antike*, t. 13, pp. 217-21.

Entrance to the stadium at Olympia.

Olympia holds in the odes by Pindar or by Bacchylides celebrating the victories that were achieved there.[14]

Considering how dry so many parts of the Greek countryside are it is easy to understand why its water made the valley of Olympia so attractive. Many rivers flowed into the Alpheius ensuring that it was well supplied, even in summer when many others were reduced to a dribble. Pausanias makes much of the amount of water in the Alpheius:[15]

> By the time you reach Olympia the Alpheius is a large and very pleasant river to see, being fed by several tributaries, including seven very important ones. The Helisson joins the Alpheius passing through Megalopolis; the Brentheates comes out of the territory of that city; past Gortyna, where is a sanctuary of Asclepius, flows the Gortynius; from Melaeneae, between the territories of Megalopolis and Heraea, comes the Buphagus; from the land of the Clitorians the Ladon; from Mount Erymanthus a stream with the same name as the mountain. These come down into the Alpheius from Arcadia; the Cladeus comes from Elis to join it. The source of the Alpheius itself is in Arcadia, and not in Elis.

The poet who composed the twenty-fifth *Idyll* of the collection attributed to Theocritus provides a poetic evocation of the land around Olympia. He describes the country of the king Augeas and paints a picture of the Elean countryside highlighting the "*acroreia* rich in springs". Numerous flocks of sheep and herds of bulls, plane trees, olives, vines, fields, and orchards give us an image of a countryside that is rich and peaceful.[16] These are the words of a peasant speaking to Heracles:

> King Augeas' fleecy flocks, good Sir, feed not all of one pasture nor all upon one spot, but some of them be tended along Heilisson, others beside divine Alpheüs' sacred stream, others again by the fair vineyards of Buprasium, and yet others, look you, hereabout; and each flock hath his several fold builded. But the herds, mark you, for all their exceeding number, find all of them their fodder sprouting ever around this great mere of river Menius; for your watery leas and fenny flats furnish honey-sweet grass in plenty, and that is it which swells the strength of the horned kine. Their steading is all one, and 'tis there upon your right-hand beyond where the river goes running again: there where the outspreading platans and the fresh green wild-olive, Sir, make a right pure and holy sanctuary of one that is graciousest of all Gods, Apollo o' the Pastures. Hard by that spot there are builded rare and roomy quarters for us swains that keep close watch over the king's so much and so marvellous prosperity: aye, we often turn the same fallows for the sowing three and four times in the year.
>
> And as for the skirts of this domain, they are the familiar place of the busy

---

14 See F. Cairns's article "Some reflections of the ranking of the major games in fifth century B.C. Epinician poetry", in *Achaie und Elis in der Antike*, t. 132, pp. 95-8.

15 Pausanias, *op. cit.*, V, 7, 1.

16 Theocritus, in *The Greek Bucolic Poets* (trans J. M. Edmonds), Loeb Classical Library, Harvard University Press, Cambridge, MA, 1969, XXV, "Hercules the lion slayer", 7-33.

View from the gymnasium to the Palaestra, Olympia.
© Sonia Halliday Photographs

vine-planters, who come hither to the vintage-home when the summer draweth to its end. Yea, the whole plain belongeth unto sapient Augeas, alike fat wheatfield and bosky vineyard, until thou come to the uplands of Acroreia and all his fountains; and in this plain we go to and fro about our labour all the day long as behoveth bondsmen whose life is upon the glebe.

Polybius[17] understood only too well how gentleness of the countryside influenced the way the sanctuary developed, but he has also noted that the ancients had introduced music into Arcadia in order to make the harshness of their region more endurable.

> Now all these practices I believe to have been introduced by the men of old time, not as luxuries and superfluities but because they had before their eyes the universal practice of personal manual labour in Arcadia, and in general the toilsomeness and hardship of the men's lives, as well as the harshness of character resulting from the cold and gloomy atmospheric conditions usually prevailing in these parts – conditions to which all men by their very nature must perforce assimilate themselves; there being no other cause than this why separate nations and peoples dwelling widely apart differ

17 Polybius, *Histories* (trans. W. R. Paton), Loeb Classical Library, Harvard University Press, Cambridge, MA, 1922, IV, 21.

so much from each other in character, feature, and colour as well as in the most of their pursuits. The primitive Arcadians, therefore, with the view of softening and tempering the stubbornness and harshness of nature, introduced all the practices I mentioned, and in addition accustomed the people, both men and women, to frequent festivals and general sacrifices, and dances of young men and maidens, and in fact resorted to every contrivance to render more gentle and mild, by the influence of the customs they instituted, the extreme hardness of the national character.

As much a historian as a geographer, Polybius gives us here the clue to the way the Games were created. They were set up to allow the participants to relax, not to set them at one another's throats. People came to the Games to compete with one another but in joy, to amuse themselves.

Pilgrims coming from the south could disembark at Gytheion, the harbour for Sparta, 46km to the south of the town. Coming back up the valley of the Eurotas they would reach the plain of Megalopolis and by the valley of the Alpheius reach Olympia. It was a long way, 193km separating Sparta from Olympia. On this journey at the foot of the mountain range of the Taygetus to arrive in the high plain of

View of the mountains around Delphi.
© André Bernand

Megalopolis provided access to a cultivated countryside that contrasted with the aridness of the mountain ranges all around. After that to go down into the valley of the Alpheius brought the magic of the running water, and the countryside spread out and became greener as the sanctuary of Olympia drew near. The pilgrims could then enjoy a well earned rest and admire the sacred wood, the temple, and the statue of Zeus described by Pausanias:[18]

> The sacred grove of Zeus has been called from of old Altis, a corruption of the word "alsos", which means a grove. Pindar too calls the place Altis in an ode composed for an Olympic victor. The temple and the image were made for Zeus from spoils, when Pisa was crushed in war by the Eleans, and with Pisa such of the subject peoples as conspired together with her. The image itself was wrought by Pheidias, as is testified by an inscription written under the feet of Zeus:
> "Pheidias, son of Charmides, an Athenian, made me."
> The temple is in the Doric style, and the outside has columns all around it. It is built of native stone. Its height up to the pediment is sixty-eight feet, its breadth is ninety-five, its length two hundred and thirty. The architect was Libon, a native. The tiles are not of baked earth, but of Pentelic marble cut into the shape of tiles. The invention is said to be that of Byzes of Naxos, who they say made the images in Naxos on which is the inscription:
> "To the offspring of Leto was I dedicated by Euergus,
> A Naxian, son of Byzes, who first made tiles of stone."
> This Byzes lived about the time of Alyattes the Lydian, when Astyages, the son of Cyaxares, reigned over the Medes. At Olympia a gilt caldron stands on each end of the roof, and a Victory, also gilt, is set in about the middle of the pediment. Under the image of Victory has been dedicated a golden shield, with Medusa the Gorgon in relief.

From the description that Xenophon gives us of the property he had received from the Spartans after he had been exiled from Athens for his pro-Spartan feelings, the charm of the countryside around Olympia can be imagined. The site of Xenophon's property is about 17km south of Pyrgos.[19]

> In the time of Xenophon's exile and while he was living at Scillus, near Olympia, where he had been established as a colonist by the Lacedaemonians, Megabyzus came to Olympia to attend the games and returned to him his deposit. Upon receiving it Xenophon bought a plot of ground for the goddess in a place which Apollo's oracle appointed. As it chanced, there flowed through the plot a river named Selinus; and at Ephesus likewise a Selinus river flows past the temple of Artemis. In both streams, moreover, there are fish and mussels, while in the plot at Scillus there is hunting of all manner of beasts of the chase. Here Xenophon built an altar and a temple

---

18 Pausanias, *Description of Greece, op. cit.*, V, 10, 1-4.

19 Xenophon, *Anabasis*, in *Xenophon in Seven Volumes*, Vol. III (trans. C. L. Brownson), Loeb Classical Library, Harvard University Press, Cambridge, MA, 1980, V, 3, 7-13.

with the sacred money, and from that time forth he would every year take the tithe of the products of the land in their season and offer sacrifice to the goddess, all the citizens and the men and women of the neighbourhood taking part in the festival. And the goddess would provide for the banqueters barley meal and loaves of bread, wine and sweetmeats, and a portion of the sacrificial victims from the sacred herd as well as of the victims taken in the chase. For Xenophon's sons and the sons of the other citizens used to have a hunting expedition at the time of the festival, and any grown men who so wished would join them; and they captured their game partly from the sacred precinct itself and partly from Mount Pholoe – boars and gazelles and stags.

The place is situated on the road which leads from Lacedaemon to Olympia, and is about twenty stadia from the temple of Zeus at Olympia. Within the sacred precinct there is meadowland and tree-covered hills, suited for the rearing of swine, goats, cattle and horses, so that even the draught animals which bring people to the festival have their feast also. Immediately surrounding the temple is a grove of cultivated trees, producing all sorts of dessert fruits in their season. The temple itself is like the one at Ephesus, although small as compared with great, and the image of the goddess, although cypress wood as compared with gold, is like the Ephesian image. Beside the temple stands a tablet with this inscription:

The place is sacred to Artemis. He who holds it and enjoys its fruits must offer the tithe every year in sacrifice, and from the remainder must keep the temple in repair. If any one leaves these things undone, the goddess will look to it.

The way to Delphi

People coming from Arcadia would go down to Olympia, but those coming by sea would go up to Delphi. In terms of rank based on reputation, the Pythian Games in the sanctuary of Delphi came second to those of Olympia. It was Apollo and not Zeus who reigned over this sacred place which was in the very centre of Greece. Strabo has noted what made its situation so special:[20]

Now although the greatest share of honor was paid to this temple because of its oracle, since of all oracles in the world it had the repute of being the most truthful, yet the position of the place added something. For it is almost in the center of Greece taken as a whole, between the country inside the Isthmus and that outside it; and it was also believed to be in the center of the inhabited world, and people called it the navel of the earth, in addition fabricating a myth, which is told by Pindar,[21] that the two eagles (some say crows) which had been set free by Zeus met there, one coming from the west and the other from the east. There is also a kind of navel to be seen in the temple; it is draped with fillets, and on it are the two likenesses of the birds of the myth.

20   Strabo, *op. cit.*, IX, 3, 6.
21   Pindar, *Pythian Odes*, in *Odes* (trans. D. Svarlien), Perseus Project, Yale, 1991, IV, 6.

Pausanias[22] describes this *omphalos* and refers to the ode by Pindar who, like Strabo, describes it as being at the centre of the earth. Strabo, however, goes further showing that men naturally sought to come together in their communal sanctuaries:[23]

> Such being the advantages of the site of Delphi, the people easily came together there, and especially those who lived near it. And indeed the Amphictyonic League was organized from the latter, both to deliberate concerning common affairs and to keep the superintendence of the temple more in common, because much money and many votive offerings were deposited there, requiring great vigilance and holiness. Now the facts of olden times are unknown, but among the names recorded, Acrisius is reputed to have been the first to administer the Amphictyony and to determine the cities that were to have a part in the council and to give a vote to each city, to one city separately or to another jointly with a second or with several, and also to proclaim the Amphictyonic Rights – all the rights that cities have in their dealings with cities.

22 Pausanias, *op. cit.*, X, 16, 3.
23 Strabo, *op. cit.*, IX, 3, 7.

The Thessalian plain near Amphissa.
© André Bernand

Pilgrims could choose between three different routes if they wanted to go to Delphi. They could come from Athens and make for Delphi via Eleusis, Thebes, Livadia, and Arachova. I have described this journey, that I undertook for the first time in 1951, in *Leçon de civilisation*.[24] Strabo in his usual way has described the countryside around Delphi in a sober fashion:

> As I have already said, Parnassus is situated on the western boundaries of Phocis. Of this mountain, then, the side towards the west is occupied by the Ozolian Locrians, whereas the southern is occupied by Delphi, a rocky place, theatre-like, having the oracle and the city on its summit, and filling a circuit of sixteen stadia. Situated above Delphi is Lycoreia, on which place, above the temple, the Delphians were established in earlier times. But now they live close to the temple, round the Castalian fountain. Situated in front of the city, toward the south, is Cirphis, a precipitous mountain, which leaves in the intervening space a ravine, through which flows the Pleistus River. Below Cirphis lies Cirrha, an ancient city, situated by the sea; and from it there is an ascent to Delphi of about eighty stadia. It is situated opposite Sicyon. In front of Cirrha lies the fertile Crisaean Plain; for again one comes next in order to another city, Crisa, from which the Crisaean Gulf is named. [25]

I cannot forget climbing up to Delphi along the road that follows the northern coast of the Gulf of Corinth from Naupactus and Antirrhon to Eratini and rises to Delphi via Amphissa. On this plain covered with olive trees the Ozolian Locrians fought the Delphians in 373 BC during the fourth holy war which was caused by Aeschines.[26] He denounced the Locrians for breaking the law when they disregarded the fact that the Amphissians were forbidden to farm their plain and were therefore defying the *amphyctyons* of Delphi. From this road it is possible to discover the western side of Parnassus and appreciate the contrast between the fertile plain of Amphissa and the harshness of the Delphic countryside.

Homer's *Hymn to Apollo*[27] evokes the Delphic sanctuary. The poet addressed the gods:

> And thence you went speeding swiftly to the mountain ridge, and came to Crisa beneath snowy Parnassus, a foothill turned towards the west: a cliff hangs over it from above, and a hollow, rugged glade runs under. There the lord Phoebus Apollo resolved to make his lovely temple, and thus he said:
>
> "In this place I am minded to build a glorious temple to be an oracle for men, and here they will always bring perfect hecatombs, both they who dwell in rich Peloponnesus and the men of Europe and from all the wave-washed isles, coming to question me. And I will deliver to them all counsel that cannot fail, answering them in my rich temple."

24 A. Bernand, *Leçon de civilisation, op. cit.,* pp. 13-4

25 Strabo, *op. cit.,* IX, 3, 3.

26 Aeschines, "Against Ctesiphon" in *The speeches of Aeschines*, (trans. Charles Darwin Adams), Loeb Classical Library, Harvard University Press, Cambridge, MA, 1989, 115-30.

27 *Hymn to Apollo,* in *Homeric Hymns and Homerica, op. cit.,* Loeb Classical Library, Harvard University Press, Cambridge, MA, 1914, verses 281-304.

View of the Tholos of the Sanctuary of Athena near Delphi.

Round Apulian plate: Helios and his four-horse
chariot.

© Photo RMN – Hervé Lewandowski, Louvre

When he had said this, Phoebus Apollo laid out all the foundations throughout, wide and very long; and upon these the sons of Erginus, Trophonius and Agamedes, dear to the deathless gods, laid a footing of stone. And the countless tribes of men built the whole temple of wrought stones, to be sung of for ever.

But near by was a sweet flowing spring, and there with his strong bow the lord, the son of Zeus, killed the bloated, great she-dragon, a fierce monster wont to do great mischief to men upon earth, to men themselves and to their thin-shanked sheep; for she was a very bloody plague.

The Delphic site is full of the divine presence as is shown by an episode related by Herodotus[28] during the expedition by Xerxes against Delphi. When the Persians sought to loot the sanctuary, a miracle occurred.

When the barbarians came with all speed near to the temple of Athena Pronaea, they were visited by miracles yet greater than the aforesaid. Marvellous indeed it is, that weapons of war should of their own motion appear lying outside in front of the shrine, but the visitation which followed was more wondrous than anything else ever seen. When the barbarians were near to the temple of Athena Pronaea, they were struck by thunderbolts from the sky, and two peaks broken off from Parnassus came rushing among them with a mighty noise and overwhelmed many of them. In addition to this a shout and a cry of triumph were heard from the temple of Athena.

The people of Delphi knew how to welcome those believers who came to adore the god. Euripides has left us a description of the sunrise over Delphi when the young sacristan, Ion, goes about the ritual purification ceremony:[29]

Now Helios bends the course of his bright chariot here toward the earth, and the stars, banished by his flame, flee into the holy night. The trackless peaks of Parnassus gleam with light and receive for mortals the sun's chariot wheels. The smoke of dry incense rises up to Phoebus' rafters. Upon her holy tripod sits the Delphian priestess, who cries aloud to the Greeks whatever Apollo utters. So, you Delphian servants of Apollo, go to the silvery streams of Castalia, and when you have bathed in the pure water, return to the temple. Keep pious silence and guard the goodness of your lips, so that to those who wish to consult the god you may utter words of good omen.

As for me, I shall perform the tasks I have ever performed since childhood: with boughs of laurel and their holy bindings I shall purify the entrance to Phoebus' house and cleanse the floor with sprinklings of water. The flocks of birds, which harm the sacred offerings, I shall put to flight with my bow. As one who is without mother or father I serve the temple of Phoebus that has given me nurture.

---

28 Herodotus, *op. cit.*, VIII, 37-8.
29 Euripides, *Ion* (ed. and trans. D. Kovacs), Loeb Classical Library, Harvard University Press, Cambridge, MA, 1999, 82-111.

Having swept the area in front of the sanctuary, Ion washes it with sacred water drawn from the spring of Castalia and chases away the birds that come to snatch the offerings that have been left. Living in the presence of a god necessitates attention to the cleanliness and purity of the place. Justin (M. Junianus Justinus), a Latin writer, contemporary of the Antonines, has described the grandiose site of the Delphic sanctuary:[30]

> The temple of Apollo at Delphi is situated at the top of the steep slopes of the Parnassus mountain. A town grew at the place where people came from everywhere to pay homage to the divine majesty. The temple and the town are protected not by walls of rock but by precipices – a natural defense and not a work of art – in such a way that it is not possible to know whether it is the strategic position of the sanctuary or the divine majesty that is the more admired. In the middle of it a rocky wall has the shape of a theatre. This is why if shouts are made and trumpets blown, the rocks normally make an echo and send back the sounds much amplified. Those who do not realize why this happens are generally filled with a religious fear and remain dumbstruck in admiration. In this crevice halfway up the mountain there is a narrow plain in which there is a deep hole giving access to the oracles. From it comes a cold breath pushed upwards by some unknown force as if by a wind and which causes the minds of the soothsayers to wander, fills them with the god, and makes them respond to those who consult them. This is the reason why there is a large number of rich *ex-votos* given by kings and by the people who have come in recognition of the divine responses they have received.

If people came from the north they would take the route from Lamia and, crossing the col of Bralos could reach first Amphissa and then Delphi. From the col at 590m and after many twists and turns there is a majestic view over the mountain ridge of Kallidromos to the southeast and over Mount Oeta to the north rising to 2,115m. This is where Dorianism was born and where the sacred places where Heracles died are to be located. The area is full of history since at the foot of the slope to the north of Kallidromos is the valley of the Sperchios and the famous pass of Thermopylae where in 480 BC the Spartan Leonidas and the Greek soldiers stopped the advance of Xerxes' army. This northern side of Parnassus is particularly imposing and the pilgrims would have been overcome by a profound emotion. From Lamia to Delphi the route is 89km long but such is the beauty of the countryside that weariness is forgotten.

Strabo[31] tells us that after the Crisean War changes were made to the competitions celebrated by the people of Delphi. The original competition, he says, was between cithara players who sang songs in honour of their god. After the war it was the *amphictyons* who organised gymnastic and horse competitions for which the prize was a Pythian crown (known as a "stephanite"). The Pythian composition was a tune for the flute, the sounds and rhythms of which represented Apollo's fight with

Columns of the temple at Delphi.
© André Bernand

30 Justin, *Epitome of Trogus' Histories*, XXIV, 6, quoted in C. Préaux *et al. Le paysage grec*, pp. 136-7.
31 Strabo, *op. cit.*, IX, 3, 10.

the dragon. Raoul Baladié has observed that every eight years until 590 BC gymnastic and horse competitions were added to the musical ones. In 582 BC, the third year of the 49th Olympiad, the feast of the Pythia was celebrated every four years in the month of Boukatios (August–September). The most spectacular event was the chariot race on the plain of Kirra. The magnificent and austere site of Delphi was a fitting setting in which the struggle between Apollo and the dragon could be imagined and the plain, once the Phocians had conquered it for the god, was ideal for the chariot competition.

The way to Isthmia

Pilgrims coming from the east or west along the south coast of the Gulf of Corinth arrived at a sanctuary that was far less impressive than the one at Delphi – the sanctuary of Isthmia.

If they came from the west and from Italy the pilgrims who came to watch or participate in the Isthmian games had the possibility of disembarking at the port of Lechaion at the base of the Gulf of Corinth: if they came from Asia and the east Strabo tells us they could cast anchor at Kenkreai in the Saronic Gulf. The difficulty of rounding the Cape of Malea was considerable. Homer[32] has said it and Herodotus has repeated it;[33] Strabo brings us a saying,[34] "But when you double Maleae, forget your home" (*Cum ad Maleam deflexeris, domesticos oblivisce*).

Not only was much time saved and danger avoided if you came by the Isthmus but traders who could not face rounding the Cape of Malea unloaded their cargoes at Corinth. The town enjoyed another attractive advantage: materials exported by sea or land from the Peloponnese were taxed and provided revenue for those who held the keys to the Isthmus. This situation encouraged a lot of people to come via the ports of the Isthmus and to bring business and religion together by frequenting the Isthmian games, which took place in the sanctuary of Poseidon deep inside a pine forest.

The route away from the Isthmus in both directions was made easy by a haulage system that Strabo calls a *diolkos*, a word which meant that things could be pulled or carried. The construction of this device went back to the time of Periander, son of Kypselis, tyrant of Corinth. Ships of a light tonnage were hoisted on to chariots or carts and pulled along a paved way between Schoinous (Kalamaki) on the Saronic Gulf and the Gulf of Corinth at a point situated a little to the west of the present canal. Excavations carried out by N. M. Verdelis between 1952 and 1962 uncovered parts of this track and allow us to trace its path. The track itself made of tuff was between 3.6 and 5m wide.[35] Its north section was straight, after which it bent round towards the northeast. The change of level was 90m. Two parallel ruts, 1.5m apart took the chariots' wheels and allowed them to negotiate the bends. In the 2nd century AD Pausanias gives us a brief description of the two harbours, Lechaion and Kenkreai, but does not mention the *diolkos*.[36] Georges Roux[37] has reproduced a photograph of this section of the track.

32   Homer, *Odyssey* (trans. Samuel Butler), Jonathan Cape, London, (2nd edition) 1922, III, 287; IX, 79-80.

33   Herodotus, *op. cit.*, IV, 179; VII, 168.

34   Strabo, *op. cit.*, VIII, 6, 20.

35   *Mitteilungen des deutschen archaologischen Instituts*, Athenische Abteilung, 73 pp 140-5 and supplement 106-118.

36   Pausanias, *op. cit.*, II, 1-15.

37   G. Roux, *Pausanias en Corinthie*, Les Belles Lettres, Paris, 1958, fig. 3.

Unlike the valley of Olympia the region of the Isthmus does not have a fertile soil. It only has two small coastal plains, one of them 1,400m wide near Lechaion, the other 690m wide near Kenkreai, as Pausanias has described them:[38]

> The Corinthian Isthmus stretches on the one hand to the sea at
> Cenchreae, and on the other to the sea at Lechaeum. For this is what makes
> the region to the south mainland. He who tried to make the Peloponnesus an
> island gave up before digging through the Isthmus. Where they began to dig
> is still to be seen, but into the rock they did not advance at all. So it still is
> mainland as its nature is to be.

The rest of the soil on this strip of land to the south of the Perachora Peninsula (an area described briefly by Pausanias) is poor, arid, badly irrigated, and windswept, its sparse vegetation being no more than a clump of pine trees.

This countryside has none of the majesty of the sanctuary of Delphi. The sanctuary of Isthmia situated to the east of Corinth was at the foot of the Gerenian mountains rising to just a few hundred metres. Today the only visitor attraction in the summer is the thermal spa at Loutraki. Twenty kilometres from there lies the antique site of the *Heraion* of Perachora. There is no road following the sea at the foot of the Citheron and the Helicon which would make it possible to reach Phocis and the harbour of Itea without having to go around the mountain ranges to the east. Today, an enormous oil refinery disfigures the countryside of the Isthmus.

Respect for the Isthmian games was in direct proportion to the importance of the festival. This did not prevent Aristophanes from making a joke that had nothing religious about it:[39] he alluded to the huts that were kept by those who took part in the Games and he played on a special sense of the word "isthmus", which designates a woman's private parts. In doing this, the games he describes cannot have been those in honour of Poseidon. Indeed, he has the servant declare: "In anticipation of the games practised in the Isthmus, I am reserving a tent... for my member."

What made this region so important was its strategic interest. In some periods there were ramparts that blocked the entrance to the Peloponnese. It was an essential crossing point as is made clear in the account that Thucydides gives of a naval operation which took place in the spring of 412 BC, the 20th year of the Peloponnesian War.[40] He tells how in the spring, the inhabitants of Chios pressed the Spartans to let the ships that were gathered in the Gulf of Corinth and which had to reassemble opposite Athens, cross the Isthmus from Corinth. In this way, 21 boats crossed the Isthmus and the Spartans' allies were eager to begin their expedition towards Chios. "They were now in a hurry [says Thucydides[41]] to make a move but it was time for the Isthmian Games and the Corinthians were hardly ready to leave before they had celebrated them. So that the sacred truce should not be broken, Agis, son of the King of Sparta, Archidamus, was ready to take personal responsibility for the expedition but the Corinthians refused." This episode is a good example of the

38   Pausanias, *op. cit.*, II, 1,5, quoted by. C. Préaux et al., *Le paysage grec*, pp. 112-3.

39   Aristophanes, *Peace* (ed. and trans. J. Henderson), Loeb Classical Library, Harvard University Press, Cambridge, MA, 1998, 879.

40   Thucydides, *op. cit.*, VII, 7-10.

41   *Ibid.*, VIII, 9.

Panhellenic Games, which were celebrated every two years and hosted by Corinth. All the Greek cities were invited to take part and it was because of this that the Athenians sent an official delegation.

A similar event occurred in 390 BC when Agesilaus, king of Sparta, led an expedition against Corinth. Xenophon tells us about it:[42]

> And first he came to the Isthmus; for it was the month during which the Isthmian games are celebrated, and the Argives chanced at the time to be offering the sacrifice there to Poseidon, as though Argos were Corinth. But when they learned that Agesilaus was approaching, they left behind both the victims that had been offered and the breakfast that was being made ready and retired to the city in very great fear, along the road leading to Cenchreae. Agesilaus, however, did not pursue them, even though he saw them, but encamping in the sacred precinct offered sacrifice himself to the god and waited until the Corinthian exiles had conducted the sacrifice and the games in honour of Poseidon. But when Agesilaus had left the Isthmus, the Argives celebrated the Isthmian games all over again. In that year, accordingly, in some of the contests individual competitors were beaten twice, while in others the same competitors were twice proclaimed victors.

Nothing allows us to understand the importance of the Isthmian Games better than the scene described by Polybius.[43] This scene took place in 196 BC when to general rejoicing the Roman consul Titus Quintius Flaminius proclaimed the freedom of Greece at the time when the Games took place:

> This having been decided and the Isthmian games being now close at hand, the most distinguished men from almost the whole world having assembled there owing to their expectation of what would take place, many and various were the reports prevalent during the whole festival, some saying that it was impossible for the Romans to abandon certain places and cities, and others declaring that they would abandon the places which were considered famous, but would retain those, which while less illustrious, would serve their purpose equally well, even at once naming these latter out of their own heads, each more ingenious than the other. Such was the doubt in men's minds when the crowd being now collected in the stadium to witness the games, the herald came forward and, having imposed universal silence by his bugler, read this proclamation: "The senate of Rome and Titus Quintius the proconsul having overcome King Philip and the Macedonians, leave the following peoples free, without garrisons, and subject to no tribute and governed by their countries' laws – the Corinthians, Phocians, Locrians, Euboeans, Phthiotic Achaeans, Magnesians, Thessalians, and Perrhaebians." At once at the very commencement a tremendous shout arose, and some did not

The stadium at Delphi.
© André Bernand

---

42 Xenophon, *Hellenica*, Vol. I (trans. C. L. Brownson), Loeb Classical Library, Harvard University Press, Cambridge, MA, 1985, I, 5, I.

43 Polybius, *Histories* (trans. W. R. Paton) Loeb Classical Library, Harvard University Press, Cambridge, MA, 1922, XVII, 46.

even hear the proclamation, while others wanted to hear it again. But the greater part of the crowd, unable to believe their ears and thinking that they were listening to the words as if in a dream owing to the event being so unexpected, demanded loudly, each prompted by a different impulse, that the herald and bugler should advance into the middle of the stadium and repeat the announcement, wishing, as I suppose, not only to hear the speaker, but to see him owing to the incredible character of his proclamation. But when the herald, coming forward to the middle of the stadium and again silencing the noise by his bugler, made the same identical proclamation, such a mighty burst of cheering arose that those who listen to the tale to-day cannot easily conceive what it was. When at length the noise had subsided, not a soul took any further interest in the athletes, but all, talking either to their neighbours or to themselves, were almost like men beside themselves. So much so indeed that after the games were over they very nearly put an end to Flamininus by their expressions of thanks.

The Isthmian Games were so important that when in September 146 BC the consul Lucius Mummius destroyed Corinth from top to bottom[44] the Games were not suppressed but transferred to Sicyon since the largest part of the territories of Corinth fell to the Sicyonians.

This is confirmed by Pausanias:[45]

The Isthmian games were not interrupted even when Corinth had been laid waste by Mummius, but so long as it lay deserted the celebration of the games was entrusted to the Sicyonians, and when it was rebuilt the honor was restored to the present inhabitants.

Polybius[46] reports that after the senatorial commission had left Achaea, Mummius repaired the installations of the Isthmia and enriched the decorations of the temples of Olympia and Delphi. Nonetheless the destruction of Corinth had been so thorough that the poet Antipater of Sidon could write:[47]

Where is thy celebrated beauty, Doric Corinth? Where are the battlements of thy towers and thy ancient possessions? Where are the temples of the immortals, the houses and the matrons of the town of Sisyphus, and her myriads of people? Not even a trace is left of thee, most unhappy of towns, but war has seized on and devoured everything. We alone, the Nereids, Ocean's daughters, remain inviolate, and lament, like halcyons, thy sorrows.

In 102 BC according to a metric inscription in Latin found among the excavations of Corinth,[48] "a fleet in control of proconsul Marcus Antonius was taken

---

44   Strabo, *op. cit.*, VIII, 6, 23.

45   Pausanias, *op. cit.*, II, 2, 1.

46   Polybius, *op. cit.*, 39, 6.

47   *Greek Anthology* (trans. W. R. Paton), Loeb Classical Library, Harvard University Press, Cambridge, MA, 1918, IX, 151.

48   R. Baladié, *Le Péloponnèse de Strabon*, Études Anciennes, Les Belles Lettres, Paris, 1980, p. 259.

Ruins of the temple of Zeus at Nemea.
© José F. Poblete / CORBIS

across the Isthmus and launched on the sea". In 44 BC Julius Caesar decided to found a colony at Corinth. In 30 BC, Octavius had his ships brought by the *diolkos*, 30 days after his arrival and stay at Brundisium (Brindisi) in January or February. Dio Cassius tells us[49]:

> he set out once more for Greece on the thirtieth day after his arrival.
> Then, because it was winter he carried his ships across the isthmus of the
> Peloponnesus and got back to Asia so quickly that Antony and Cleopatra
> learned at one and the same time both of his departure and of his return.

On 29 August on his way back from Asia, Strabo comes to present a petition to Octavius who was then at Corinth before going to Actium where he would celebrate his triumph.[50] All these dates underline the remarkable historic importance of the route leading to the Isthmus.

The way to Nemea

The way to Nemea could not give rise to the same emotions. The site had neither the charm of Olympia, nor the grandeur of Delphi, nor the strategic importance of the Isthmus. Ancient Nemea must not be confused with the modern Nemea (in ancient times Haghios Georgios), which is in a nearby valley situated further west and into which the small river Asopos flows. The upper basin of this river constituted the region of Phliasia, where the town of Phleious was located. This plain is full of vines and the Iraclion village people today produce a heady red wine called "the blood of Periclus". Ancient Nemea is 5km east of today's Nemea and is situated between the mountains of Spiria (725m) and Apesas (873m) at the source of the river Nemea. Ancient Nemea is about 30km to the south of Corinth.

Pilgrims going to Nemea would recall the story of how in this place Heracles had overcome a lion. Rather than hypothesise that there were lions in pre-ancient Greece, I think that the legend owes its origin to a curious topographical feature. Erosion by the weather has carved a rock into the shape of a lion to the point where village people still identify a cave with the one where Heracles supposedly killed the monster. In his first *Nemean*, Pindar celebrates the exploits of Heracles, the god who is dear to athletes and their admirers, since, with Hermes, he presided over the physical exercises practised at the institutes of higher education.

At the junction of Corinthia, Argolis, and Arcadia, Nemea was a place where neighbouring people could come together on a route that joined the Corinthian and Saronic Gulfs. From what Pausanias[51] witnessed, we learn that the following local towns were involved in the Nemean Games:

> From Cleonae to Argos are two roads; one is direct and only for active
> men, the other goes along the pass called Tretus ("Pierced"), is narrow like the
> other, being surrounded by mountains, but is nevertheless more suitable for

49 Dio Cassius, *Roman History*, Vol. VI (trans. E. Cary and H. B. Foster), Harvard University Press, Cambridge, MA, 1969, 51, 5.

50 Strabo, *op. cit.*, X, 5, 3.

51 Pausanias, *op. cit.*, II, 15.

carriages. In these mountains is still shown the cave of the famous lion, and the place Nemea is distant some fifteen stades. In Nemea is a noteworthy temple of Nemean Zeus, but I found that the roof had fallen in and that there was no longer remaining any image. Around the temple is a grove of cypress trees, and here it is, they say, that Opheltes was placed by his nurse in the grass and killed by the serpent. The Argives offer burnt sacrifices to Zeus in Nemea also, and elect a priest of Nemean Zeus; moreover they offer a prize for a race in armour at the winter celebration of the Nemean games.

According to G. Roux, there is a general consensus that the emperor Hadrian created these winter games. Ruins uncovered by the University of California have revealed a stadium, a sanctuary to Zeus, water channels, a vaulted gallery, spas, a public arena, "treasures", a temple with six lines of 12 Doric columns built on the ruins of another temple which dates from the beginning of the 6th century and was destroyed towards the end of the 5th century BC. There is no doubt that it was a sanctuary where pilgrims to the Nemean games would have gone, all the more so because the remains of what seems to have been a hostelry have also been discovered.

The pilgrims' journey to the Games was also therefore a pathway to the gods who reigned over regions that were very different from one another. Invested with a glorious past and with important gods as their patrons, these sites were the places where people came together in peace and not in battle or in the lists of murderous tournaments. What animates the Games is a desire for peace and conviviality.

Chapter III
Congregation of the Greeks

Coming together

Among the arguments that Lucian offers Solon to convince him about the usefulness of the athletic Games is the idea that the exercises took place in front of citizens all of whom enjoyed the spectacle, shared the pleasure they provided and in whose name prizes for bravery and boldness were awarded. Solon declares to the Scythian Anacharsis:

> You are not yet used to our customs, I tell you. But your opinion is sure to change when you attend our ceremonial gatherings and you witness the immense crowds flocking to see the Games, the amphitheatres packed with thousands of spectators, the athletes applauded and the victor honoured as an equal of the gods.

Everyone shared in the same admiration and pleasure. Solon insisted[1] on this so that it could not be thought that he was using the argument of the greatest number. What matters is the combination of competition and happiness:

> If the Olympic Games were happening now, Anacharsis, or the Isthmian Games, or the Panathenaea, you would appreciate when you saw what went on there, that there is a good reason these events have become so popular. The pleasure that they give is indescribable. You need to sit amongst the spectators to experience for yourself the bravery of the athletes, the beauty and the superb condition of their bodies, their prowess, their invincible strength, their resilience, their emulation, their insurmountable resolve and their unquenchable thirst for victory. I am sure that you could not help not only being impressed, but shouting and cheering.

The fact that the prizes are awarded in the presence of all the Greeks gives these Games a universal value and involved the spectators in a decision based on the criteria and guidelines of the Greek *paideia*. Solon again emphasises:[2]

> In our opinion their enthusiasm [young people's] will increase when they see that those who do well are honoured and their names proclaimed in front of all the Greeks. Also, since they must appear naked before so many spectators, they should ensure they stay fit, so as not to be ashamed and to make themselves as worthy as possible of victory. And the prizes, as I have already mentioned, are not to be sniffed at, as they include receiving the praise of the spectators, being remarked upon and singled out, and known as being

---

1   Lucian, *Anacharsis or Athletics*, Vol. IV (trans. A. M. Harmon), Loeb Classical Library, Harvard University Press, Cambridge, MA, 1925, 12.

2   *Ibid.*, 36.

one of the best among your peers. That is why many spectators still young enough to exercise come away from these Games with a high opinion of virtue and hard work. In truth, Anacharsis, if the love of glory were to be abolished, what would be left of any worth? For who would bother to undertake anything truly noteworthy?

The Games have nothing to do with individual actions nor are they for the satisfaction of personal ambition. They are collective activities taking place under the eyes of everybody and for which the prizes are awarded by everybody. If there is any struggle it is in a healthy desire to reach the same level and has a distinct ethical and civic objective. Thanks to three institutions closely associated with the Games – *panegyris, theoroi,* and *proxenis* – it was possible to bring Greeks together in a joyful, communal ceremony.

The *panegyris*

The *panegyris* is when all people come together on the occasion of a solemn festival and particularly when the Games are being held. In his ninth *Olympian*[3] Pindar talks of the "great gathering in honour of Zeus Lykaios" when he describes the festival that took place on the mountain called Lycea (*Lukaion*) in the southwest region of Arcadia where there was a temple dedicated to Zeus. The speech that Isocrates[4] gave on the occasion of the 100th Olympiad in 380 BC is called a *panegyric* because in it he invites the Greeks to gather together and forget their struggles and hatred:

> Now the founders of our great festivals are justly praised for handing down to us a custom by which, having proclaimed a truce and resolved our pending quarrels, we come together in one place, where, as we make our prayers and sacrifices in common, we are reminded of the kinship which exists among us and are made to feel more kindly towards each other for the future, reviving our old friendships and establishing new ties. And neither to common men nor to those of superior gifts is the time so spent idle and profitless, but in the concourse of the Hellenes the latter have the opportunity to display their prowess, the former to behold these contending against each other in the games; and no one lacks zest for the festival, but all find in it that which flatters their pride, the spectators when they see the athletes exert themselves for their benefit, the athletes when they reflect that all the world is come to gaze upon them.

For Isocrates what matters is not athletic performance but the fact that the Greeks come together thereby acquiring strength to confront any invaders and in particular the Persians. At the beginning of his speech he shows himself to be amazed at the fact that athletes are awarded prizes, since for him the Games should provide people with the chance to share the same cultural and civic ideals:

> I am often amazed that the founders of solemn festivities and gymnastic

Zeus or Poseidon, in the National Archaeological Museum of Athens.
© 1990, Photo Scala, Florence
National Archaeological Museum of Athens

---

3   Pindar, *Olympian Odes*, in *Odes* (trans. D. Svarlien), Perseus Project, Yale, 1991, IX, 145.
4   Isocrates, *Panegyricus* (trans. G. Norlin), Harvard University Press, Cambridge, MA, 1969, 43-4.

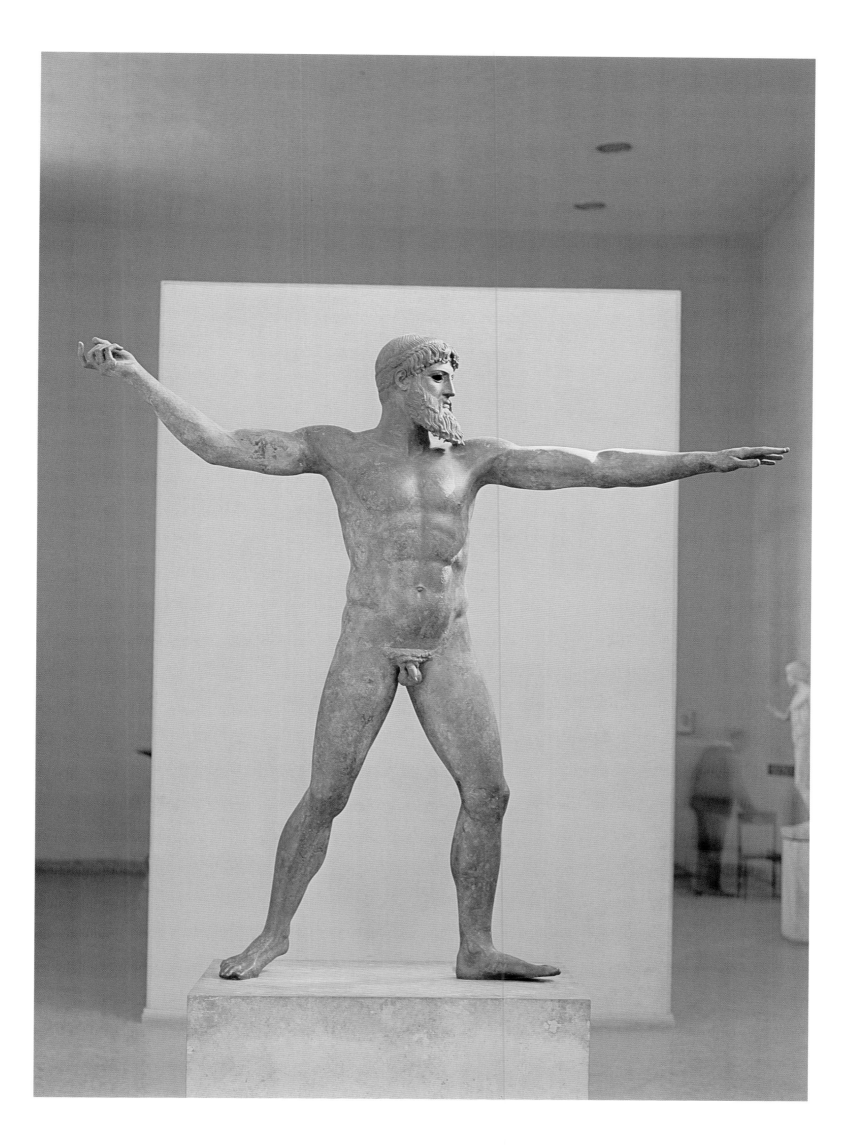

competitions should award physical competitions so richly, while they give nothing to those men they should really be interested in, namely those who have worked for the common good and have raised their souls so as to be fit to serve others. Even if the athletes were twice as strong it would be of no benefit to other men, but when an individual has noble thoughts it can be of value to all those who want to share his ideas.

In his speech *Antidosis*,[5] Isocrates refers again to the link between thinking and physical activity: real culture is a fusion of mind and body. In his *To the Rulers of the Mytilenaeans*[6] he again expresses surprise at the fact that prizes should be awarded to athletes and not to men of learning:

I marvel that so many cities judge those who excel in the athletic contests to be worthy of greater rewards than those who, by painstaking thought and endeavor, discover some useful thing, and that they do not see at a glance that while the faculties of strength and speed naturally perish with the body, yet the arts and sciences abide for eternity, giving benefit to those who cultivate them.

Aristotle[7] mentions a speech by Gorgias in which he develops the same idea:

In epideictic speeches, the sources of the exordia are praise and blame, as Gorgias, in the Olympiacus, says, "Men of Greece, you are worthy to be admired by many," where he is praising those who instituted the solemn assemblies. Isocrates on the other hand blames them because they rewarded bodily excellences, but instituted no prize for men of wisdom.

In fact, Isocrates does not criticise the Games but rather what is made of them. According to him their merit is to bring people together, thereby strengthening the sense of community. He knows that Greek culture will only spread if the Greeks are united.[8] For them, the Games are precisely a chance to meet in festive circumstances and strengthen panhellenism when threatened by foreigners.

Before Isocrates, in 384 BC, Lysias[9] had celebrated the foundation of the Olympic Games which had had the happy result of bringing Greeks together inspired by a common ideal. He begins his address by praising Heracles, the founder of the Games:

I have not come here to talk trivialities or to wrangle over words: I take that to be the business of utterly futile professors in straits for a livelihood; but

5   Isocrates, *Antidosis* (trans. G. Norlin), Harvard University Press, Cambridge, MA, 1969, 185.

6   Isocrates, *To the Rulers of the Mytilenaeans*, in *Letters* (trans. La Rue Van Hook), Harvard University Press, Cambridge, MA, 1969, 5.

7   Aristotle, *The Art of Rhetoric* (trans. J. H. Freese), Loeb Classical Library, Harvard University Press, Cambridge, MA, 1959, 14, 30-34.

8   This element of Isocrates has been examined by the author in detail in a previous book, *Leçon de civilisation*, Fayard, 1994, pp. 52-3, 132-3, 153, 163, 166-9, 171-5, 178, 314, 382.

9   Lysias, *Olympic Speech*, in *Lysias* (trans. W. R. M. Lamb), Loeb Classical Library, Harvard University Press, Cambridge, MA, 1930, 1-6.

Temple of Heracles at Agrigento, Sicily.
© James Marshall / CORBIS

I think it behoves a man of principle and civic worth to be giving his counsel on the weightiest questions, when I see Greece in this shameful plight, with many parts of her held subject by the foreigner, and many of her cities ravaged by despots. Now if these afflictions were due to weakness, it would be necessary to acquiesce in our fate: but since they are due to faction and mutual rivalry, surely we ought to desist from the one and arrest the other, knowing that, if rivalry befits the prosperous, the most prudent views befit people in a position like ours. For we see both the gravity of our dangers and their imminence on every side: you are aware that empire is for those who command the sea, that the King has control of the money, that the Greeks are in thrall to those who are able to spend it, that our master possesses many ships, and that the despot of Sicily has many also. We ought therefore to relinquish our mutual warfare, and with a single purpose in our hearts to secure our salvation; to feel shame for past events and fear for those that lie in the future, and to compete with our ancestors, by whom the foreigner, in grasping at the land of others, was deprived of his own, and who expelled the despots and established freedom for all in common.

Isocrates' thinking goes further than that of Lysias. The latter saw the Games as a way of reconciling the different factions within Greek cities so as to be able to withstand their enemies, in particular the Persians. Isocrates thought that the differences between the Greeks and the barbarians could only be abolished by having someone, like Philip II of Macedonia, in a position of authority and by creating a single panhellenic culture beyond Greece.

As a result of wars and trading, and the consequent intermingling of peoples, persons of mixed race appeared in the ancient world. This meant that everyone who subscribed to the values of Greek culture would be considered Greek. The Games brought Greeks and barbarians together to share in a celebration of the prowess of both athletes and artists[10] whatever their origin. It is for this reason that the Games were so successful during the reign of Alexander and the Ptolemaic dynasty.

In the Classical period the cities where the Games were to be held had special envoys, like itinerant ambassadors, called *theôroi*. They ensured regular contact between the different cities likely to take part.

Sacred ambassadors

These official envoys responsible for announcing that the Games were to take place enjoyed a religious status and were received and lodged by their official counterparts called *theôrodokoi* or "those who welcomed the *theôroi*". At Delphi, envoys were called *theares* and their hosts, *thearodokoi*, but their roles were the same.

The *theôria* designated either the sending of *theôroi* for a religious festival or simply the fact of having the status *theôros*. Since the word also meant "the act of seeing, watching, and investigating", from Plato onwards it signified "reflection and meditation" and from this later in Polybius' work for example there developed the idea of "theory and theoretical speculation".

The boat that carried the *theôroi*, at Delos in particular, was called a *theôris* (*naus*

---

10   This process is described by the author in *Leçon de civilisation, op. cit.*, section 3, "L'apparition du métis", pp. 295-393.

being understood) and according to Pindar[11] the *thearion* was the place where the *theôroi* would meet and he refers to the existence of the noble reunion of Pythian Apollo at Aegina.

Pausanias[12] tells us that at Troezen there existed a cult to Apollo called *Thearos*. According to Pierre Chantraine's *Dictionnaire étymologique de la langue grecque* (Etymological Dictionary of the Greek Language) the denominative verb *theoreo* links the idea of travelling with that of observing, because *theôros* can also mean "spectator". Herodotus[13] uses this verb to mean "to be a spectator at the Olympic Games" ("*theôrein ta Olympia*"). The job of the *theôros* therefore is both to advertise the Games and to be present at them. In his translation of Thucydides,[14] Denis Roussel renders "*theôrein kata ta patria*" as "to send official delegations to the festivities". The dictionary informs us that according to Achaeus, a tragic poet from Eretrea in the 5th century BC, *theôros* (spectator) was the opposite of *agônistés* (participant) at the Games.

Good illustrations of the roles played by the *theôroi* are provided by the decrees issued in Magnesia on the Meander in the 3rd century BC. According to these the cities willing to host new Games would recognise what was required in the way of festivities and accept privileges – and especially the right to *asylia* – requested by all well-meaning participant cities.

That is the case for example in a decree issued by the confederation of the Epirotes recognising the Games and the *asylia* of the sanctuary of Artemis Leukophryene at Magnesia on the Meander in Asia Minor.[15] In the traditional manner the decree sets out the invitation of the people of Magnesia and tells of the organisation of the Games, the oracle at Delphi, the account of the goddess's appearance, the good relations between the people of Magnesia and the Epirotes:

> Considering that the people of Magnesia on the Meander who have
> friendly and special relations with the Epirotes, have sent a decree and the
> delegates Arstodamos, son of Diokes, Aristeus, son of Gorgasos, and Antanor,
> son of Kolotion, to renew these ties and invite the Epirotes to accept the
> Games[16] which the city of Magnesia hold every four years in honour of
> Artemis Leukophryene, Games with music, gymnastics, and horse events, on a
> par with the Pythian Games on account of its honours that conform to the
> divine oracles at Delphi; considering too that the delegates have made it
> known that according to the oracle it would be preferable to advantage and
> to honour Apollo Pythian and Artemis Leukophryene and declare the city
> and lands of Magnesia sacred; and considering that they have also reported the
> appearance of the goddess and the help and benefits the people of Magnesia

11 Pindar, *Nemean Odes*, in *Odes* (trans. D. Svarlien), Perseus Project, Yale, 1991, III, 70.

12 Pausanias, *Description of Greece* (trans. W. H. S. Jones and H. A. Ormerod), Loeb Classical Library, Harvard University Press, Cambridge, MA, 1988, II, 31, 6.

13 Herodotus, *Histories* (trans. A. D. Godley), Loeb Classical Library, Harvard University Press, Cambridge, MA, 1920, I, 59.

14 Thucydides, *History of the Peloponnesian War* (trans. C. F. Smith), Loeb Classical Library, Harvard University Press, Cambridge, MA, 1930, V, 18, 2.

15 O. Kern, *Inschriften von Magnesia*, 32. Reproduced, with translation and commentary by J. Pouilloux, *Choix d'inscriptions grecques*, p. 84-88, 22.

16 Translated as "competition" ("concours") by J. Pouilloux.

have brought to the Greeks; and considering that they asked and begged the Epirotes to accept and to help increase the honours offered to the goddess and that by acting like this they will be both honouring the oracle and showing friendship to the people, may it please the Epirotes to renew the special bond of friendship with the people of Magnesia and accept the Games in honour of Artemis Leukophyrene, in which a crown will be awarded and which will be equal in terms of honours to the Pythian Games, and may they consider the city and lands of Magnesia as sacred and untouchable. They will have more *theôrodokoi* to welcome the *theôroi* whenever they come from Magnesia and announce the sacrifice to be made for the Games; they will, for their part, send *theôroi* to share in the sacrifices and increase the honours to the goddess; they will show to the people of Magnesia with whom there are such close ties of friendship the recognised rights of the *proxenoi* of the Epirotes; so that these decisions are always known they will transcribe the decree to Dodon in the sanctuary of Zeus Naos on a base that is an offering of the Athenians and they will make sure that it goes to the strategist Crison and his colleagues; they will ask Charopidas, the secretary of the council who is taking office to pay all expenses. Moreover, they will praise the delegates Aristodamos, Aristeus, and Antanor because they have come and stayed in a way that is worthy of Magnesia and the Epirotes. For this reason they will make them and their descendants *proxenes* forever and grant them citizens' rights as well and protection along side the Epirotes in times of war or peace. They will be exempt from taxes and have all the rights and advantages enjoyed by the Epirotes. Charopidas, the secretary of the council will give them the same amount of money as is given to those who announce the Pythian Games, an amount fixed by law.

The people of Kassope agreed the same terms.

Such a document as this shows how, thanks to the Games, people at the opposite ends of the Greek world could confidently join with one another. The region of Epirus is to the northeast of mainland Greece, Magnesia on the Meander is a town to the south of Ephesia on the right bank of the lower Meander. Under the protection of Delphi that gave Magnesia the right to hold the "Isopythian" Games, in other words, equal to the Pythian Games, and with the approval of Kassope, a town in the south of Epirus, the Epirotes gave the people of Magnesia substantial privileges: protection afforded by the town and region, a welcome by those prepared to receive the *theores* from Magnesia, and the granting of the status of *proxenes* to their envoys, and citizens' rights and protection. The agreement between the god of Delphi and Artemis Leukophryene is made official by the transcription of the Epirotes' decree in the great sanctuary of Zeus at Dodone. This document shows us how a local festivity became a panhellenic one. The same happened earlier for the Panathenaea, the festival of the "mysteries" observed in Eleusis and the Asklepieion of Epidaurus, as well as for other local festivities at that time.

In certain cases the *theôroi* would move around, often over great distances in a procession. The religious enthusiasm was increased by the presence of local dignitaries – principal and ordinary magistrates, people with religious responsibilities, representatives of the people, tribes or noble families, beautiful young men, Dionysian artists and horsemen who would lead the procession. Thanks to the inscriptions, for

The archaeological site at Olympia.
© Yann Arthus-Bertrand / CORBIS

Decrees bestowing *promanteia* (the right to consult the oracle at Delphi).
© André Bernand

the most part on a wall of the sanctuary at Delphi, we know the composition of the *theôroi* sent by the Athenians to Delphi to celebrate Pythian Apollo and the Games in his honour at the end of the 2nd century BC.[17] A certain number of decrees issued by the people of Delphi supporting a person or group of persons from Athens allow us to imagine what the atmosphere of this festivity was like and what form it took. It was called the *Pythiad* and those taking part the *Pythiasts*. According to G. Colin, they had a more active role than the *theôroi* who were there chiefly as spectators. The *theôriai* coincided with periods of magistrature. The nine chief magistrates, the highest ranking of the city, were at the head of the *theôria* and the Games were named after the most important one among them. The herald of the Areopagus, a high-ranking civil servant, went with them. In Roman times, he would become more important because he modified the decisions taken by the popular assemblies.

Important epigraphic documents contain lists of the *thearodokoi* as they were called at Delphi or *theôrodokoi* elsewhere. These lists reveal the proper names of the countries and of certain cities that we cannot situate precisely. Onomastics and historical geography are both enriched by these documents, which also allow us to

---

17 The text of these inscriptions is taken from G. Colin, *Le culte d'Apollon Pythien à Athènes*, BEFAR, Paris, 1905.

see how far afield Games took place. In the sanctuary at Delphi, there are several lists, a fragment of one from the end of the 5th century BC, another, much more extensive, from the late 3rd century BC, and other fragments from the following century.

Far from benefiting from advantages, the *theôrodokoi* had an expensive duty since the *theôroi* had to be received appropriately and in keeping with Greek hospitality. Brothers and sisters would share this obligation. From the lists at Delphi published by André Plassart[18] we can identify the brothers who undertook this duty: three at Aigion, three and their sister at Kynaitha, two at Sicyon, three at Kallistai, two at Kleitos, and three at Telpousa. Plassart observes that in this list, 95 examples show two or more *theôrodokoi* as opposed to double that number when the *theôrodokia* was the responsibility of a single person. There were also women: the daughter and sister of Nikomedes were involved at Kos; at Kynaitha we find Aristomena, daughter of Pelopidas with her three brothers (unless it is a widow with her three sons); at Opous a woman's name, Kleito, can be read after that of Antendros Agemonos. Other lists exist, such as the one at Epidauros[19] or the one containing the names of the *theôrodokoi* in Argos published by P. Charnaux.[20]

Thanks to the Delphic list we can follow the route taken by the *theôria* sent to Ionia. First it went to the Euboea (Chalcis, Eretria, Karystos), then to Andros, Keos (Koresia, Ioulis), Kos, the coast of Caria by way of Halicarnassus, Bargylia, and Iasos. Before listing the towns of the inner Caria, there is Cnidos to the south of the Ceramic Gulf and the towns on the edge of the Lycean lands, Kaunos, and Kalyndos. After that comes Kallipolis to the northeast of the Ceramic Gulf and then in order from south to north after Theangela, east of Halicarnassus, come Mylasa, Stratonikeia, and Antioch.

As far as the *theôroi* sent into the Peloponnese are concerned, Plassart shows that according to the list of the *theôrodokoi* at Delphi, they marched from north to south by way of western Arcadia,[21] visiting Kynaitha, Kleitos, Paia, Telpousa, and Heraia, from there they went to Lepreion in Triphylia, and Phialeia (or Phigalia in Arcadia), and Doureon in Messenia. Before Kyparrisia, a western harbour of Messenia, are Phrixa to the south of the Alpheius and Samikon on the coast of Triphylia but according to Plassart these have been mislocated. This sort of thing happens because these lists have constantly been updated and altered. Sometimes there are blank spaces, sometimes names are added in the margins so the route is not always clear. Moreover, given the condition of the stone, they are not always easy to decipher. To welcome the heralds from Delphi, coming to announce the *Pythia* and the *Sôtéria* Games at Athens was expensive, but it was also an honour. That is why the people of Delphi granted privileges to the *thearodokoi*, and some of the decrees describing these have been preserved. Other benefactors are simply *proxenoi*. Copying these texts is a monotonous business because they always list the piety of the beneficiaries and their devotion to Delphi. The privileges awarded are always the same: *proxenia* (the right to welcome foreign visitors and act as an ambassador), *promanteia* (to consult the oracle

18 A. Plassart, "Inscriptions de Delphes : la liste des théorodoques", in *Bulletin de Correspondance Hellénique*, (1921) 45, pp. 1-85.

19 *Inscriptiones Graecae* (*IG*) IV, 1504. Study by G. de Sanctis, « I thearodokoi d'Epidavro alla meta del IV sec. av. Cr. » in *Atti della R. Acc. di Torino*, (1911-1912), 47, pp. 290-8.

20 P. Charnaux, "Liste argienne des théarodoques", in *Bulletin de Correspondance Hellénique*, 90 (1966): 156-239.

21 Plassard is referring to the map fig. 8, in *IG* V 2.

at Delphi), *asylia* (immunity), *prodikia* (priority in disputes), *ateleia* (exemption from taxes), and *proedria* (the right to sit in the first row of the assembly) and it is generally made quite clear that the descendants of the beneficiaries will continue to receive them. These texts are so repetitive that we need only quote two of them.

One of them concerns Thrasykles, the *hieromnémôn* (keeper of the sacred archives) invited to Delphi to join the jury for the Pythian Games. He won a crown in a competition for new tragedies and, on return to Athens, paid tribute to the people of Delphi by giving them the crown he had won.

> During the magistrature of Architimos at Athens to Thrasykles, keeper of the archives, son of Archikles, an Athenian from the area of Lachiades. Considering that Thrasykles, son of Archikles, keeper of the archives, residing in a proper manner in our city, has accomplished sacrifices in the name of the Athenian people according to our ancient customs, and was a pious and fair judge at the Pythian Games and is devoted to us, and considering that having won the competition for new tragedies, he has given his crown to our people, hail to the god of fortune: may it please the city of Delphi to pay tribute to Thrasykles, son of Archikles and to decree to him and to his descendants *proxenia, promanteia, asylia, prodikia*, exemptions from taxes, *proedria* in all the Games Delphi organises, and all the benefits awarded to other *proxenoi* and benefactors of our city. And may this decree be inscribed in the sanctuary of Apollo.
>
> In the magistrature of Antigenes, son of Archias, in the month of Heracles, at the council of Philleas, son of Damenes, and Athanion, son of Kleoxenidas.

Another decree (number 66) records other quite special circumstances. It is about one Apollodoros who acted judge in a trial involving certain sanctuaries and some land over which there was a dispute. Having satisfactorily carried out his duties, the Athenian deputy was awarded not only the usual privileges over and above the *proxenia*, but the honour of receiving the heralds who would come from Delphi to announce to the Athenians the Games known as *Pythia* and *Sôtéria*.

> Hail to the god of fortune! The full assembly of the city's delegates is pleased. Considering that Apollodoros, son of Olympiodoros, and Athenian having been designated as a member of the *theôria* sent by our city has fully made the case for our city in the trial concerning the sanctuaries and the contested land. He has shown his deep piety and his devotion to our city and coming to our help he settled this dispute sparing nothing of his zeal and friendship. His stay with us was correct and he demonstrated his preference for our city much to the appreciation of our magistrates.
>
> Hail to the god of fortune! Considering all this, may it please us officially to praise Apollodoros, son of Olympiodoros, the Athenian for his devotion and his zeal towards us and invite him to have the same feelings for us in the future in the knowledge that we know how to demonstrate our gratitude towards our friends and benefactors by giving him and his descendants *proxenia, promanteia, asylia, prodikia, ateleia*, and *proedria* in all the Games organised by our city. He will have the right to acquire land and a house and have all the privileges accorded to other *proxenoi* and benefactors of our city.

Roman marble statue of Heracles, in the style of the Polyclitus school. Sculptor unknown; 125 AD. © The J. Paul Getty Museum (inv. 70.AA.109). Gift of J. Paul Getty

It pleases us to make him the *theôrodokos* of those sent to announce the *Pythian* and *Sôtérian* Games, to give him hospitality, and have the magistrates watch over his return so that he will be under a good escort, and may the secretary, according to our law, to register the *proxenoi* in the council chamber and inscribe the decree on the wall of the building of the Athenians.

Other people had a role to play in the gathering of Greeks at the time of the Games in all cities. These people were the *proxenes*.

Official hosts

The citizens of a Greek city who were delegated by another Greek city to look after the interests of its people when they arrived in their town were called the *proxenoi*. They were named by a decree issued by the towns who gave them the responsibility of welcoming the citizens who came from friendly cities, lodging them, and assisting them in matters to do with law, politics, or finance. The *proxenia* was a responsibility but also an honour and a way in which the person who provided hospitality could receive privileges from the city of the person he was welcoming. The *proxenos* was obliged to welcome into his home delegations from the city that had honoured him, but had to take care of them during their stay. We have seen the privileges awarded to the citizens of Magnesia on the Meander by the Epirotes.

Proxenoi have frequently been compared to modern day consuls; in Rome, under the Republic, their title designated the two magistrates who had the highest authority. Under the Roman Empire the posts of these consuls were only honorific.

Nowadays, consuls are simply diplomats charged by a government to defend the interests of its people in a foreign country and to carry out various administrative tasks. In antiquity, the *proxenia* was much more complex. It commits the one who is honoured by it to an alliance and to friendly relations that are truly profound, especially since they involve religion – as is the case for the *theôroi* – since the arrangements are sanctioned by the gods.

From the time of Homer until the time when Greece was divided into different regions, the notion of hospitality had different meanings, but we should not forget that the *xenia* was overseen by Zeus Xenios (protector of foreigners) nor that the *proxenia* contained within it some of the features of the *xenia*.[22] As P. Gauthier has written in his excellent study:[23]

> The *proxenia* inherited the usual, daily functions of the *xenia* in the city. We know that beyond anything demanded by the ties between two cities, the *proxenos* is the citizen who looks after those arriving from a foreign city in the way the *xenos* has duties towards an individual or a foreign family. Reciprocity is assured by important honours awarded to the *proxenos* when he has

---

22 P. Gauthier, an historian specialising in the study of institutions, has devoted much time to the proxeny, first in "Symbola : les étrangers et la justice dans les cités grecques", in *Annales de l'Est* (II, 42), Université de Nancy, Nancy, 1972, then in *Les cités grecques et leurs bienfaiteurs*, École française d'Athènes, Athènes, 1985, pp. 129-49. He provides a rich bibliography, particularly quoting from P. Monceaux, *Les proxénies grecques* (1986); H. Francotte, *Mélanges de droit public grec* (1910); Busolt-Swoboda, *Gr. Staatskunde*, 1926, II; G. Klaffenbach, *Gr. Epigraphik*, 1966, 2; and also many observations by Louis Robert.

23 P. Gauthier, "Symbola : les étrangers et la justice dans les cités grecques", *op. cit.*, pp. 24-5.

occasion to stop in the city that has chosen him. Thus, it is quite legitimate to speak of "public hosts" when talking of the *proxenoi*: they take in foreigners who are passing through, they help them materially as far as they are able; thanks to their position within the city and to their status as citizens they protect them by deed and in law. In fact, in his city, the *proxenos* is an ordinary person who acts for his own reasons without mandate or official privilege (this is one of the reasons why a comparison with modern consuls does not work). It is only in the foreign city that he benefits from honours and a privileged position. Therefore, a good *proxenos* must be rich and have influence (just as the ties of *xenia* were of interest above all to the aristocracy, so the *proxenoi* in the 5th and 6th centuries often belonged to aristocratic families). Since he has no legal power attached to a function that would be official in his own city, the *proxenos* is only worth what his fortune, influence, and prestige are worth.

There are many ways of understanding the privileges enjoyed by the *proxenoi*. The essay *Proxenie und Evergesie* by Adolf Wilhem[24] is essential reading. The analyses of P. Gauthier[25] are detailed and subtle. It is useful to refer to the Delphic inscriptions dealing with the *proxenoi*[26] to understand the privileges awarded to them. (Unfortunately, as is usual in the publication where these essays have appeared, these texts have not been translated.) These included *promanteia*, *proedria*, *prodikia*, *asylia*, *ateleia*, *empasis* or *ekthesis tés kai oikias* (the right to acquire land and lodging). The texts often indicate clearly that these privileges are awarded "in the same way and under the same conditions as they are to other benefactors." All of these privileges encourage the *proxenes* in their tasks and promote mutual aid and friendship between cities.

The transformation of local games into panhellenic Games (they were called "sacred") created a network of tight relations of reciprocal friendship throughout the country, which, in a Greece that was often plagued by wars abroad or at home, made life happier for the population as a whole. For a little while, though the time was short and threats still present, people could live in peace thanks to the promotion of local games to the level of "Stephanite" Games (in which the rewards were not of silver but a simple crown) that people wanted to become Isolympic (equal in honour to the Olympic Games), Isopythian, etc. According to Louis Robert:[27]

> From the second half of the 3rd and even more so in the 2nd century, cities
> that celebrated Games in this way were not rare: Asklepieia in Kos, Didymeia
> in Miletus, Heliaia in Rhodes, Eleutheria in the Thessalanian Confederation,
> and Leukophryene in Magnesia on the Meander. The description of these last
> Games carved on the walls of the public assembly rooms shows how the
> transformation came about. At first an oracle, then the agreement of the cities
> as well as of the kings who, solicited by the *theôroi*-ambassadors, sent *theôroi*
> acting as representatives to offer sacrifices in the name of the town. At Cos we

24   A. Wilhem, "Proxenie und Evergesie", in *Att. Urkunden*, (1942), V, pp. 11-86, is excellent.

25   P. Gauthier, *Les cités grecques et leurs bienfaiteurs, op. cit.*, see index entry for "Proxénies".

26   J. Pouilloux, *Fouilles de Delphes*, vol. III, Epigraphie, fasc. IV, Paris, 1930-70: *Les inscriptions de la terrasse du temple et de la région nord du sanctuaire*, 373-450.

27   *Acts of the Eighth International Congress of Greek and Latin Epigraphy, Athens, 3-9 October 1982*, Athens, 1984, p. 36.

have the replies received from cities in Sicily and from greater Greece, including Macedonia and Thrace and from the kings of Bithynia and the Cimmerian Bosphorus.

These Games grew in number during the Hellenistic period and again later during the Roman period. L. Robert refers to the *Pythia* of Sicyon, the *Asklepieia* of Epidaurus, the *Poseidaia* in Mantinea, the *Aleaia* in Alea Athena at Tegea, the *Hemerasia* of Artemis at Lousoi, the *Koriasia* of Artemis in Cleitor, the *Lykaia* of Zeus Lykaios on the mountain of Lycea, the *Chtoneia* of Demeter at Hermione. All of these festivities and many others attached to certain cities were places where Greeks could come together regularly to show their skill before the gods and their compatriots. There was no better way to increase a sense of pride in being Greek and to develop a unique culture.

Chapter IV
Training the body, enriching the mind

The festivities bringing all Greeks together had two objectives: to train the body and to enrich the mind.[1] The pleasures afforded by the dual exercise of mind and body aimed at producing a holistic culture whose richness is difficult to imagine today.[2]

In Lucian's *Anacharsis, or Athletics*[3], Solon gives a long explanation of this dual training that the Greeks enjoyed:

> Then you must first let me tell you briefly what our ideas are about a city and its citizens. We consider that a city is not the buildings, such as walls and temples and docks. These constitute a firm-set, immovable body, so to speak, for the shelter and protection of the community, but the whole significance is in the citizens, we hold, for it is they who fill it, plan and carry out everything, and keep it safe; they are something like what the soul is within the individual. So, having noted this, we naturally take care of the city's body, as you see, beautifying it so that it may be as fair as possible, not only well furnished inside with buildings but most securely fenced with these external ramparts. But above all and at all hazards we endeavour to insure that the citizens shall be virtuous in soul and strong in body, thinking that such men, joined together in public life, will make good use of themselves in times of peace, will bring the city safe out of war, and will keep it always free and prosperous.
>
> Their early upbringing we entrust to mothers, nurses, and tutors, to train and rear them with liberal teachings; but when at length they become able to understand what is right, when modesty, shame, fear, and ambition spring up in them, and when at length their very bodies seem well fitted for hardships as they get firmer and become more strongly compacted, then we take them in hand and teach them, not only prescribing them certain disciplines and exercises for the soul, but in certain other ways habituating their bodies also to hardships. We have not thought it sufficient for each man to be as he was born, either in body or in soul, but we want education and disciplines for them by which their good traits may be much improved and their bad altered for the better. We take example from the farmers, who shelter and enclose their plants while they are small and young, so that they may not be injured by the breezes: but when the stalk at last begins to thicken, they prune away the excessive growth and expose them to the winds to be shaken and tossed, in that way making them more fruitful.
>
> Their souls we fan into flame with music and arithmetic at first and we

---

1   See the bibliography given by H. I. Marrou, *A History of Education in Antiquity* (trans. George Lamb), Sheed and Ward, New York/London, 1956, pp. 353-8.

2   The teachers also aimed to instil a respect for morality and justice.

3   Lucian, *Anacharsis or Athletics* (trans. A. M. Harmon), Loeb Classical Library, Harvard University Press, Cambridge, MA, 1925, 20-21.

teach them to write their letters and to read them trippingly. As they progress, we recite for them sayings of wise men, deeds of olden times, and helpful fictions, which we have adorned with metre that they may remember them better. Hearing of certain feats of arms and famous exploits, little by little they grow covetous and are incited to imitate them, in order that they too may be sung and admired by men of after time. Both Hesiod and Homer have composed much poetry of that sort for us.

When they enter political life and have at length to handle public affairs — but this, no doubt, is foreign to the case, as the subject proposed for discussion at the outset was not how we discipline their souls, but why we think fit to train their bodies with hardships like these.

Lucian's long account gives us a better understanding of how the Games were organised; some were physical or involved horses, others were musical and their organisation was based on the dual education that citizens had to undergo. As Juvenal[4] would say in the 2nd century, "Our prayers should be for a sound mind in a healthy body".

The philosophers' counsel

Greek Philosophers before Lucian were preoccupied with this dual system of education for young people. Plato is quite clear about it, though Aristotle, who was often inclined to correct his master, had some reservations.

In *Protagoras*[5] the Sophist defines the kind of education young people should receive. After having reminded us that in his early years the notion of good and bad are taught to the child by his nurse, mother, tutor, and father, Protagoras defines the dual training that will make a good citizen of him. The master watches over the good behaviour of his pupil who then undergoes a dual education:

[…] the children, when they have learnt their letters and are getting to understand the written word as before they did only the spoken, are furnished with works of good poets to read as they sit in class, and are made to learn them off by heart: here they meet with many admonitions, many descriptions and praises and eulogies of good men in times past, that the boy in envy may imitate them and yearn to become even as they. Then also the music-masters, in a similar sort, take pains for their self-restraint, and see that their young charges do not go wrong: moreover, when they learn to play the harp, they are taught the works of another set of good poets, the song-makers, and they insist on familiarizing the boys' souls with the rhythms and scales, that they may gain in gentleness, and by advancing in rhythmic and harmonic grace may be efficient in speech and action; for the whole of man's life requires the graces of rhythm and harmony. Again, over and above all this, people send their sons to a trainer, that having improved their bodies they may perform the orders of their minds, which are now in fit condition, and that they may

---

4   Juvenal, "Satires", in *Juvenal and Persius*, (trans. G. G. Ramsay), Harvard University Press, Cambridge, MA, 1969, X, 356 : "*Orandum est ut sit mens sana in corpore sano*".

5   Plato, *Protagoras* (trans. W. R. M. Lamb), Loeb Classical Library, Harvard University Press, Cambridge, MA, 1924, 325-6.

not be forced by bodily faults to play the coward in wars and other duties. This is what people do, who are most able; and the most able are the wealthiest. Their sons begin school at the earliest age, and are freed from it at the latest.

Another Sophist, Hippias, who boasted that he knew everything, took advantage of the Olympic Games to sell his knowledge to anyone who was interested:[6] "I always go up to Olympia to the festival of the Greeks from my home at Elis, and entering the sacred precinct, offer to speak on anything that anyone chooses of those subjects." It can be seen, therefore, that a sporting event could be accompanied by education on various subjects.

Plato often insisted that the young should be initiated to physical exercise and to music:[7]

> [The guardians of the Republic] are in training for the greatest contest of all [...] And will the habit of body of our ordinary athletes be suited to them? [...] a habit of body such as they have is but a sleepy sort of thing, and rather perilous to health. Do you not observe that these athletes sleep away their lives, and are liable to most dangerous illnesses if they depart, in ever so slight a degree, from their customary regimen?

Those who only go in for physical exercise without caring about music are excessively brutal, Plato concludes.[8]

> Those who do not interest themselves in music become excessively brutal... and yet this brutality is natural enough and if it is well controlled, it is transformed into courage, but if not it ends up naturally by becoming an inflexible harshness.

Plato came back on a number of occasions to the need to ally physical exercise and music. In *The Republic* he declares,[9] "After music, it is through physical exercise that young people should be formed. It should be practised carefully, from childhood and throughout life".

But, he goes on:[10]

> I am quite aware that the mere athlete becomes too much of a savage, [...] if he do nothing else, and holds no converse with the Muses, does not even use that intelligence which there may be in him, having no taste of any sort of learning or enquiry or thought or culture, grow feeble and dull and blind, his mind never waking up or receiving nourishment, and his senses not being purged of their mists? [...] And he who mingles music with gymnastic in the

---

6   Plato, *Lesser Hippias* (trans. H. N. Fowler), Loeb Classical Library, Harvard University Press, Cambridge, MA, 1969, 363.

7   Plato, *The Republic* (trans. Benjamin Jowett), Prometheus Books, New York, 1986, III,403-4.

8   *Ibid.*, III, 403.

9   *Ibid.*, III, 410-2.

10 *Ibid.*, III, 410.

fairest proportions, and best attempers them to the soul, may be rightly called the true musician and harmonist in a far higher sense than the tuner of the strings. [...] And as there are two principles of human nature, one the spirited and the other the philosophical, some God, as I should say, has given mankind two arts answering to them (and only indirectly to the soul and body), in order that these two principles (like the strings of an instrument) may be relaxed or drawn tighter until they are duly harmonised.

Aristotle will also reflect on the parts played by physical exercise and music in education[11] recommending there should be a happy balance between these disciplines. For him, music is the source of happiness:[12]

Our first inquiry is whether music ought not or ought to be included in education, and what is its efficacy among the three uses of it that have been discussed – does it serve for education or amusement or entertainment? It is reasonable to reckon it under all of these heads, and it appears to participate in them all. Amusement is for the sake of relaxation, and relaxation must necessarily be pleasant, for it is a way of curing the pain due to laborious work; also entertainment ought admittedly to be not only honourable but also pleasant, for happiness is derived from both honour and pleasure; but we all pronounce music to be one of the pleasantest things, whether instrumental or instrumental and vocal music together (at least Musaeus says, "Song is man's sweetest joy," and that is why people with good reason introduce it at parties and entertainments, for its exhilarating effect).

As far as physical exercises are concerned, Aristotle warns against excessive training, remarking that, "the Lacedemonians end up by making brutes with their exhausting exercises". But he recognises that physical exercise is good for children to whom it gives a balanced body. Up to puberty they should be trained in such a way that this is achieved. Aristotle is much more reticent than Socrates about the benefits of physical education. In fact, if Xenophon is to believed:[13]

On noticing that Epigenes, one of his companions, was in poor condition, for a young man, he said: "You look as if you need exercise, Epigenes."

"Well," he replied, "I'm not an athlete, Socrates."

"Just as much as the competitors entered for Olympia," he retorted. "Or do you count the life and death struggle with their enemies, upon which, it may be, the Athenians will enter, but a small thing? Why, many, thanks to their bad condition, lose their life in the perils of war or save it disgracefully: many, just for this same cause, are taken prisoners, and then either pass the rest of their days, perhaps, in slavery of the hardest kind, or, after meeting with cruel

11 Aristotle, *Politics* (trans. B. Jowett), Dover Publications, New York, 2000, VIII 4, 8-9 (on gymnastics) and VIII 5, 9-11 (on music). Aristotle's idea's about education are discussed in A. Hourdakis, *Aristote et l'éducation*, Presses universitaires de France, Paris, 1998.

12 Aristotle, *Politics, op. cit.*, VIII, 5, 9-11.

13 Xenophon, *Memorabilia* (trans. E. C. Marchant and O. J. Todd), Loeb Classical Library, Harvard University Press, Cambridge, MA, 1923, III 12, 1-4.

Music and sport: three naked young athletes train to the accompaniment of a flute played by a musician wearing a long tunic. Red-figure vase from the Department of Classical and Near Eastern Antiquities in the National Museum of Denmark (Chr VIII 805).
© National Museum of Denmark

sufferings and paying, sometimes, more than they have, live on, destitute and in misery. Many, again, by their bodily weakness earn infamy, being thought cowards. Or do you despise these, the rewards of bad condition, and think that you can easily endure such things? And yet I suppose that what has to be bourne by anyone who takes care to keep his body in good condition, is far lighter and far pleasanter than these things. Or is it that you think bad condition, healthier and generally more serviceable than good, or do you despise the effects of good condition? And yet the results of physical fitness are the direct opposite of those that follow from unfitness. The fit are healthy and strong; and many, as a consequence, save themselves decorously on the battle-field and escape all the dangers of war; many help friends and do good to their country and for this cause earn gratitude; get great glory and gain very high honours, and for this cause live henceforth a pleasanter and better life, and leave to their children better means of winning a livelihood.

Paideia: the complete man

Those responsible for education agree then that physical training and spiritual reflection should complement one another. The *paideia* does not justify the reputation of savagery and brutality that some have given to the Olympic ideal. The debate is

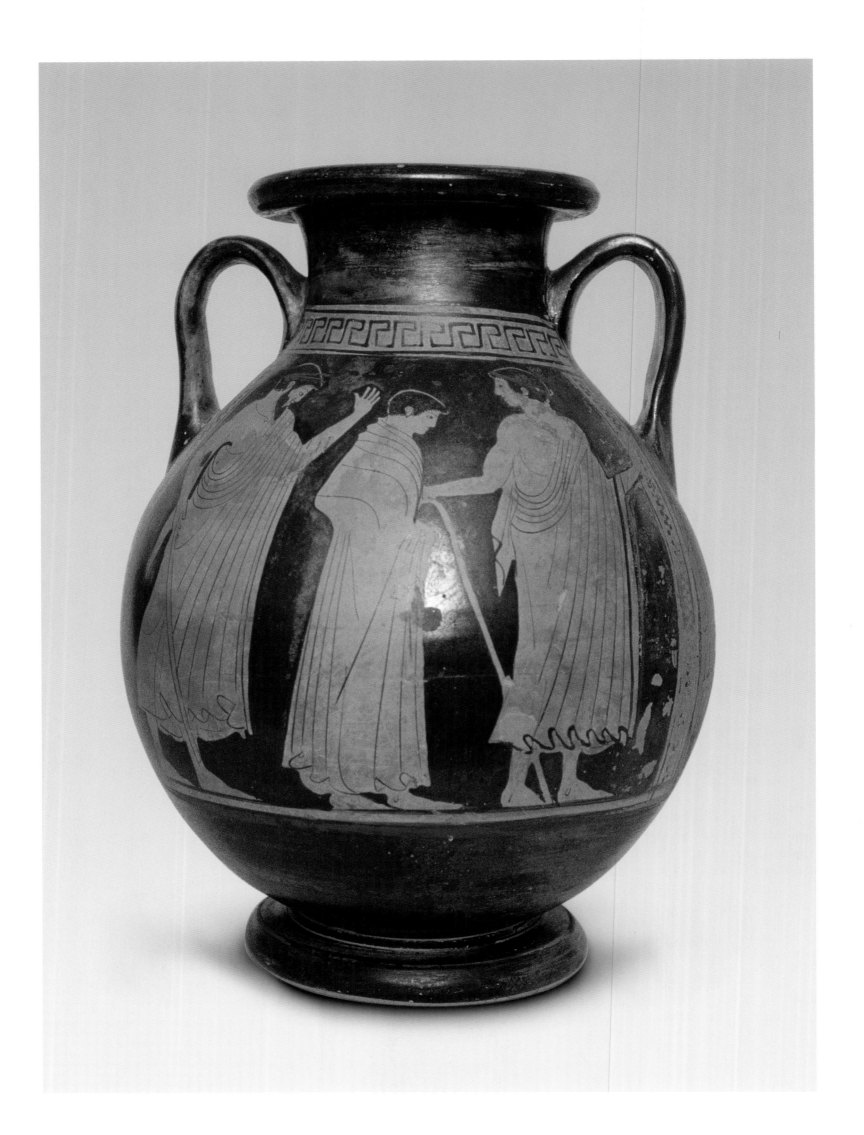

not new, since a care to temper physical strength by reflection is one of the lessons Isocrates gave to Demonikos:[14]

> you must consider that no athlete is so in duty bound to train against his competitors as are you to take thought how you may vie with your father in his ways of life. But it is not possible for the mind to be so disposed unless one is fraught with many noble maxims; for, as it is the nature of the body to be developed by appropriate exercises, it is the nature of the soul to be developed by moral precepts.
>
> Give careful heed to all that concerns your life, but above all train your own intellect; for the greatest thing in the smallest compass is a sound mind in a human body. Strive with your body to be a lover of toil, and with your soul to be a lover of wisdom, in order that with the one you may have the strength to carry out your resolves, and with the other the intelligence to foresee what is for your good.

This wise advice allows us to understand that the Greeks would not have been happy at the Games to see brutes full of hate unleashed against one another. Like music, morality had to restrain the abuses of strength. This lesson had famous guarantors. Pericles, in his funeral oration, for example, condemned the excesses of Spartan education and praised the reflection and moderation of the Athenians:[15]

> And again, in the matter of education, whereas they from early childhood by a laborious discipline make pursuit of manly courage, we with our unrestricted mode of life are nonetheless ready to meet any equality of hazard.

The Attic orators emphasised the originality of the *paideia*, which brought together mind and body. In his speech, *Panegyricus* celebrating the merits of Athens, Isocrates states:[16]

> Besides, it is possible to find with us as nowhere else the most faithful friendships and to enjoy the most varied social intercourse; and, furthermore, to see contests not alone of speed and strength, but of eloquence and wisdom and of all the other arts — and for these the greatest prizes.

According to him, the fact that these festivities continued in Athens shows how superior this city was to others. These regular meetings brought people together and helped diffuse the values of Greek culture. He gives a fine definition of universal hedonism that was revolutionary for its time:[17]

> And so far has our city distanced the rest of mankind in thought and in

---

14 Isocrates, *To Demonicus* (trans. G. Norlin), Harvard University Press, Cambridge, MA, 1969, 12 and 40.

15 Thucydides, *History of the Peloponnesian War* (trans. C. F. Smith), Loeb Classical Library, Harvard University Press, Cambridge, MA, 1930, II, 39, 1.

16 Isocrates, *Panegyricus* (trans. G. Norlin), Harvard University Press, Cambridge, MA, 1969, IV, 45.

17 *Ibid.*, IV, 50.

Red-figure *pelikos* from Corinth, circa 470 BC. The bearded man leans on a stick, gesturing with his left hand. The child is enveloped in a cloak up to his neck.

© National Archaeological Museum of Athens

speech that her pupils have become the teachers of the rest of the world; and she has brought it about that the name Hellenes suggests no longer a race but an intelligence, and that the title Hellenes is applied rather to those who share our culture than to those who share a common blood.

This idea recalls the words Thucydides gave to Pericles:[18]

> In a word, then, I say that our city as a whole is the school of Hellas, and that, as it seems to me, each individual amongst us could in his own person, with the utmost grace and versatility, prove himself self-sufficient in the most varied forms of activity.

The many Games at Athens maintained an atmosphere of joy that contrasted with the anguish too often caused by war. According to Thucydides, Pericles emphasises this:[19]

> Moreover, we have provided for the spirit many relaxations from toil: we enjoy games and sacrifices regularly throughout the year, and homes fitted out with good taste and elegance; and the delight we each day find in these things drives away sadness.

There is no better way of saying that the Games took place in Athens in a climate of happiness, joy, and relaxation. According to Thucydides, these festivities ensured that local people would look after their dwellings with taste and bring to Athens riches from all over the world. The gods could rejoice but men also found profit in them.

The culture of the gymnasium

The dual nature of Greek culture, which was both the formation of the body and the development of the mind, is best seen in the role played by the gymnasium. Only the privileged could frequent this institution – sons of citizens on the local register, who had originally formed part of the old landed aristocracy who enjoyed such pastimes as befitted free men. Certainly, these institutions gradually became more democratic, but they always denied access to those who earned little – peasants, artisans, and shopkeepers. What is more, women were excluded. It is certain that the education provided by the gymnasium was only for an elite.

Gradually, the gymnasium became a place not only of physical exercise, but a centre of artistic expression and debate. The most ancient ones known were at Athens, the Academy and the Lyceum, whose foundation is attributed to Pisistratus and his sons. It is here that young people prepared themselves to enter into competitions and become champions. The setting of the gymnasium was pleasant and welcoming and training took place in gardens replete with trees and flowing water. It is difficult to imagine this delightful countryside today, where Phaedrus and Socrates conversed together at the foot of the Ardettos hill, by the small River Ilisos, listening to the singing of the cicadas.

---

18 Thucydides, *op. cit.*, II, 41.
19 *Ibid.*, II, 38.

One of the baths in the changing rooms of the Palaestra at Olympia.
© Sonia Halliday Photographs

It is the height of summer, the river is almost entirely dry and it will soon be midday. Phaedrus, barefoot, is enjoying himself walking in the trickle of water. A tall plane tree provides shade, there is a gentle breeze, and some grass to sit on. Socrates is enchanted with the place: [20]

> Ah! By Hera, this is a marvellous place to stop! This plane tree covers as
> much area as it is high. And how tall and magnificently shady is this wild
> pepper. Given that everything is in flower, this place could hardly be more
> fragrant. And again, the unparalleled charm of this spring that flows beneath
> the plane tree and the freshness of its water. I must put my foot in it to
> believe it! If I judge by these small figures and these statues of gods this spring
> is no doubt consecrated to the nymphs, and in particular to Achelous. And
> what is more, is not the atmosphere enviable and hugely pleasant? This is a
> clear song of summer, echoing the chorus of the cicadas! But what is most
> exquisite about it is the turf, which is so naturally soft that it is possible to

---

20 Plato, *Phaedrus* (trans. H. N. Fowler), Loeb Classical Library, Harvard University Press, Cambridge, MA, 1980,
    229-30.

The Stoa of Attalus, Athens.
© André Bernand

have one's head perfectly at ease when lying down. I can see that a foreigner can have no better guide than you, my dear Phaedrus.

The gymnasium, always situated in a rural area, had buildings for different purposes, which were laid out according to the topography of the sanctuary and the nature of the exercises. The events that the participants trained for together, like boxing, wrestling and physical exercises, took place in the palaestra, the word *palaestra* literally meaning "area for wrestling [or *palé*]".[21] Excavations have revealed many examples in Greece as well as in Asia Minor and epigraphic texts such as the inventories of Delos[22] which allow us to verify the descriptions given by Vitruvius (Marcus Vitruvius Pollio), a Roman architect of the 1st century BC.[23] H. I. Marrou has reproduced the plan of the palaestra at Priene and furnished us with a description of it.[24] We can see that the square sports ground, is surrounded by a number of rooms where the athletes could meet, undress, wash themselves, and apply the oil and sand necessary for the contests.

21 On the difference between the gymnasium and the palaestra, see J. Delorme, *Gymnasion : Études sur les monuments consacrés à l'éducation en Grèce*, De Boccard, Paris, 1960, pp. 253-71.

22 See *Bulletin de Correspondance Hellénique*, 1930, 54, pp. 97-8.

23 Vitruvius, *On Architecture* (trans. Frank Granger), Loeb Classical Library, Harvard University Press, Cambridge, MA, 1969, V, 11.

24 H. I. Marrou, *op. cit.*, pp. 128-30.

The palaestra of Olympia benefited from the fact that the river Kladeos was nearby. It was constructed at the end of the 3rd century BC and corresponds well to the specifications given by Vitruvius, who was perhaps inspired by this model. The *ephébeion* was the room where athletes could meet, the *loutron* was a bathroom, the *apodytérion* was the changing room, the *korukeion* was the boxing room, the *elaiothesion* was the oil shop, and the *konistérion* was the shop that stocked sand. At Delphi, the gymnasium built in the 4th century BC was on a terrace constructed near the edge of the Pleistos Gorge and the palaestra was on a lower terrace. While in many cities the gymnasium and the palaestra were near the stadium, at Delphi the stadium was on the slope above the theatre.

These establishments built for strengthening the body were also notable for their teaching and discussion, since the verbal contests were preparation for the "musical" Games. One of the privileged places for discussion was the portico, a covered terrace where one could walk about whilst holding conversations. To understand the real charm of these places it is necessary, after having been to the assembly room on a summer's day, to find a shaded and airy spot. The best example of this kind of building is the marble Stoa of Attalus in Athens. Plato has described the portico of a private house where the Sophist Protagoras would walk about, surrounded by his disciples. Not without irony, Plato describes his walk:[25]

> We came upon Protagoras as he was walking round in the cloister, and
> close behind him two companies were walking round also; on the one side
> Callias, son of Hipponicus and his brother on the mother's side, Paralus, son of
> Pericles and Charmides, son of Glaucon, while the other troop consisted of
> Pericles' other son Xanthippus, Philippides, son of Philomelus, and
> Antimoerus of Mende, who is the most highly reputed of Protagoras' disciples
> and is taking the course professionally with a view to becoming a sophist. The
> persons who followed in their rear, listening to what they could of the talk,
> seemed to be mostly strangers, brought by the great Protagoras from the
> several cities which he traverses, enchanting them with this voice like
> Orpheus, while they follow where the voice sounds, enchanted; and some
> of our own inhabitants were also dancing attendance. As for me, when I saw
> their evolutions I was delighted with the admirable care they took not to
> hinder Protagoras at any moment by getting in front; but whenever the
> master turned about and those with him, it was fine to see the orderly
> manner in which his train of listeners split up into two parties on this side
> and on that, and wheeling round formed up again each time in his rear
> most admirably.

Callias, the owner of the house, had other ways of retaining Protagoras' pupils and many of the Sophists who visited him there. He had turned a shop into a room for his guests, where beds were available. Plato tells us that whilst Prodicos buried himself under furs and blankets, near him a man with hotter blood, Pausanias, from the area of Kerameis, was lying down with "a young adolescent who was well-endowed, if I am not mistaken and, in any case, very beautiful. I believe I heard it said

---

25 Plato, *Protagoras, op. cit.,* 314-5.

that his name was Agathon and would not be surprised if he was not loved by Pausanias." It is not surprising that the "handsome Alcibiades" as Socrates called him should come wandering by here.

Lysias (circa 440–380 BC) recognised that recourse to intelligence as well as physical strength was a method of asserting the primacy of the Greeks over other populations. In his *Olympic Speech*[26] he recalls that Heracles, when he founded the Olympic Games, insisted on this ideal, at once physical and intellectual.

In addition to the Lyceum and the Academy, Athens had another gymnasium, the *Kynosarges* to which both Herodotus[27] and Demosthenes refer. Towards the end of the 3rd century BC, two more were added — those of Ptolemy and Diogenes — no doubt built in honour of private benefactors.[28] Both of these served not only for physical exercises but as a place where philosophers, rhetoricians, and sometimes even doctors and astronomers would teach.

The part played by the gymnasium in the Greek *paideia* could be seen in all countries whenever and wherever Greece dominated. During the Hellenistic period the number of gymnasia increased, even in countries where the civilisation was quite different. I am thinking in particular of Egypt, not only in Alexandria[29] but throughout the country.[30]

The Ancient Greeks' first concern was for education. In the word *paideia* we have *pais* meaning "child". What is important, then, is education of young people. But for the Greeks, man is always young. That is why the advice given by writers, philosophers, or politicians to adults anxious to perfect themselves by improving their physiques and sharpening their minds is full of freshness and spontaneity. Plotinus, who lived between 204–270 AD and originally came from Egypt, gives this piece of advice which can be taken in a moral or physical sense: "Never stop shaping your own statue."[31] In the palaestra of Taureas at Athens all the boys and young men, so Plato tells us, look at Charmides as though they were looking at a statue and, as Chairephon says to Socrates, it is not only the face but the body of the adolescent we must admire and then judge the beauty of his soul:[32]

> Chaerephon called me and said: What do you think of him, Socrates? Has he not a beautiful face?
> Most beautiful, I said.
> But you would think nothing of his face, he replied, if you could see his naked form: he is absolutely perfect. And to this they all agreed.
> By Heracles, I said, there never was such a paragon, if he has only one other slight addition.

26 Lysias, *Olympic Speech, op. cit.,* 1-6. See A. Bernand, *Leçon de Civilisation,* Fayard, Paris, 1994, p. 170.

27 Herodotus, *Histories* (trans. A. D. Godley), Loeb Classical Library, Harvard University Press, Cambridge, MA, 1920, V, 63.

28 G. Cambiano, "Devenir homme" in *L'Homme grec,* éditions du Seuil, Paris, 1993, pp. 130-1.

29 A. Bernand, *Alexandrie la Grande,* Hachette, Paris, 1996, pp. 103 and 160-4.

30 See the references given by A. Bernand under the index entry for *gymnasion,* in *La prose sur pierre dans l'Égypte hellénistique et romaine,* t. I, p. 185, which refer to the texts and translations given in that volume.

31 Plotinus, *Enneads* (trans. A. H. Armstrong), Loeb Classical Library, Harvard University Press, Cambridge, MA, 1969-1988, I, 6, 9.

32 Plato, *Charmides* (trans. W.R.M. Lamb), Loeb Classical Library, Harvard University Press, Cambridge, MA, 1955, 153.

Copy of the statue of Heracles (bronze) by Lysippus, dating from the Hellenistic period (330-20 BC). Housed in the Louvre, Paris.

What is that? said Critias.

If he has a noble soul; and being of your house, Critias, he may be
expected to have this.

This concern for both body and soul is at the heart of Greek culture. We would
be wrong to imagine that this text only contains a bawdy allusion. Rather, it is in the
agreeable formula of the anecdote that the dual concern of the *paideia* is defined. Thus
arises the ideal of the *kalokagathia* (the state of being both handsome and good): *kalos*
refers to physical beauty with an erotic connotation, *agathos* refers to the qualities of
the mind. Students at the gymnasium maintain that this is where these two qualities
were acquired. That is why Aristophanes in *Clouds* quotes the advice that Just Reason
gives to the young Pheidippides:[33]

> No, you'll be hale and glistening and pass your days in gymnasia, not in
> the agora chattering about the thorny subjects currently in vogue, or being
> dragged into court about some trifling, obstinatious, disputatious, ruinatious
> case. No, down to the Academy you shall go, and under the sacred olive trees
> you shall crown yourself with white reed and have a race with a decent boy
> your own age, fragrant with woodbine and carefree content, and the catkins
> flung by the popular tree, luxuriating in spring's hour, when the plane tree
> whispers to the elm.
>
> If you follow my recommendations, and keep them ever in mind, you will
> always have a rippling chest, radiant skin, broad shoulders, a wee tongue, a
> grand rump and a petite dick. But if you adopt current practices, you'll start
> by having a puny chest, pasty skin, narrow shoulders, a grand tongue, a wee
> rump and a lengthy edict.

In a recent book,[34] I wrote of the excessive preoccupation with sexual parts, as
illustrated by different texts and statues. Valerie Visa-Ondarçuhu, considering the issue
of small penises, wonders whether it is not "an allusion to sexual continence, indeed,
abstinence on the part of certain competitive athletes about whom we have already
spoken in the chapter on Hippocratic doctors".[35] In other words, this anatomical
detail does not simply record a physical reality but is a warning that we should not
expect sexual performances from these athletes.

Not wishing to shy away from the truth, I have come to the conclusion that the
beautiful Greek man was not a reality but an ideal. Because of my love for Greece, I
have been tempted to describe the Greek as unpleasant and mean, so as to exorcise
that picture of Greece in which rhetoricians have delighted, but which has never
existed. This fairytale Greece is so far from reality, so far removed from the concerns
of today's youth that I am certain it has turned our contemporaries, and in particular,
the young, from a study of Greece.

This imaginary Greece, dreamed up by those on the margins of historical study,

33 Aristophanes, *Clouds* (ed. and trans. J. Henderson), Loeb Classical Library, Harvard University Press, Cambridge,
    MA, 1998, v. 1002–1019.

34 A. Bernand, *Guerre et violence dans la Grèce antique*, Hachette Littératures, Paris, 1999, pp. 32-3.

35 Quoted in V. Visa-Ondarçuhu, *L'image de l'athlète d'Homère à la fin du ve siècle avant J.–C.*, Les Belles Lettres,
    Paris, 1999, p. 379-80.

An athlete cleaning himself with a strigil.
© 2003 Kunsthistorisches Museum, Wien

no longer attracts young people of today who have their feet on the ground, rather than their heads in the clouds. Travel to and around Greece today is easy and those who have eyes to see may learn that, like many other regions of the world, this country offers evidence of both harrowing conditions of existence and tragic episodes of history. The pastoral idyll is a far cry from the real mountains and islands of Greece. This country is not a puppet theatre, "a chosen land" to use Verlaine's phrase, where the soul of Greece expresses itself.

I for one have "embarked for Kythera" and I can confirm, having roamed all over the island, that there is only one spot where magnificent trees shelter a waterfall which runs into a pond where Watteau's shepherds would be happy. This admirable island only has arid moorlands, and harsh mountains between which stretch long, high plains often beaten by the winds. I have known Kythera under a black sky, in a sandstorm, and when the setting sun casts terrifying rays of light, as in a painting by Dürer. When you see the harbour of Haghia Pelagia stand out against the Pelopponnesian mountains and the fearsome Cape of Malea, it is easy to understand the dangers faced by ancient sailors trying to land on this island, most of whose coasts drop vertically into the sea.

Strabo[36] tells us that the opposing winds made the passage around the Cape so difficult that "traders coming by sea, some from Italy, others from Asia, were happy not to have to pass the cape and would unload their cargo at Corinth". Navigation in the Aegean Sea was difficult and dangerous. What would be thought of a person who said it was like navigating an enchanted river?

Let us retain the lessons that Ancient Greece has given to the world and that form the basis of our civilisation. The idea of combining physical and spiritual culture is one of which we can only approve. But we should know that those who constructed this philosophy have not exemplified it by deeds. It was a constant effort but a joyful one because it measured the distance between the Greeks as they were and what they wanted to be and also because it bore witness to the confidence they had in human nature. To study the reality of Greece is not to ride on a flying carpet and look down from on high at the deeds and achievements of men. If we want to understand the true lessons of Greece we must abandon our illusions. All the rest is only literature.

Thanks to the Olympic ideal, the *paideia* had the merit of uniting generations of fathers and sons. By creating Games for children and modelling them on those for adults, children could have a more precise idea of the efforts and exploits of their fathers and aim to emulate them.

---

36   Strabo, *op. cit.*, VIII, 6, 20.

Chapter V

Bridging generations

Fathers and sons

Not only was an Olympic victory an honour for a father and for his city, but it was also a matter of pride for his son. In the same way, when a son won it filled his father with happiness. Sophocles[1] summarised the situation well: "Is there for children a greater matter for pride than the successes of a father, as for a father those of his son?"

But before we look at this mutual admiration, what was the relationship between a son and his father in antiquity? We should not forget that the father was largely absent from the home for more than two years out of three and the home remained under the control of the ever-present mother.[2] In Athens, for example, men were called to war between the ages of 19 and 49 and after that served for ten years in the reserve. As the average life expectancy was 45 years, sons did not have their fathers around for very long.

Happily or unhappily, a son's early education did not depend directly on his father. To the extent that it can be possible given family life, job, and day-to-day living, familiarity, complicity even, between father and son is a feature of modern civilisation. There was nothing like it in Ancient Greece.

Up to about the age of 10, the education of a son did not depend on his father. Until the age of seven, the child remained in his family surrounded by women. The baby was first a *paidion*, then, from 7 to 14 a *pais*, and from 14 to late adolescence, which varied according to different cities but was usually between 14 and 21 years, a *meirakion*. This succession of three periods, each of seven years, went back to Hippocrates, according to the *Onomasticon* by Pollux of Naucratis, a grammarian living around 180 AD. According to Aristotle,[3] from his very first years the small baby must learn to move his limbs and to withstand the cold. The philosopher gives as an example the barbarians who threw their newborn children into a cold river or, like the Celts, only allowed them a few clothes. It was not the fathers who were responsible for this shock therapy, but mothers and nurses. After this first period of childhood (*prôté hélikia*) the following three years were under the control of the *paidonomos*.[4] The decent behaviour of children and young adolescents was the responsibility of the magistrates belonging to the oligarchy. Fathers handed responsibility for this first period of the child's education to inspectors of education. According to Aristotle, they had to oversee games, put up with the shouts and noisy tears of the children,[5] make sure that they should be with slaves as infrequently as possible, and avoid bad examples and indecent paintings or images.

---

1   Sophocles, *Antigone* (trans. H. Lloyd-Jones), Loeb Classical Library, Harvard University Press, Cambridge, MA, 1994, 703–4.

2   A. Bernand, *Guerre et violence dans la Grèce antique*, Hachette Littératures, Paris, 1999, p. 214-6.

3   Aristotle, *Politics* (trans. B. Jowett), Dover Publications, New York, 2000, VII, 1335.

4   *Ibid.*, VII, 1336.

5   See J. Aubonnet's notes in Aristotle, *Politics, op. cit.*, p. 318-9.

Plato said the same thing when he warned:[6] "There never will be a good man who has not from his childhood been used to play amid things of beauty and make of them a joy and a study." In *Laws*,[7] Plato argues the principle of a full and proper education: "There ought to be no bye-work interfering with the greater work of providing the necessary exercise and nourishment for the body, and instruction and education for the soul."

When the child was old enough to go to school, he was taught by the master of the school, the *didaskalos*. Neither the father nor the mother was involved in this since it was a source of possible family disagreement. It was a servant called a pedagogue (*paidagôgos*) who, as the name suggests, "led the child" to school, and this mentor who often carried a long stick did not go in for jokes. Aristophanes has Just Reason describe the trail of children making their way to school:[8]

> The first rule was that not a sound, not even a mutter, should be heard
> from a boy. Furthermore, the boys of each neighbourhood had to walk
> through the streets to the music master's all together and in good order,
> without coats even if the snow was coming down like chaff. Then he would
> teach them to memorize a song – while keeping their thighs apart! – "Pallas,
> Dire City Sacker," or "A Cry Sounds From Afar," and to tune their voices to
> the mode their fathers handed down. And if any of them clowned around or
> jazzed up the song with the sort of riff today's singers put in, these irritating
> riffles in the style of Phrynis, he'd get a hiding, with plenty of lashes laid on
> for effacing the Muses.

Unlike the *didaskalos* who was badly paid and not respected, the gymnasium teacher, the *paidotribés*, enjoyed a salary and status. A true educator, he knew the difficulties of the traditional sports as described in the 3rd century AD by Philostratus (*On Gymnastics*, 28-42).

It was this teacher and not the father who taught young boys the correct way to behave:[9]

> At the trainer's the boys had to cross their thighs when sitting, so they
> wouldn't reveal anything that would torment the onlookers; and when they
> stood up again, they had to smooth the sand and take care not to leave
> behind an image of their pubescence for their lovers to find. And in those
> days, no boy would oil himself below the navel, and so his privates bloomed
> with dewy down like apricots. Nor would he liquefy his voice to a simper for
> his lover and walk around pimping for himself with his eyes. At dinner he
> wasn't allowed to help himself to a head of radish, or to snatch his elders' dill
> or celery, or to eat the tasty tidbits, or giggle, or sit with his legs crossed.

The *paidotribés* was not immune to sexual temptation as is shown, for example,

---

6   Plato, *The Republic* (trans. B. Jowett), Prometheus Books, New York, 1986, VIII, 558.

7   Plato, *Laws* (trans. B. Jowett), Prometheus Books, New York, 2000, VII, 788.

8   Aristophanes, *Clouds* (ed. and trans. J. Henderson), Loeb Classical Library, Harvard University Press, Cambridge, MA, 1998, 963-72.

9   *Ibid.*, 973-83.

A young athlete trains with a ball. Marble relief, in the National Archaeological Museum of Athens.
© National Archaeological Museum of Athens

by the epigrams of Strato of Sardis, a poet of the first half of the 2ⁿᵈ century AD.[10] I have quoted one of these in *Guerre et violence dans la Grèce Antique*.[11] I will quote the other one here:[12]

> A. "If you are minded to do thus, take your adversary by the middle, and laying him down get astride of him, and shoving forward, fall on him and hold him tight." B. "You are not in your right senses, Diophantus. I am only just capable of doing this, but boys' wrestling is different. Fix yourself fast and stand firm, Cyris, and support it when I close with you. He should learn to practise with a fellow before learning to practise himself."

These passages play on the double sense of words meaning both wrestling holds and erotic positions. It is known that the verb *tribein* (to exercise) was used with the obscene meanings of "to screw" and "to rub". I will leave it to the reader to imagine the meaning that can be given to this verb and to the etymology of *paidotribés*.

When the child was of an age to go to the gymnasium, an extra supervision was carried out by the head teacher (*gymnasiarchos*), who was normally a honourable, rich and worthy person. To have this position of authority, it was necessary to be at least 40 years old, an age that was supposed to put the person beyond temptation in a place frequented by so many young and handsome boys clothed with only their beauty.

As the places for training, the gymnasium and the palaestra, were public, the master in charge had the responsibility of watching out for attempts at seduction by visitors who were more interested in those boys taking part than in the sports. Socrates and his friends would not come to the gymnasium to take exercise but to pick someone up. In the 4ᵗʰ century, there were 10 "wise men" (*sophronistai*), each one elected from a tribe, who were concerned with the good behaviour of the young people.

Plato, who saw in education a way of making good soldiers and who was an admirer of Spartan education, believed in military regulations to reinforce the control exerted over the young men. At the beginning of *Laches*[13] Plato shows us two fathers who have come to consult Socrates about the education of their sons since their own education had been neglected. They say: "We resent what our fathers did when they left us free to do as we pleased in our youth since they were so occupied themselves by the affairs of others."

The Spartan mirage

In *The Republic* Plato refers to Spartan education in order to outline what form the education of the guardians of the future should take.[14] According to him, morally strong men should be chosen. They should be put to work, made to suffer, undergo terrifying tests, and prove that they could resist being tempted and seduced throughout their lives. They would be made to enter competitions that would prepare them for future ones.

---

10 *Greek Anthology* (trans. W. R. Paton), Loeb Classical Library, Harvard University Press, Cambridge, MA, 1918, XII, 206 and 222 among others.

11 *Ibid.*, 222.

12 *Ibid.*, 206.

13 Plato, *Laches* (trans. W. R. M. Lamb), Loeb Classical Library, Heinemann, London, 1924, 179.

14 Plato, *Republic*, op. cit., III, 16, 7-9.

The communal aspect of this education and the toughness of the tests are underlined by the picture Plutarch gives us when he praises the way the young Spartans are trained. At best, the part the father plays in the education of his son is that of a witness; it is the local community that takes this in hand. In the *Life of Lycurgus* the meals, which could have presented an opportunity for fathers to speak privately to their sons, were communal events and, in any case, a frugal bowl of slops was hardly an incentive. "When he had a child, the father was not in charge of his upbringing," Plutarch tells us.[15] He goes on that according to Lycurgus:[16]

> By the time they were come to this age there was not any of the more
> hopeful boys who had not a lover to bear him company. The old men, too,
> had an eye upon them, coming often to the grounds to hear and see them
> contend either in wit or strength with one another, and this as seriously and
> with as much concern as if they were their fathers, their tutors, or their
> magistrates; so that there scarcely was any time or place without someone

Attic red-figure skyphos from the workshop of the Brygos Painter, 500-480 BC. A child runs across one side of the vase, *chlamys* thrown off to reveal his naked torso, while looking back over his shoulder. In his right hand he holds a hoop and stick, in his left, a basket of fruit. Has he stolen the basket from a suitor, or is it a present from an admirer from whom he is fleeing?

© National Archaeological Museum of Athens

15 Plutarch, *Lycurgus*, in *Lives* (trans. J. Dryden), Modern Library Classics, New York, 1992, 16, 1.
16 *Ibid.*, 17, 1.

present to put them in mind of their duty, and punish them if they had neglected it.

Furthermore it was not always possible to know who the father was since, according to Lycurgus, there were practices that aimed simply at producing healthy children. The elderly husband of a young woman could ask a young man to make his wife pregnant with a child of "generous blood". And a man could find himself hired by an indulgent husband to "put seed into his wife as it is put into fertile earth and to have with her fine children born of good blood and a good race".[17] Thus, "children did not belong solely to their fathers but to the community as a whole".

Contrary to the custom in the majority of Greek cities, where women were excluded from the gymnasia and did not attend the Games, the young Spartan women, according to Lycurgus,[18] had to practise – naked – running, wrestling, and throwing the discus and javelin. Dressed very simply, they danced and sang songs called Parthenaia written for them by Alcman, a lyric poet of the 7th century BC. These displays by young girls were a way of encouraging young men to look forward to marriage; as Plato says, "they felt themselves led by a force that was quite different from anything to do with geometry".

These Spartan practices incensed those cities where women had to remain decent and reserved. In *Andromache*, Euripides has Peleus, the father of Achilles, say:[19]

> No! a Spartan maid could not be chaste, e'en if she would, who leaves her
> home and bares her limbs and lets her robe float free, to share with youths
> their races and their sports – customs I cannot away with. Is it any wonder
> then that ye fail to educate your women in virtue?

The eugenics recommended by Plutarch made the father more a stud than a husband. The children Plato recommended to be guardians in *The Republic*[20] had no communication whatsoever with their fathers whom they did not know:

> The wives of our guardians are to be common, and their children are to be
> common, and no parent is to know his own child, nor any child his parent.

This idea of a community of children destined to be guardians and evoked by Plato drew from Aristotle sharp criticism, particularly in the second book of his *Politics*. He considers Socrates' formula to be ambiguous since, as he says:[21]

> [...] every citizen will call the same boy his son and also the same woman
> his wife, and will speak in the same way of property and indeed of everything
> that falls to his lot; but *ex hypothesi* the citizens, having community of women
> and children, will not call them "theirs" in this sense, but will mean theirs
> collectively and not severally.

---

17 Plutarch, *Lycurgus, op. cit.,* 15, 12-4.

18 *Ibid.,* 15, 14-5.

19 Euripides, *Andromache* (trans. E. P. Coleridge and W.-A. Landes), Players Press, London, 1999, 595-601.

20 Plato, *Republic, op. cit.,* V, 57.

21 Aristotle, *Politics, op. cit.,* II, III, 2.

Two young boxers from the Minoan period. Fresco from the West House in Santorini.

© National Archaeological Museum of Athens

According to him,[22] natural similarities would give clues allowing identity to be revealed as would any behaviour that would not be tolerated by parents even though it might be acceptable in front of strangers:[23]

> Moreover it is not easy for those who institute this communism to guard against such objectionable occurrences as outrage, involuntary and in some cases voluntary homicide, fights, abusive language; all of which are violations of piety when committed against fathers, mothers and near relatives as if they were not relatives; but these are bound to occur more frequently when people do not know their relations than when they do, and also, when they do occur, if the offenders know their relationship it is possible for them to have the customary expiations performed, but for those who do not no expiation is possible.

Finally, Aristotle points to the difficulties involved with transferring children:[24]

> Again, as to the transference of some of the children at birth from the Farmers and Artisans to the Guardians and of others from the Guardians to

Two naked horsemen, wearing red ribbons in their hair and riding bareback, whipping their horses. Black-figure vase, kept in the British Museum.
© The British Museum

22 Aristotle, *Politics, op. cit.*, I, 8-9.

23 *Ibid.*, I, 10.

24 *Ibid.*, I, 18.

the Farmers and Artisans, there is much confusion as to how it is to be done and the parents who give the children and the officials who transfer them are bound to know which they give to whom.

The weaknesses of the Spartan education system or the suggestions in *The Republic* show us that Greek children needed to have a framework and a paternal example to give them a model and a sense of direction. It was precisely the Olympic system that helped them to understand their place in the social hierarchy, giving them a way of relating to their fathers.

The hierarchy of children

On the metaphorical chessboard represented by the Games, the Olympic system gave to children the "squares" that corresponded to their ages and potential. Children were not left without supervision, but had to undertake a series of tests that stimulated their enthusiasm and drew them closer to adults. The competitive instinct, natural in children, was reinforced by a wish to emulate adults by performing in the same way as their fathers. By taking part in competitions children could integrate into the official life and the world of their elders.

The word "child" is much too vague to translate the different categories of children involved in athletics in the ancient world. For the Spartans, there were many distinctions, as there are in scouting today, between cubs, scouts, and rovers, and children were divided up into groups (*ilai* or *agelaî*) similar to the ones we have today. H. I. Marrou has drawn up a table of these different categories based on their age:[25]

Eight to eleven: the little boy	*rôbidas* (meaning unknown) *promikkizomenos* (the very little boy) *mikkizomenos* (the little boy) *propais* (the young adolescent)
Twelve to fifteen: the "adolescent"	*protopampais* (adolescent, first year) *atropampais* (adolescent, second year) *melleirén* (future *ephebe*) *melleirèn* (future *ephebe*, second year)
Sixteen to twenty: the *ephebe* (in Sparta, *irene*)	*eirèn* (first year *ephebe*) *eirèn* (second year *ephebe*) *eirèn* (third *ephebe*) *eirèn* (fourth *ephebe*) *prôteiras* (senior *eirèn*)

No matter what discussion may be provoked by this picture, we have to remember that these different grades were based on age and formed a hierarchy.

Outside Sparta, two categories of young men were distinguishable: *meirakion* from 14–17 years made up of the *ageneios* (beardless) followed by the *ephebes*, 18–20 years. These divisions based on age varied slightly according to different cities. The ancient Attic *ephebe* corresponds to modern military service. Aristotle's *The Athenian Constitution* (XLII) explains how it worked. Forgetting the *ephebes* for a moment, let us listen to the songs of praise addressed to children.

---

25 H. I. Marrou, *A History of Education in Antiquity* (trans. G. Lamb), Sheed and Ward, New York/London, 1956, pp. 20-21 and p. 264, note 23. The table and comments are from Marrou.

Victorious children

Pindar and Bacchylides have celebrated the victories claimed by children. In a beautiful ode in which he evokes the Olympian countryside, Pindar celebrates the young Alcimedon of Aegina who won at wrestling in the boys' competition and whose brother Timosthenes had won at Nemea:[26]

> Well-wooded grove of Pisa beside the Alpheus, welcome this victory procession and the garland we bring to the victor; the man who is attended by your splendid prize of honor has great glory forever. Some good things come to one man, some to another; with the favor of the gods, there are many paths of success. Timosthenes, fortune has allotted you and your brother to the care of your ancestor Zeus, who made you renowned at Nemea, and made Alcimedon an Olympic victor beside the hill of Cronus. He was beautiful to look at, and his deeds did not belie his beauty when by his victory in wrestling he had Aegina with her long oars proclaimed as his fatherland. There the savior Themis, seated beside Zeus the god of hospitality, is honored more than among all other men.

In his tenth *Olympian* he sings the praises of Hagesidamus of western Locris, who won at boxing. The fourteenth *Olympian* praises Asopichus of Orchomenus, who won in the boys' stadium. Echo carried the news of his glory to his father in his tomb:[27]

> For I have come to sing the praise of Asôpichus with Lydian tune and with meditated lays, because, thanks to thee, the house of the Minyae is victorious in Olympia.
> Now! hie thee, Echo, to the dark-walled home of Persephonê, and bear the glorious tidings to the father, so that, when thou hast seen Cleodâmus, thou mayest tell him that, beside the famous vale of Pisa, his son hath crowned his youthful locks with garlands won from the ennobling games.

The tenth *Pythian* is consecrated to the Thessalian, Hippocleas, who won the double race (*diaulodromon*) for boys. It was in the valley of Parnassus, at Delphi, that he achieved this. But at Olympia his father Phricias had won in the armed race (*hoplitodromos*). This song of praise is a good example of the way a son would emulate his father, love of fame linking one with the other.

The eleventh *Pythian* praises the Theban Thrasydaeus who won in the boys' stadium at Delphi and "revived the memory of the paternal household which he enriched with a third crown". Here, once again, we have that exchange of glances between a son and father, uniting them in the same quest for glory.

In the second *Nemean* in honour of Timodemus, son of Timonous from Acharnae who won at physical combat, Pindar hopes that this champion will be victorious at both the Isthmian and Pythian Games. In the fifth stanza he recalls that Timodemus' descendants carried off numerous crowns and gathered many victories for themselves: four at the Pythian Games, eight at the Olympic Games, and seven at the Nemean Games. It can be seen that sons followed the example set by their fathers.

Marble statue of Antinous. From Delphi, dating from just after 138 AD.
© The Archaeological Museum of Delphi

---

26 Pindar, *Olympian Odes*, in *Odes* (trans. D. Svarlien), Perseus Project, Yale, 1991, VIII, 12-29.
27 *Ibid.*, XIV, 25-35.

The fourth *Nemean* celebrates the victory at wrestling in the boys' competition of Timasarchus from Aegina. His father, Timocritus, who was a fine cithara player, was dead and not able to see his son win. Pindar insists on showing how in disciplines very different from one another, father and son were at one. Timasarchus' maternal uncle, Callicles, won a victory at Isthmia. In this way, the Theandrides, the name of the family to which Timasarchus belonged, set an example to the youngest.

The fifth *Nemean* is in honour of Pytheas from Aegina, who won at physical combat in the category of the "beardless ones" (*ageneioi*). This, as we know, was the category between young boys (*paides*) and fully-grown men (*andres*). Pytheas' maternal uncle Euthymenes had won a crown at Aegina and his grandfather Themistius had won at Epidaurus. These two crowns were laid in the portico of the sanctuary of Aeacus. As we can see, victories were often a family affair. This same victory by Pytheas is celebrated in the thirteenth song of praise by Bacchylides.

The sixth *Nemean* is in praise of Alcimidas from Aegina, a wrestler who won in the competition for young boys. In his first *antistrophe* Pindar uses a turn of phrase that is a good way of illustrating the role the family plays in the making of champions: "Alcimidas gives visible proof that his hereditary qualities are like the fruitful fields." Theon, Alcimidas' father, is not mentioned but the grandfather Praxidamas, of the same family, won once at Olympia, five times at Isthmia, and three times at Nemea. Pindar observes that "no other family has been proclaimed by the boxing contest in the center of all Greece as the guardian of more garlands".

The seventh *Nemean* informs us that yet another *pais*, Sogenes from Aegina, was victor in the boys' pentathlon; neither his father nor any of his ancestors had achieved this. When he celebrates the wrestler Theaeus of Argos in the tenth *Nemean*, Pindar lists his many successes at Delphi, Isthmia, and Nemea and devotes the third triad to the victories of his maternal family in numerous local games and on four occasions at Isthmia. "It is no wonder that it is innate in their race to be good athletes."

From all these songs of praise, it emerges that the glory acquired at the major Games is not just for the person who wins, but also for his family. One became a champion, not because one was the son of one's father, but because one was the offspring of a family of victors.

The poet Bacchylides of Ceos, who, by his mother, was a nephew of the poet Simonides and a contemporary of Pindar, although younger than he, lived from around 507–430 BC.[28] Of the 14 songs of praise, more or less intact, that he composed, six are dedicated to children who won at the Games. Once again, we find in these texts the complicity between fathers and sons that pushes the latter to emulate their father or grandfather or other relations in an effort to bring glory to the family by victories. For Bacchylides, the celebration in a triumphal ode of victories by children seems to be a favourite theme. His uncle, Simonides, had often treated this theme and had composed so many songs of praise, that the publishers in Alexandria had to bind them in seven books according to the Games with which they dealt.

The first song, the manuscript of which is badly damaged, was composed for Argeius of Ceos, a child who won at boxing in the Isthmian Games. The poet calls him "Argeius, who has a strong hand and the spirit of a lion," but there are so many

---

28   According to J. Duchemin and L. Bardollet in Bacchylides, *Dithyrambes, Épinicies, Fragments*, Les Belles Lettres, 1963, pp. x-xi.

A champion of the Isthmian Games.
© Vanni Archive / CORBIS
Photographer: Ruggero Vanni

gaps in the text that we can learn nothing else. The second song, reduced to a triad, evokes "the battle of bold hands" carried out by the boy and recalls his earlier 70 victories at the Games. The sixth song, which only has two stanzas, celebrates the victory of the child, Lachon of Ceos, in the stadium where the Olympic Games were held. The victory of this "wind-footed" boy is one in a long series won by the Ceans. The seventh song, also badly damaged, is addressed to the same child. It is possible, but not certain, that one Chairolas, quoted in the ode, may have been his grandfather.

The eleventh song is for Alexidamus of Metapontum, a city in greater Greece near Sybaris. In the category of the *paides* this "marvellous son of Phaiscus", as the poet calls him, won at wrestling in Pythian Games. He was honoured by the *phyllobolia*.

"Many garlands of flowers fell around Alexidamus on the plain of Cirrha, because of his all-conquering powerful wrestling." On a previous occasion at the Olympic Games, this child had been deprived of the most prestigious award because he had been the victim of an accident, no doubt caused by someone who was jealous.

In the thirteenth song, we come across Pytheas again who won in the general combat competition for the category of the *ageneioi* at the Nemean Games and in whose honour Pindar had written the fifth Nemean. Evoking the crowns of flowers, the festive songs, and the choirs of young girls, Bacchylides reminds us how glory at athletics could please a proud young girl and would reflect on all the family. In the third *antistrophe* he evokes, and this is unusual, Pytheas' financée:

> And a proud maiden [...] often lightly springing with her feet like a carefree
> fawn on the flowery hills with her far-famed [companions] who live nearby. The
> maidens wear garlands of crimson blossoms and rushes, the native decoration,
> and sing of your child, mistress of the all-hospitable land.

These texts remind us that a victor was not alone; all his family are involved in his triumph. The loneliness of the Greek child was relieved by exercises which he learned from his *paidotribés* and which he practised for the delights of all his family. In this way, the Games would bring happiness to the family as a whole. These young people were taught not to hate their opponent, but to want to be the best in these official contests.

The *paidotribés* tried to inculcate in his pupils the ideal of *arété*, not of "virtue" as it is often translated, but of "valour". As the Spartan poet Tyrtaeus, who lived at the time of the Second Messenian War (around 650 BC) tells us:[29]

> I should not consider a man worthy to be remembered, nor think highly of
> him, merely because he was a good runner or wrestler, even though he was as
> big and strong as the Cyclops, swifter than Boreus the Thracian, more handsome
> than Titho, richer than Midas or Cinyras, stronger than King Pelops, son of
> Tantalus; though his speech was softer than Adrastus' and he enjoyed every kind
> of fame – unless he was also valorous in arms, unless he could stand fast in
> battle... that is the true valor – *arété* – the highest reward that a man can obtain
> from his fellows. It is a good common to all, a service to the city and the people
> as a whole, when every man can stand firm on his two feet in the front line and
> rid his heart of all idea of flight.

29 Tyrtaeus, *Fragments*, 12, 1-10. Quoted by H. I. Marrou, *op. cit.*, p. 16, and notes 8-9 p. 362.

To this military valour, Greek education adds an ideal that is much more demanding. Equally important, it is more complete because it embraces all the values of a Greek community – respect for rules and the law, belief in everything that makes sense of a citizen's life, a quest for perfection and performance. To give only one example, I will refer here to the funeral epigram coming from Hermoupolis Magna (Touna el-Gebel) in Egypt[30] in which the *paidotribés* Hermocrates, son of Hermaios, talks of his role in the gymnasium and in the education of young people, referring to himself as the one "who rewarded many adolescent winners each year." This text from the end of the 2nd century or the beginning of the 3rd century AD and from a foreign country, illustrates the pride a teacher felt at having educated many pupils and shows how aware he was at having put his talent to the service of the collective interest and glory of the gymnasium. Such teaching and training for future competitions was fundamental to Greek civilisation. In this way, pride at following the example of their fathers or, inversely, the happiness fathers felt at the successes of their children, were transmitted from generation to generation. A sense of a bond between families counted for a great deal, to the point where the Greeks would not allow the barbarians to compete with them even if there existed already in their own country a tradition of selective competition. This was so in Egypt where Alexander, subsequently named "The Great", saw his right to take part in the Games challenged. Herodotus recounts this incident:[31]

> Now that these descendants of Perdiccas are Greeks, as they themselves say, I myself chance to know and will prove it in the later part of my history. Furthermore, the Hellenodicae who manage the contest at Olympia determined that it is so, for when Alexander chose to contend and entered the lists for that purpose, the Greeks who were to run against him wanted to bar him from the race, saying that the contest should be for Greeks and not for foreigners. Alexander, however, proving himself to be an Argive, was judged to be a Greek. He accordingly competed in the furlong race and tied for first place. This, then, is approximately what happened.

Herodotus relates this as a rumour, not wanting to take responsibility for it himself. It is certainly true that Alexander's name does not appear in the list of victors, perhaps because he was one of many. Here we have a fine example of the kind of racism that the Greeks did not hide.[32]

Training for and participation in the Olympic and other Games, then, was reserved for an elite based on the examples set by fathers and relatives and reserved for families of Greek origin. Different generations could come together but not people from different countries. Today, when we see the number of different national teams taking part, such caution seems inconceivable and it leads us to be less than fulsome in our praise of the benefits of the ancient Games.

30 This text has been published in French with a commentary by E. Bernand, *Inscriptions métriques de l'Égypte gréco-romaine,* Les Belles Lettres, Paris, 1969, p. 22.

31 Herodotus, *Histories* (trans. A. D. Godley), Loeb Classical Library, Harvard University Press, Cambridge, MA, 1920, V, 22.

32 See A. Bernand, *Leçon de civilisation,* Fayard, Paris, 1994.

2
PLAYING THE GAME

Chapter VI

Ritual

The Games took place in a sacred atmosphere that is difficult for the modern mind to imagine. To take part in the Games was a religious undertaking and we should not take Thucydides' (II, 38) declaration in the wrong way: "We can guarantee relaxation; we have contests (*agônes*) and sacrifices (*thusiai*) all the year."

Whether they were cultural or physical, these games were tributes to the gods. First, because man's destiny – his misfortune as well as his success – was considered to be the result of divine intervention. Secondly, because the sanctuaries and competitions that took place in them were founded on religious myths. For example, if we consider the Olympic Games, the contests go back to the decision of King Oenomaous of Pisa, to have a chariot competition to test his daughter's suitors.

The king always won because of his divine horses, a present from his father, Ares. But one of these suitors, Pelops, won thanks to the love of the king's daughter, Hippodamia who, having fallen in love with him, obtained the help of the king's driver, Myrtilos. He sabotaged the axle of Oenomaous' chariot, replacing the spokes of the king's chariot's wheels with spokes of wax that did not take long to give way. Having got rid of her father, who, it was said, was in love with her, Hippodamia married the handsome Pelops. He had been the cup bearer and soothsayer for Poseidon, though that did not prevent him from having many children with Hippodamia.

These edifying myths link Pelops' name to the foundation of the Olympic Games. After not being celebrated for some time, the Games were then reintroduced by Heracles in memory and in honour of Pelops. It was Heracles who set out the limits of the sanctuary of Olympus and renewed the tradition of the Games once he had cleaned the Augean stables by altering the course of the river Alpheius. In all the other sanctuaries where Games took place, mythology has it that the competitions are associated with the gods. That is why religion has such an important place in their organisation; it is not only rules but also rituals that define the greatest moments of the Games.

The Olympic oath

The Olympic oath was a particularly important ceremony and created a climate of solemnity, sobriety, and calm. For the Olympic oath we have precise information given to us by Pausanias, the historian whose work appeared in the third quarter of the 2nd century AD. He is, therefore, a contemporary of the great emperors Trajan, Hadrian, Antoninus, and Marcus Aurelius. Religious rituals were ever present and allowing for the fact that certain variations survived into the Classical period, Pausanias allows us to imagine the ceremony of the oath and the stages in the celebration of the Games. Here he describes the Olympic oath:[1]

Image on previous page:

The *Doryphorus* (spear carrier). Bronze statue of an athlete by Polyclitus embodying his treatise, the *Canon* (The Rule of Perfection), in Munich University.

© AKG London

Vase showing three long distance runners. Housed in the British Museum.

© The British Museum

---

1   Pausanias, *Description of Greece* (trans. W. H. S. Jones and H. A. Ormerod), Loeb Classical Library, Heinemann, London, 1988, V, 24, 9-11.

But the Zeus in the Council Chamber is of all the images of Zeus the one most likely to strike terror into the hearts of sinners. He is surnamed Oath-god, and in each hand he holds a thunderbolt. Beside this image it is the custom for athletes, their fathers and their brothers, as well as their trainers, to swear an oath upon slices of boar's flesh that in nothing will they sin against the Olympic games. The athletes take this further oath also, that for ten successive months they have strictly followed the regulations for training. An oath is also taken by those who examine the boys, or the foals entering for races, that they will decide fairly and without taking bribes, and that they will keep secret what they learn about a candidate, whether accepted or not. I forgot to inquire what it is customary to do with the boar after the oath of the athletes, though the ancient custom about victims was that no human being might eat of that on which an oath had been sworn. Homer proves this point clearly. For the boar, on the slices of which Agamemnon swore that verily Briseis had not lain with him, Homer says was thrown by the herald into the sea.

"He spake, and cut the boar's throat with ruthless bronze;
And the boar Talthybius swung and cast into the great depth
Of the grey sea, to feed the fishes."

Such was the ancient custom. Before the feet of the Oath-god is a bronze plate, with elegiac verses inscribed upon it, the object of which is to strike fear into those who forswear themselves.

This ceremony described in such detail by Pausanias shows us precisely how solemn the Olympic oath was. As Anne Jacquemin has observed, we find it in lots of official acts to do with Greek communities.[2] This oath taken on the *tomia* (literally, pieces) of sacrificed boar recalls the oath made by Heracles to the children of Nelea (Pausanias IV, 15,8) at the place subsequently called The Boar's Tomb, near Stenycleros in Messenia on the first flanks to the northeast of Mount Ithoma. A similar oath was taken when treaties were signed as Aristophanes tells us (*Lysistrata* 186-192), at the moment of elections (Plato, *Laws* VI, 753d), when the Athenian magistrates took office (Aristotle, *The Athenian Constitution*, LV, 5): "Having passed the examination the magistrates go to the stone on which the cut-up parts of the victims have been placed [*pros ton lithon eph'ou ta tomi' estin*]."

Anne Jacquemin notes that the same oath on the "cut-up pieces" was used in Athens at murder trials (Antiphon, *On the Murder of Herod*, 88; Demosthenes, *Against Aristocrates*, 67-69; Aeschines, *On the Unfaithful Embassy*, 87). It is clear, therefore, that this is a solemn act carried out in serious circumstances and indicates the importance of the Olympic oath.

Much has been written in an attempt to understand the term *tomia*. Where they *splankna* (intestines) or were they the animal's genitals? The word *tomia* is too vague for us to be precise. What is certain is that the oath pronounced over a sacrificial victim reduced to pieces was a pious act and this explains this practice at the moment of the Olympic oath.

Red-figure vase showing an award ceremony. On the right a bearded man, probably the *agônothete*, ties a red ribbon around the head of a smiling young man, who wears long woollen ties round his left arm and leg and holds a sprig of olive.
© Staatliche Antikensammlungen und Glyptothek München / Photo: R. Kuehling

2   A. Jacquemin, *Commentaire à Pausanias*, Collection des universités de France, Paris, 1999, V, 24, 9.

Discipline

A group of superintendents responsible for preventing violence and irregularities assured discipline at the Olympics. They were responsible for maintaining order and preventing any conflicts. They were called *hellanodikai* and this gives a good indication of their role. As Pindar says (*Olympian Odes,* III, 22) the *hellanodikai* watched over "the way the Great Games… and the way the quinquennial festivity took place on the holy banks of the Alphea". This responsibility for judging was given to a body of several people. The number of *hellanodikai* varied according to the different periods, Pausanias informs us:[3]

> But at the ninety-fifth Festival nine umpires were appointed. To three of them were entrusted the chariot-races, another three were to supervise the pentathlum, the rest superintended the remaining contests. At the second Festival after this the tenth umpire was added. At the hundred and third Festival, the Eleans having twelve tribes, one umpire was chosen from each. But they were hard pressed in a war with the Arcadians and lost a portion of their territory, along with all the parishes included in the surrendered district, and so the number of tribes was reduced to eight in the hundred and fourth Olympiad. Thereupon were chosen umpires equal in number to the tribes. At the hundred and eighth Festival they returned again to the number of ten umpires, which has continued unchanged down to the present day.

This text does not take account, perhaps, of the way this duty underwent certain modifications but it allows us to understand the flexibility of this institution and the constant concern that the organisers had on these feast days to avoid any calls for conflict which would have offended the gods.

Zeus, the god of Olympia, was ever present in the sanctuary. Pausanias has counted the number of statues dedicated to him pointing out that they were offered by grateful cities. The presence of the lord of the sanctuary and the Games made all the participants remember that their contests were offerings to the gods.

Pictures carved on the pediments in the temple to Zeus do in fact warn us against cheating in what should be open and honest games. The eastern pediment shows the preparations for the chariot race opposing Oenomaus and Pelops. As we know the latter won, having violated the Olympic ideal – the race was rigged. The monumental figure of Zeus in the centre of the pediment gives the god the role of judge and dispenser of justice. To the west, the pediment pictures the brutalities committed by the drunken Centaurs who wanted to carry off the women and young boys on the occasion of Pirithous's wedding. Pirithous was a friend of Theseus and of Deidamia, daughter of Atrax, king of Lapithes. As Mathurin Régnier wrote: "At Atracia, where the drunken Centaurs/Their loins on fire, wanted to make like dogs". Again it is naked uncontrolled physical strength that is depicted under the eyes of Apollo. We are a long way from the joy of the Games.

Inside the temple of Zeus, the metopes also glorify strength since they represent the 12 labours of Heracles in their chronological order, according to legend: the struggle with the lion of Nemea; his fight with the hydra at Lerna; hunting the

---

The abduction of Ganymedes by Zeus. Terracotta statue in the museum of Olympia.
© The Archaeological Museum of Olympia

Stymphalaian birds; victory over the Cretan bull; his capture of the Ceryneian deer; the blow of his club that conquered the Amazon Hippolyteus; the pursuit of the boar of Erymanthus, which he brought back alive to Eurysthea; his breaking-in of Diomedes' mares; slaying the giant Geryon; his search for the Hesperidean apples; his capture of the monstrous Cerberus; and cleaning the Augean stables. All of these exploits are mortel struggles, but they illustrate and glorify prowess, acceptance of danger, and the search for fame – values idealised by the Games. As a large number of inscriptions indicate, this is the reason why Heracles, with Hermes, will be one of the protectors of the athletes.

Calendar of the games

The calendar of the games ritually followed an order that sought to preserve the role of each of the main panhellenic sanctuaries. The Olympic Games, which were the most prestigious, took place every four years. The festivity was called the *pentaetéris*, because it was celebrated after four years had gone by in the third year of each Olympiad. In the same way, the Pythian Games took place every four years in the third year of the Olympiad and in the second month of the Delphic calendar, *Boukatios*, which corresponded to the Attic *Metageitniôn* at the height of summer (August-September). The Isthmian and Nemean Games took place every two years, alternating with those of Olympia and Delphi. In this way, neither Apollo who reigned at Delphi, nor Poseidon, Lord of Isthmia, nor Zeus at Nemea could take offence since the greatest fame went to the winning athletes of the whole "season" covering the four Games and who earned the title of *periodoniké*.[4]

The finest example of a *periodoniké* that we can cite is Theagenes of Thasos. Jean Pouilloux has devoted a long study to him.[5]

We know this person above all because of what Pausanias has written. In VI, 6, 5, he briefly describes the disputes between the Thasian and his rival Euthymos and the *hellanodikai*. Pausanias tells the story of Theagenes and his many victories.[6] The text is long but worth quoting in full.

> Not far from the kings mentioned stands a Thasian, Theagenes the son of Timosthenes. The Thasians say that Timosthenes was not the father of Theagenes, but a priest of the Thasian Heracles, a phantom of whom in the likeness of Timosthenes had intercourse with the mother of Theagenes. In his ninth year, they say, as he was going home from school, he was attracted by a bronze image of some god or other in the marketplace; so he caught up the image, placed it on one of his shoulders and carried it home. The citizens were enraged at what he had done, but one of them, a respected man of advanced years, bade them not to kill the lad, and ordered him to carry the image from his home back again to the market-place. This he did, and at once became famous for his strength, his feat being noised abroad throughout Greece. The achievements of Theagenes at the Olympian games have already – the most famous of them – been described in my story, how he beat

---

4   The list of periodonics was compiled by R. Knab, *Die Periodoniken, ein Beitrag zur Geschichte der gymnischen Agone an den 4 griechischen Hauptfesten*, Diss, Giessen, 1934.

5   J. Pouilloux, *Recherches sur l'histoire et les cultes de Thasos*, De Boccard, Paris, 1954, I, II, pp. 62-105.

6   Pausanias, *op. cit.*, VI, 11, 2-9.

Heracles wrestles the lion at Nemea. Red-figure amphora, circa 520 BC.
© The British Museum

Euthymus the boxer, and how he was fined by the Eleans. On this occasion the pancratium, it is said, was for the first time on record won without a contest, the victor being Dromeus of Mantineia. At the Festival following this, Theagenes was the winner in the pancratium. He also won three victories at Pytho. These were for boxing, while nine prizes at Nemea and ten at the Isthmus were won in some cases for the pancratium and in others for boxing. At Phthia in Thessaly he gave up training for boxing and the pancratium. He devoted himself to winning fame among the Greeks for his running also, and beat those who entered for the long race. His ambition was, I think, to rival Achilles by winning a prize for running in the fatherland of the swiftest of those who are called heroes. The total number of crowns that he won was one thousand four hundred. When he departed this life, one of those who were his enemies while he lived came every night to the statue of Theagenes and flogged the bronze as though he were ill-treating Theagenes himself. The statue put an end to the outrage by falling on him, but the sons of the dead man prosecuted the statue for murder. So the Thasians dropped the statue to the bottom of the sea, adopting the principle of Draco, who, when he framed the Athenians laws to deal with homicide, inflicted banishment even on lifeless things, should one of them fall and kill a man. But in course of time, when the earth yielded no crop to the Thasians, they sent envoys to Delphi, and the god instructed them to receive back the exiles. At this command they received them back, but their restoration brought no remedy of the famine. So for the second time they went to the Pythian priestess, saying that although they had obeyed her instructions the wrath of the gods still abode with them. Whereupon the Pythian priestess replied to them :

But you have forgotten your great Theagenes.

And when they could not think of a contrivance to recover the statue of Theagenes, fishermen, they say, after putting out to sea for a catch of fish caught the statue in their net and brought it back to land. The Thasians set it up in its original position, and are wont to sacrifice to him as to a god. There are many other places that I know of, both among Greeks and among barbarians, where images of Theagenes have been set up, who cures diseases and receives honors from the natives. The statue of Theagenes is in the Altis, being the work of Glaucias of Aegina.

Plutarch, in *Political Thought*, summarises Theagenes's career and describes how "at a dinner of a party for heroes after some funeral sacrifice, he jumped up just at the moment when, according to tradition, everyone had been served, and he knocked over all who were there in a general brawl, as though no one else should be proclaimed victor in his presence".

An epigram by Poseidippos of Pella told by Athenaeus (X, 41) indicates that the champion drugged himself on meat as he readily admitted: "Despite a well-established convention, I once ate a bull from Meonia. Thasos, the land of my fathers, could not provide enough to nourish Theagenes. When I had eaten it all, I requested more. That is why the bronze statue in my image shows me holding out my hand." The inscriptions in Thasos allow us to complete the picture of this celebrity of the ancient world.

Red-figure neck amphora showing a *hoplitodromos* (a race in full armour) about to start. Berlin Painter, circa 480-470 BC. Kept in the Louvre.
© Photo RMN – Hervé Lewandowski, Louvre

Timetable of events

The contests took place following a ritual that hardly varied. The festivity lasted for six days, the first day being taken up by the Olympic oath and religious ceremonies. The games known as *gymnikoi* got their name from the fact that the athletes were naked (*gumnoi*). This was a matter of pride to the Greeks for they were unlike the barbarians who wore loin cloths. Strictly speaking, there were 13 contests. Ten were reserved for adult men: the simple, or one-lap race (*stadion*), which could become a double, two-lap race (*diaulos*), a long race (*dolichos*), the race in which the competitors carried arms and wore helmets, shin-guards, and shields (*hoplitodromos*), wrestling with bare hands (*palê*), boxing (*pygmê*), the pancratium (*pankration*), and the pentathlon combining five tests: jumping (*halma*) which could be a double or triple jump, with or without weights, discus (*diskos*), javelin (*akôn*), running, and wrestling. There were three tests for children. It seems that the oldest of these was a simple running race. The winner was called the *olympionikés* after which the Olympiad is named.

Prize giving

On the sixth and last day, winners were given an olive wreath ornamented with bands. The winners and the priests formed a procession and gathered in front of the altars. The ceremony was finished with prayers and sacrifices. After that, a large banquet was given to the winners and to the priests in the Prytaneum.[7] Wreaths varied according to the sanctuaries.[8] According to Pausanias (V, 15, 3) the branches were taken from "the olive tree intended for fine crowns" (*kallistephanos*) which was found in the Altis behind the temple of Zeus. Again, according to Pausanias (X, 7, 8), the wreath at Delphi was made of laurel and at Isthmia and Nemea of parsley. The ancient wreaths, whatever they were made of, had three advantages: they were decorative, they gave off an agreeable smell, and were a protection from the sun. The athletes were naked and did not use the vine leaf, which became so prominent in the Christian era. The simplicity of these natural trophies matched the austerity of the Games. Once more, according to Pausanias (VIII, 48, 2), the winners were given "a palm to hold in their right hand". Here we have a noble origin indeed for the academic palms that are awarded today to those who have given good service to the French educational system. Sometimes, rewards in silver were made. At Athens, a ruling by Solon meant that 500 drachmas were given to the Olympic winner and 100 to the Isthmian winner. But the *stephanitai* Games (those where the prize was a wreath) were more highly regarded than the *thematikai* or *chrématitai* Games (where the rewards were of a material value). Plutarch's testimony is enlightening:[9]

> The king had always about his person someone who had been crowned in the Olympic games; and upon this account a Lacedaemonian is said to have refused a considerable present, which was offered to him upon condition that he would not come into the lists; and when he had with much to-do thrown his antagonist, some of the spectators saying to him, "And now, Sir Lacedaemonian, what are you the better for your victory?" he answered, smiling, "I shall fight next the king."

7   See L. B. Zaidman and P. Schmitt, *La religion grecque*, Armand Colin, coll. Cursus, Paris, 1989, pp. 85-6.
8   M. Jost, *Aspects de la vie religieuse en Grèce*, SEDES, Paris, 1992, pp. 209-10.
9   Plutarch, *Lycurgus*, in *Lives* (trans. J. Dryden), Modern Library Classics, New York, 1992, 22, 8.

Starting line of the stadium's running track at Olympia.

© Dave Bartruss / CORBIS

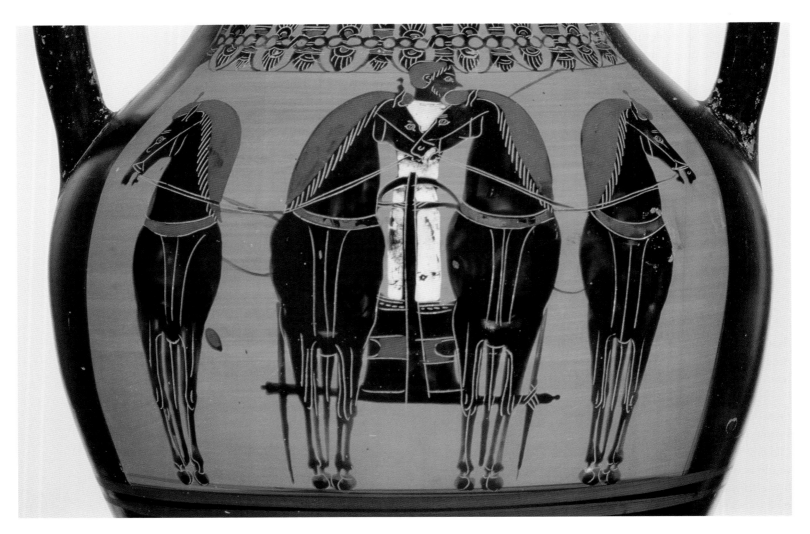

Frontal view of a four-horse chariot (*tethrippon*). Black-figure vase, with hair and manes in red. The charioteer, who is standing, wears a white tunic. Circa 268 BC.

© Staatliche Antikensammlungen und Glyptothek München / Photo: R. Kuehling

The city honoured by the winner gave him further rewards depending on where he was. In Athens winners were given the right for life to eat with the highest officials at the state's expense and when there were sacrifices, they received a double ration of meat: hence the expression "to crown with meat", which is found in inscriptions. Theoretically, the winner had the right to enter the city through a gap in the wall.

The Game was called *eiselastikos* and a sort of triumphal entry was organised in his honour. Dressed in purple, he would then cross the town on a chariot and a vote could be taken to have a statue of him erected either in the public assembly room or in the sanctuary. Unlike on the modern podium, there were no prizes for second or third.

Horse trials

The contests involving horses to which Homer refers are physical tests of a special kind and pose particular questions as we can understand from the songs of praise written by Pindar or Bacchylides. The owners of the horses and chariots did not normally ride or drive them themselves. It is generally thought that they financed the race and kept the horses and chariots in good condition. The matter is not quite so simple, however, and in her remarkable thesis, Valérie Visa-Ondarçuhu shows that in

Pindar's work it is sometimes difficult to know whether the owner of a chariot had driven it in the arena himself. She writes:[10]

> Only five precise indications are given to us on this subject about the contestants praised by Pindar. The explanatory notes tell us that the chariot race in which victory is attributed to Arcesilas of Cyrenea, had been achieved by his brother-in-law, Carrhotos (*Pyth.* 5 and 6). In the sixth Olympian, Pindar mentions Phintis, the driver from the Agesias of Syracuse (*Ol.* 6,22). In the second Isthmian in honour of Xenocrates from Agrigente, he recalls a victory prior to the Panathenaic Games in which the driver Nikomaque was in charge overall (*Isth.* 2, 19-21). Moreover, in the sixth Pythian, in honour of another victory by Xenocrates, the regular references to his son Thrasybulus can lead us to suppose that on this occasion it was he who drove for his father. Finally, Pindar himself tells us that Herodotus of Thebes was both owner and driver of the winning team.

Therefore, we can conclude that in most cases praise was for the stable-owner, though on occasions dignitaries like the tyrants of Sicily were not unwilling to show off their riding talents in these prestigious riding competitions. Only people with money had horses, and wars gave them the opportunity to demonstrate their riding talents.

The documentation we can get from the Delphic decrees related to the Pythiad provides us with detail about the Games with horses. For the horse, there was a race simply called *hippios*, without epithet, the straight race (*akamptos*), and the double race (*diaulos*) that involved a complete lap. The war horse (*hippos polemistés*) would do the single or double race. Texts talk as well of a race for war horses with both rider and horse fully armed, giving us the expression *en hoplois* (in arms). A particularly popular race consisted in driving the chariot in such a way that one of the team members, called *apobatés*, could get on and off (*harmati ekbibazon*). Some of these Games were called *ek pantón*, if everyone, Athenians and foreigners, could take part. Others were reserved for members of the cavalry and their officers (*ek tôn hippeôn, ek tôn phylarchôn*).

These races took place in the hippodrome or if the terrain was not suitable, on the nearest plain. That was the case in Delphi where they raced on the plain of Crisa.

Musical competitions

Alongside the physical games were games which were called "musical" and which allowed the disciplines of the Muses to be practised – not only music but also poetry and the dramatic arts. In particular, the Pythian Games, which took place at Delphi, had lots of contests of this kind. Among his many talents, Apollo was a master of song, poetry, and all aspects of the Muses because he was the conductor of the Muses (*Mouségétés*).

The thymelic Games were about music and bore the name of the altar (*thumelê*) which the choir danced around while the scenic Games (*skénikoi*) involved the dramatic actors. Music was for the cithara (*kithara*) and the flute (*aulos*). The *aulétés pythikos* was a musician playing the special rhythm of the Pythian nome. The struggle

---

10   V. Visa-Ondarçuhu, *L'image de l'athlète*, Les Belles Lettres, Paris, 1999, pp. 113-4.

between Apollo and Python formed the background of these musical competitions. The flautist had to play his instrument without changing his expression.

In addition to the physical exercises, the Pythiad regularly held competitions in literature, tragedy, comedy, poetry, and music to the great pleasure of the actors and spectators. Above all, it was the group of Dionysiac artists from Athens who organised these musical Games. In two decrees in Delphi are preserved the names and merits of these artists. Having reminded us in the traditional way of the pious nature of these artists and their concern to increase the splendour of these festivities, the decree (no. 48) tells us how they were rewarded:

> May it please the city of Delphi to praise the group of Dionysiac artists from Athens for their devotion to our city and for their reverence for the gods and to award them as is the custom at Delphi the crown of the gods. And as well, let us award these artists who have journeyed at their own expense and have carried out their activities in public, *promanteia*, *asylia*, as was awarded to their ancestors, and all the other advantages awarded to *proxenoi* and benefactors of our city. These decrees shall be written in the sanctuary of Apollo on the treasure of the Athenians, and be sent to the Assembly and to the people of Athens as well as to the artists themselves.

These rewards show how valuable artists' performances were considered to be. The artists sent representative members to the procession. G. Colin has observed that there was no magistrate but a senior *theôros* and sometimes as many as four or seven *theôroi*. In inscription no. 49, G. Colin has pointed out the profession of all of these delegates: the chief *theôros* is a comic poet, and among the ordinary *theôroi* are to be found two tragic poets, two actors, an assistant instructor for tragedies, and two tragic actors playing secondary roles. All of these members of the procession made offerings and were present at sacrifices. Professional singers sang paeans but also gave concerts, dramatic representations and poetry recitals. Choruses sang and danced around the altar. We can see, therefore, that in these Games, "musical" competitions held as important a place as the physical ones. To be certain of the quality of the choruses in the Hellenic period, they were sung by professional artists called *Dionysiac* singers. These groups appeared in Greece toward the time of Alexander the Great and homage is paid to them in numerous inscriptions. To take the example of one country I have often visited, I can quote the decree of the artists of Dionysus, son of Mousaios. This is an inscription found in Egypt found at Ptolemais and dating from the end of the reign of Ptolemy II Philadelphus, who reigned in Egypt from 285-246 BC.[11]

> It has pleased the artists who are servant of Dionysus and Brotherly Gods and those in charge of the association to reward Dionysus, son of Mousaios, by making him a magistrate for life, and crowning him with ivy according to the ancestral laws for his devotion to the city of Ptolemais and the artists who serve the great Dionysus and the Brotherly Gods, to award this crown to the Dionysiacs and to inscribe this decree on a stele and to erect it in front of Dionysus' temple. The money for the cost of the stele will be given by the treasurer Sosibios.

Attic Panathenaic amphora with lid showing a scene from the race of the *apobatés*. Attributed to the Marsyas Painter, Athens 340-339 BC. The charioteer is dressed in white, on his left an armed competitor, with helmet and shield prepares to jump from the moving chariot and run alongside it, before jumping back on.

© The J. Paul Getty Museum (inv. 79.AE.147)

11 A. Bernand, *La prose sur pierre*, CNRS éditions, Paris, 1992, p. 3.

This decree dates from the reign of Ptolemy II Philadelphus, between 269 BC, date of the creation of the cult of the Brotherly Gods, and 246 BC, the date of the king's death.

From Ptolemais there comes as well a decree for the artists of Dionysus in honour of Lysimachos, son of Ptolemaios, chief cavalry officer and magistrate for life:[12]

> It has pleased the artists who serve Dionysus and the Brotherly Gods: given that Lysimachos, son of Ptolemaios, living in Sostratos, cavalry officer and magistrate for life, has shown himself to be devoted to the king and to his parents not only in the past but even more now and given that he is full of piety and devotion for Dionysus and the other gods, and given that he is full of generosity for the artists, not only individually, but for all of them as a whole, and that he has put his passion and energy into helping advance their profession, and given that it is proper to distinguish and honour men of this kind with suitable honours, let it please the company of Dionysiac artists whose names are inscribed below to crown Lysimachos with a crown of ivy, according to the ancient custom, on the eleventh day of the month of Peritios, for his valour and piety towards King Ptolemy, Dionysus, and other gods and for his devotion to the king, his parents, and the artists. Praise to the god of fortune! May his portrait in the entrance hall to the magistrates chamber be consecrated; may Demarchos, the secretary of the company, inscribe this decree on a stele and erect it in front of Dionysus's temple and may the money for the expense of this be given both by the treasurer Sosobios Zopyros, responsible for the sacred transactions of the triennial and annual festivals and by his two brothers.

The names of the members of the company follow. We find two tragic poets, two comic poets, a singer who accompanies himself with the cithara, a dancer or a pantomime performer. On the second column, we find the actors: a tragedian, six players: four responsible for secondary roles and a choir master. On the third column, the list of musicians is completed with mention being made of a flautist for the tragedies, a trumpeter and a costume designer. There is also mention of the protectors of this association: five *proxenoi*, no doubt responsible for public relations and six of the artists' benefactors. This gives us an almost complete picture of a theatrical company that had the religious and cultural role to make the Greek repertory known. In doing this, it also played a political role.

It is difficult to imagine the splendours that accompanied these Games. A text by Xenophon[13] gives us an idea:

> Now when the Pythian festival was approaching, Jason sent orders to his cities to make ready cattle, sheep, goats, and swine for the sacrifice. And it was said that although he laid upon each city a very moderate demand, there were

12 A. Bernand, *La prose sur pierre, op. cit.*, p. 6.

13 Xenophon, *Hellenica*, in *Xenophon in Seven Volumes* (trans. C. L. Brownson), Vol. III, Loeb Classical Library, Heinemann, London, 1980, VI, 4, 29-38.

contributed no fewer than a thousand cattle and more than ten thousand of the other animals. He also made proclamation that a golden crown would be the prize of victory to the city which should rear the finest bull to lead the herd in honour of the god. Furthermore, he gave orders to the Thessalians to make preparations for taking the field at the time of the Pythian festival; for he was intending, it was said, to be himself the director both of the festal assembly in honour of the god and of the games. What he intended, however, in regard to the sacred treasures, is even to this day uncertain; but it is said that when the Delphians asked the god what they should do if he tried to take any of his treasures, Apollo replied that he would himself take care of the matter.

We have to believe that the ambitions and intention of Jason were not pure, since the young men came to cut his throat on his throne. The gods had predicted it.

Victory songs

The victory songs called *epinikia* extended and amplified the glory surrounding the winners. These triumphal odes were sung at the banquets and formed a literary genre perfected by Pindar and Bacchylides. Before them, Tyrtaeus, a poet and war-leader living at the time of the second Messenian War, in the second half of the 7th century BC, sang of the bravery of the Spartans in a number of war poems. Whether he was originally from Athens as tradition has it or a flautist from Miletus as Suidas has suggested, he composed some military songs of which Plutarch speaks (*Life of Lycurgus* 22, 4-5). He describes the Spartan adolescents with their long, glowing and plaited hair, because Lycurgus said that long hair enhances beauty and makes them appear more fearsome. Plutarch then adds:[14]

> When their army was drawn up in battle array, and the enemy near, the
> king sacrificed a goat, commanded the soldiers to set their garlands upon their
> heads, and the pipers to play the tune of the hymn to Castor, and himself
> began the paean of advance. It was at once a magnificent and a terrible sight
> to see them march on to the tune of their flutes, without any disorder in their
> ranks, any discomposure in their minds, or change in their countenances,
> calmly and cheerfully moving with the music to the deadly fight.

Marching songs were called *embatéria* and, in his *Exhortations*, Tyrtaeus reminds the young men to show themselves to be worthy of their country and of "the invincible race of Heracles".[15]

> You young men, keep together, hold the line, do not start panic or
> disgraceful rout.
> Keep grand and valiant spirits in your hearts, be not in love with life – the
> fight's with men!
> Do not desert your elders, men with legs no longer nimble, by recourse to
> flight: it is disgraceful when an older man falls in the front line while the

---

14 Plutarch, *Lycurgus, op. cit.*, 22, 4-5.

15 Tyrtaeus, *Fragments* (trans. M. L. West), Greek Lyric Poetry, Oxford World Classics series, 1999, 10.

young hold back, with head already white, and grizzled beard, gasping his valiant breath out in the dust and clutching at his bloodied genitals, his nakedness exposed: a shameful sight and scandalous. But for the young man, still in glorious prime, it is all beautiful: alive, he draws men's eyes and women's hearts; felled in the front line, he is lovely yet.

Let every man then, feet set firm apart, bite on his lip and stand against the foe.

These patriotic songs, inspired by Heracles, the god of the physical Games, show the link that exists between the Olympic and military ideals. Pindar and Terpander, Plutarch tells us (VI, 21, 6), "portray therefore Spartans who are both passionate about music and about war". Praise given to the warrior is the same as that given to the victor. The actions of both of them increase the prestige of the city and pay homage to the gods.

The poet Bacchylides, younger than Pindar, was born at Ioulis on the island of Ceos which was famed for the number of victories in the Great Games.[16] It is thought that he was born around 507 BC and that he died around 430 BC. He not only celebrated Hieron of Sicily, victor in the chariot race (*Epinician Odes* III, IV, V) but also victorious children (*Epinician Odes* I, II, VI, VII, XI, XIII). His eulogy of Automedes, son of Timenos of Phleious, a city near Nemea,[17] informs us that in the pentathlon this athlete carried off three of the five trophies:

[...] for he stood out among the pentathletes as the shining moon in the mid-month night sky outshines the light of the stars. In such a way, amid the vast circling crowd of the Greeks, did he display his marvellous body, hurling the wheel-shaped discus, and raise a shout from the people as he flung the shaft of the dark-leaved elder-tree from his hand into the steep sky.

He executed the flashing movement of wrestling, and brought strong-limbed bodies down to the earth with such high-spirited strength, then returned to the dark-whirling waters of the Asopus, whose fame has reached every land, even the farthest reaches of the Nile.

16 See the introduction to Bacchylide, *Dithyrambes, Épinicies, Fragments*, (ed. J. Irigoin and trans. J. Duchemin and L. Bardollet), Les Belles Lettres, Paris, 1963.

17 Bacchylides, *op. cit.*, IX.

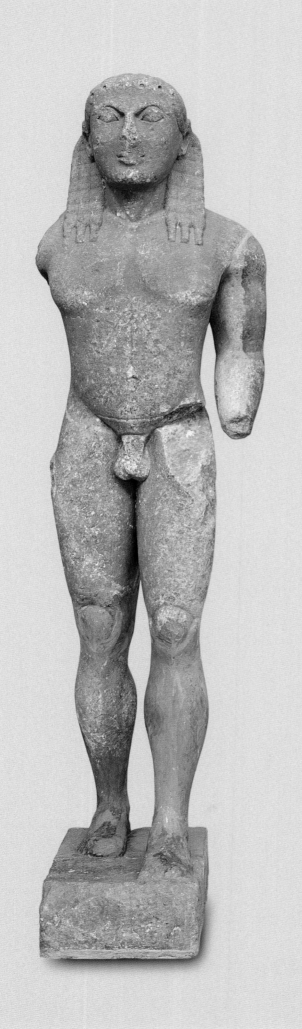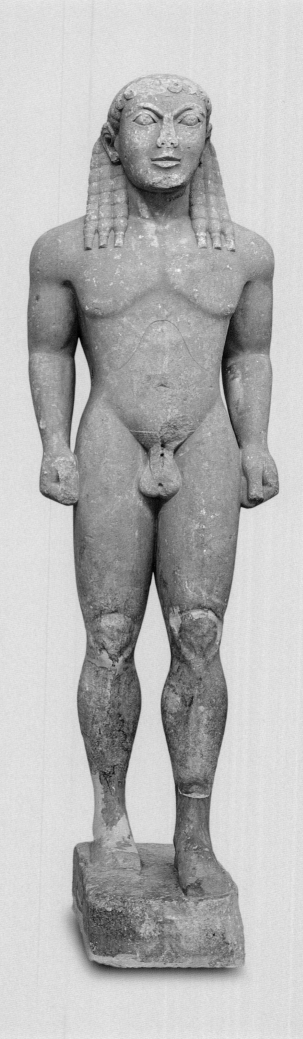

Chapter VII
Peace, prowess, perfection

The Olympic truce

The Games had to take place in peacetime as pilgrims and participants had to be able to travel to the meetings without danger. The truce (*ekecheiria; ekechéria* in Dorian), was a rare break in the continual wars of Ancient Greece.

Thucydides (IV, 58-64)[1] has Syracusan Hermocrates, son of Hermon give a speech highlighting the advantages of a truce in the conflict which opposed the Sicilian towns of Camarina and Gela in the eighth year of the Peloponnesian War (March 424-February 423 BC). This man, whom Thucydides admired a great deal and of whom he often talks, knew how to find the right words at a congress held at Gela and at which all the Sicilian towns were represented. Citizen of one of the biggest cities on the island, he wanted to protect the interests of the island as a whole, all the more so since it was under threat from Athens. Hermocrates' arguments were as follows: "What is the point of reviewing all of the misfortunes that war brings, since what you could learn from these will teach you nothing?" Or again: "Do not forget that it is internal conflicts that cause the loss of states." Or: "All men are agreed that peace is the most desirable thing in the world. Why then should it not be re-established between us?" Or: "Does not peace, too, allow us to have honours and become famous but with fewer risks?"

It was not simply a matter of making a truce. It was also necessary that it should not be broken. In his account of the 12th year of the Peloponnesian War (March 420-February 419 BC), Thucydides (V, 49-50) tells how in the course of that summer at the Olympic Games when the Arcadian Androsthenes had carried off his first victory, the Lacedemonians saw themselves forbidden by the Eleans to have access to the sacred arena and could neither sacrifice nor take part in the Games. "They had not paid the fine that the Eleans had imposed on them, invoking the Olympic law, for having attacked their fort at Phyrkos. Moreover, they had sent a body of armed infantry men to Lepreon during the Olympic truce." The Eleans tried in vain to have the Lacedemonians promise over the altar to Zeus to settle the fine later. They refused and the situation worsened. This is Thucydides' account:[2]

> Access to the sanctuary therefore was forbidden to the Lacedemonians and they had to make their sacrifices at home while all the other Greeks, apart from those from Lepreon, took part in the Games. However, fearing that they would have recourse to force so that they could make their sacrifices in the temple, the Eleans kept a number of their young men armed and put them on guard. They were reinforced by a thousand Argiens and by the same number of Mantineans and by horsemen from Athens who were waiting for the Games to open at Harpina. The Greeks quickly became anxious since

---

1 Thucydides, *History of the Peloponnesian War* (trans. C. F. Smith), Loeb Classical Library, Heinemann, London, 1930, IV, 58-64.
2 *Ibid.*, V, 50-1.

Cleobis and Biton (*kouroi*), in the museum at Delphi.
© 1990, Photo Scala, Florence

they feared they would see the Lacedemonians arrive bearing weapons, especially after the Spartan Lichas, son of Arkesilaos had been beaten by the rod bearers on the track. His carriage had indeed won but since he had not had the right to take part, the people were declared winners. Lichas had come onto the track, therefore, and crowned his driver to show that the chariot belonged to him. After this, the spectators became even more uneasy, expecting some strong reaction but the Lacedemonians did not react and the Games finished without incident.

Truces were sometimes advanced as a reason for not taking part in a military expedition. Xenophon[3] records that the people of Phleious refused to march with the Lacedemonians, saying that they had a truce.

Athletic competitions were sometimes used as a strategem to empty a town's garrison in wartime. Thus, in his account of the 14th year of the Peloponnesian War (March 418-February 417 BC) Thucydides[4] tells us how the Athenian general Demosthenes, son of Alkisthenes, at the request of the Argives, had the soldiers leave the garrison at Epidaurus for the athletic competitions he was organising and this gave him an excuse to completely empty the garrison. He then shut the gates.

Truces, like treaties, were always unpredictable. In the *Hellenica*[5] Xenophon tells how, in 385 BC when the Spartan Agesipolis led his expedition against the town of Mantinea, the Spartans ignored the truce signed during the winter of 418-417 BC. Breaking promises in this way was common. According to Plutarch, the idea of an Olympic truce (*hé Olympiaké ekecheiria*) could only be proposed by a gentle and peace-loving man. The Sophist Hippias refused to see these qualities in the legislator Lycurgus but Demetrios of Phalera did. He was a peripatetic philosopher who was governor of Athens from 317 to 307 BC and who had written a book entitled *On Peace*. The introduction of the Olympic truce could only have been divinely inspired.[6]

> Lycurgus came only as a spectator, and that by mere accident too. Being there, he heard as it were a man's voice behind him, blaming and wondering at him that he did not encourage his countrymen to resort to the assembly, and, turning about and seeing no man, concluded that it was a voice from heaven, and upon this immediately went to Iphitus and assisted him in ordering the ceremonies of that feast, which, by his means, were better established, and with more repute than before.

It is difficult to imagine the glory that Olympic victories brought. Herodotus offers us an anecdote on this:[7] Solon reminds us of two young Argive men, Cleobis and Biton, who had been winners at the Great Games. When the festivities in honour of Hera were celebrated, their mother was due to go to the temple in a chariot drawn

3   Xenophon, *Hellenica*, in *Xenophon in Seven Volumes*, Vol. III (trans. C. L. Brownson), Loeb Classical Library, Harvard University Press, Cambridge, MA, 1985, IV, 2, 16.

4   Thucydides, *op. cit.*, V, V, 80.

5   Xenophon, *Hellenica*, *op. cit.*, V, 2, 2.

6   Plutarch, *Lycurgus*, in *Lives* (trans. J. Dryden), Modern Library Classics, New York, 1992, 23, 3-4.

7   Herodotus, *Histories* (trans. A. D. Godley), Loeb Classical Library, Harvard University Press, Cambridge, MA, 1920, I, 31.

by oxen. When the oxen failed to appear, the two young men took the yoke and pulled the chariot 45 *stades* (8km), such was their strength. Everyone congratulated them for it and praised their strength. People crowded round the statue of Hera and their mother asked the goddess to reward them with the greatest happiness a mortal could have. After taking part in the sacrifice and the banquet, the two young men fell asleep in the sanctuary and never woke up.

That was the prestige given to physical strength: "To win, and then to die" would have been the motto of champions. The two statues erected by the people of Delphi in honour of the two young men were later found in the sanctuary at Delphi: at 2.35 m high, they were in the ancient style of statues honouring beautiful adolescents.[8]

Not all Olympic champions aspired to such a radical peace. A truce allowed a period of peace so that competitions could take place. This truce is described in epigraphic texts. Peace was necessary for the accomplishment of the prowess demanded of the participants in the Games.

Feats and achievements

Only individual achievements mattered. In antiquity, team competitions did not exist. Moreover, some of our modern competitions were unknown – for example, the steeple chase, cross-country, relay, swimming and diving competitions, and of course, the winter events and aquatic competitions. Pausanias (II, *Corinth.*, 35,1) informs us that swimming and diving (*kolymbos*) competitions occurred at the sanctuary of Dionysus near to the place known as Hermione in Argolis. We know that regattas took place at the Panathenaic Games in Corcyra, at Nicopolis, from the reign of Augustus. The Athenian *ephebes* sometimes held canoe races in the Salamine and the Mounychia rivers.[9] But these were local competitions and had no place in the major panhellenic Games.

It is not unreasonable to think that these unusual competitions were organised and based on ones that occurred in foreign countries. Thus, Herodotus tells how at Abydos, Xerxes took pleasure in participating in a nautical race organised in his honour:[10]

> When they were at Abydos, Xerxes wanted to see the whole of his army. A lofty seat of white stone had been set up for him on a hill there for this very purpose, built by the people of Abydos at the king's command. There he sat and looked down on the seashore, viewing his army and his fleet; as he viewed them he desired to see the ships contend in a race. They did so, and the Phoenicians of Sidon won; Xerxes was pleased with the race and with his expedition.

Pierre Briant[11] draws on another text by Herodotus[12] to underline the

8   A. Barguet refers to C. Picard, *Manuel d'Archéologie grecque*, Paris, 1973, I, p. 495 and to the article by B. A. Van Groningen, "L'exploit de Cléobis et Biton et la véracité d'Hérodote", collection *Mnémosyne* (vol. XII), pp. 34-43.

9   See V. Vanoyeke, *La naissance des Jeux olympiques et le sport dans l'Antiquité*, Les Belles Lettres, Paris, 1992, pp. 51-2.

10   Herodotus, *op. cit.*, VII, 44.

11   P. Briant, *Histoire de l'Empire perse de Cyrus à Alexandre*, Fayard, Paris, 1996, pp. 209-10.

12   Herodotus, *op. cit.*, VII, 100.

Black-figure vase showing a ball game called "kings and donkeys". An adult sitting on a folding chair gets ready to throw the ball. Three youths, sitting on the shoulders of three others, stretch their arms out towards the trainer. Those who drop the ball carry those who catch it. The vase is housed in the British Museum.
© The British Museum

importance of the review of troops. He recalls that in Doriskos, in Thrace, Xerxes organised a new review once the number of soldiers had been counted:

> When his army had been numbered and marshalled, Xerxes desired to ride through and view it. Then he did this; as he rode in a chariot past the men of each nation, he questioned them while his scribes wrote it all down, until he had gone from one end to the other of the cavalry and infantry. After he had done this, the ships were drawn down and launched into the sea. Xerxes alighted from his chariot into a Sidonian ship and sat under a golden canopy while he was carried past the prows of the ships, questioning the men in the same way as the army and having the answers written down. The captains put out and anchored in line four hundred feet from the shore, with their prows turned landward and the marines armed for war; Xerxes viewed them by passing between the prows and the land.

Briant rightly notes that "Xerxes was reviewing not the military strength of his empire, but its ethnic and cultural diversity". When we bring these texts together, we can understand that the nautical jousts were a way of giving Hellenic quality to these Games with the prestige attached to them in the Greek world. We will see that in the Hellenic period, descriptions of processions of champions and their trophies was really a review of troops and intended to confirm their superiority over those of neighbouring kingdoms.

One thing is certain, balls had no place in the Games. Greek has the term *sphaira* to designate round objects (from which we have the modern word, "sphere"). Games with balls existed for training purposes.[13] Wall ball (*aporraxis*), for example, an ancient form of pelota, played with bare hands; sky ball (*ourania*); *harpaston* in which some people would like to see a similarity to rugby and which was played with a small, hard ball. Athenaeus of Naucratis,[14] a writer of the first half of the 3rd century AD, tells us that this ball was called a *phaininda* and that he was an enthusiast.

As we can see from the *Odyssey*, engaging in ball games was something girls could do. Nausicaa and her friends did so after they had been bathing in the sea and after having rubbed one another with oil.[15]

> When they had done dinner they threw off the veils that covered their heads and began to play at ball, while Nausicaa sang for them.

The squeals when one of the women accidentally threw the ball off at an angle woke Ulysses.

Athletes did not bring back victories to their fathers and cities by playing ball or team sports. A spirit of ambition that was characteristic of the Hellenic ideal — emulation — moved them. Since Homer's time, the aim of well-born persons was constantly to improve through competition with equals. By doing this it ensured that they would live on in the memory of men. In her own way, this is what Helen wanted

---

13 See E. Norman Gardiner, *Athletics of the ancient world*, Clarendon Press, Oxford, 1930, pp. 230-8.

14 Athenaeus, *The Deipnosophists* (trans. C. Burton Gulik), Harvard University Press, Cambridge MA, 1928, I, 14.

15 Homer, *Odyssey*, (trans. S. Butler), Jonathan Cape, London, (2nd edition) 1922, VI, 99-100, 115-6.

to do. The desire to achieve was inseparable from a desire for glory and this attitude would not disappear with the emergence of Christianity. Marie-Françoise Baslez[16] in her fine book on St Paul observes that in Pauline writings as in earlier works of praise, there are references to the effort, to the race, to the crowns, and prizes carried off by winners. We find the same theme in the works of Philon of Alexandria and in those of many of the Church Fathers.

Victory odes

These hymns, also called epinician odes, celebrated the glory brought by athletic or artistic competitions. This is the leitmotiv of odes by Pindar or Bacchylides, which, as we have seen, were written in celebration of children and young people. One section of the *Olympian Odes* celebrates the Sicilian tyrants Hieron of Syracuse (*Ol.*I), and Theron of Agrigentum (*Ol.* II and III), winners of the chariot races. But they also celebrated others less important like Psaumis of Camarina, winner in the mule chariot race (*apéne*) (*Ol.* IV and V), and Agesias from Syracuse, who also won in the same competition (*Ol.* VI). Diagoras from Rhodes, a boxer (*Ol.* VII), Alcimedon from Aegina, a child wrestler (*Ol.*VIII), the boxer Epharmostas, from Opuntian Locris, and his two compatriots (*Ol.*VIII, IX, X, XI), Ergosteles, a Sicilian from Himera, a winner of the *dolichos* (*Ol.* XII), Xenophon, a rich Corinthian winner both in the stadium and the pentathlon (*Ol.*XIII). Finally there is the child from Orchomenus, who won in the stadium (*Ol.*XIV). All of these texts exalt the love of glory. Members of rich families supported these athletes and poets sang their glory. This can explain why poets often make no mention of their brutality and cruelty. Pindar himself celebrated the athlete Hieron:[17]

> A god who hath this care, Hieron, watcheth and broodeth over thy desires; but, if he doth not desert thee too soon, I trust I shall celebrate a still sweeter victory, even with the swift chariot, having found a path that prompteth praises, when I have reached the sunny hill of Cronus.
> Howsoever, for myself, the Muse is keeping a shaft most might in strength. Some men are great in one thing; others in another: but the crowning summit is for kings. Refrain from peering too far! Heaven grant that thou mayest plant thy feet on high, so long as thou livest, and that I may consort with victors for all my days, and be foremost in the lore of song among Hellenes in every land.

We find the same theme in the second Olympian:[18]

> Ye hymns that rule the lyre! What god, what hero, aye and what man shall we loudly praise? Verily Zeus is the lord of Pisa; and Heracles established the Olympic festival, from the spoils of war; while Thêrôn who is just in his regard for guests, and who is the bulwark of Acragas, the choicest flower of an auspicious line of sires, whose city towers on high.

---

16 M.-F. Baslez, *Saint Paul*, Fayard, Paris, 1991, p. 42.

17 Pindar, *Olympian Odes*, in *Odes* (trans. D. Svarlien), Perseus Project, Yale, 1991, I, 171-88.

18 Pindar, *Olympian Odes*, op. cit., II, 1-14.

Red-figure amphora by the Douris Painter, circa 490 BC. Victorious athlete holding an olive sprig and wearing on his right arm and right leg a long red woollen ribbon.
© The State Hermitage Museum, St. Petersburg (inv. B. 5576)

As Pindar says, victory at Olympia ensures eternal fame:[19] "Come now, holy arena of Pisa and banks of the Alphea, shaded by magnificent trees, welcome this triumphal procession! Whoever receives your dazzling reward will have fame forever."

According to Pindar, celebrating Hieron of Aetna, winner of the chariot race at Delphi, such a victory was no less glorious.[20] "To sum up, then, in the future this town will be celebrated for the prizes won by its horses and will be famous for the beautiful songs with which its festivities resound."

In the fourth Pythian, written for Arcesilas of Cyrenea, winner of the chariot race, Pindar[21] recalls how people who originated from the island of Thera founded Cyrenea. They "exchanged dolphins for horses, oars for reins, and drove chariots like the wind." In other words, from being island-dwellers and sailors, they became mainland-dwellers and farmers. The achievement of Arcesilas at Delphi served to perpetuate the daring achievement of Battos, "coloniser of the fertile Libya".

Perfection

In order for their performances to earn them the glory for which they strove, the athletes' and artists' movements had to be perfect and their bodies had to glow with strength and beauty. Flautists were not meant to contort their faces when blowing their instruments, for example.

We should note, in passing, that the flute was an important instrument. In Sparta, it accompanied the rhythm of soldiers marching to an attack in the same way that the British army used bagpipes during the last war. The *triéraulés* and *aulos* were also used to help rowers keep stroke.[22] At feasts, flautists were women who combined their talent with their charms, though these were less sought after at these all-male affairs than those of young boys.

Paintings from the Tomb of the Diver, preserved in the museum at Paestum, highlight scenes of masculine beauty. On one of the smaller sides of a panel there is a mature man dressed in a cloak and leaning on a stick, following a young naked man who is pointing to the female flautist in front of him. On the longer sides we can see couples of cup bearers and soothsayers. The former have beards, the latter do not. All wear crowns of leaves, are lying together in couples feasting on chaises longues (*kliné*), courting one another quite openly. A man, eyes shining and mouth greedy, pulls an *ephebe* carrying a cithara towards him; elsewhere we see a couple playing at *kottabus* (see p. 230). On the same divan, a man is playing a double flute with his back turned towards a bearded man, adjusting his crown.[23]

Among many others, Pindar has sung the praises of these beautiful adolescents when he composed an ode for Xenocrates of Agrigentum, who had been the victor in the chariot race:[24]

The men of old, O Thrasybulus, who mounted the car of the golden-

---

19 Pindar, *Olympian Odes, op. cit.,* VIII, 12-5.

20 Pindar, *Pythian Odes, op. cit.,* I, 69-72.

21 *Ibid.,* IV, 1-41.

22 Demosthenes, *De Corona* (trans. J. H. Vince, C. A. Vince), Loeb Classical Library, Heinemann, London, 1969, line 129, mentions the "flutist of the *trier*", who rescued Æschines' mother from a life of prostitution.

23 M. Cipriani and G. Avagliano, *Art et Histoire de Paestum,* Casa editrice Bonechi, Florence, 1999, pp. 62-5.

24 Pindar, *Isthmian Odes, op. cit.,* I.

wreathed Muses, taking up the sounding lyre, lightly shot forth their honey-sweet songs in honour of their loves, whensoever one fair in form had that precious bloom which turneth the thoughts to Aphrodite on her beauteous throne.

Plato has described how desire (*himeros*) was awakened by the bodily contacts which took place in the gymnasium:[25]

As times goes on, his youth and destiny cause him to admit him to society. For it is the law of fate that evil can never be a friend to evil and that good must always be friend to good. And when the lover is thus admitted, and the privilege of conversation and intimacy has been granted him, his good will, as it shows itself in close intimacy, astonishes the beloved, who discovers that the friendship of all his other friends and relatives is as nothing when compared with that of his inspired lover. And as this intimacy continues and the lover

Lovers at a banquet, circa 480 BC. The fresco, from the Tomb of the Diver at Paestum, is from an interior wall of the sarcophagus, so this happy memory was intended for the occupant's contemplation only.

© 1990, Photo Scala, Florence – courtesy of the Ministero Beni e Att. Culturali. Paestum Museum

25 Plato, *Phaedrus* (trans. H. N. Fowler), Loeb Classical Library, Heinemann, London, 1980, 255.

comes near and touches the beloved in the gymnasia and in their general intercourse, then the "fountain of that stream which Zeus, when he was in love with Ganymedes, called desire flows copiously upon the lover; and some of it flows into him, and some, when he is filled, overflows outside".

Plato then goes on to describe what this love can lead to for the one who is loved:[26]

> [...] but he calls it, and believes it to be, not love, but friendship. Like the lover, though less strongly, he desires to see his friend, to touch him, kiss him, and lie down by him; and naturally these things are soon brought about. Now as thy lie together, the unruly horse of the lover has something to say to the charioteer, and demands a little enjoyment in return for his many troubles; and the unruly horse of the beloved says nothing, but teeming with passion and confused emotions he embraces and kisses this lover, caressing him as his best friend; and when they lie together, he would not refuse his lover any favour, if he asked it.

These meetings were made easier if those who frequented the gymnasium could shine. But how did you become handsome? Obviously, by training in the way any athlete or artist should. But in order to reach the highest point of beauty (*aglaia*) there were tricks that young men took advantage of. Not only was olive oil in this country a way of slipping out of your opponents grasp or of protecting yourself against the sun, it also gave a lustre to the skin. Oil also made massaging after physical effort easier, softening muscles and overcoming tiredness. Those in charge at the gymnasium spent a lot of money answering to these needs. Vases often depict the tiny phial of oil that young athletes always had ready.

The funerary stele of a certain Diodorus, son of Theophilus, a teacher at the gymnasium who died at the age of 53, depicts the equipment he had. Below the epitaph from left to right we can make out a crown, three tablets – each one bearing a portrait – a pointed hat, an axe, three strigils, and two palms at either side of a container of oil decorated with three ladles for its distribution. This evidence was discovered at Prusa in Asia Minor and dates from the Roman era. It allows us to see the full range of what the gymnasium teacher needed.[27]

Coins cast at the festivals show us which one is being commemorated by presenting a monumental crown with two palms above it. This design was often thought to depict a funerary urn but when it appears on coins it shows an athlete wearing it like a hat. In Artemidorus's *The Key to Dreams* there is the story of an athlete dreaming that he was washing his feet in this monumental crown, which he had mistaken for a bucket.

Another way of improving one's appearance and of demonstrating that there was a festival was to put on a crown. This was worn at feasts and in the open air had the advantage of protecting you from the sun. A crown made from the olive tree (*elaias stephanos*) was the commonest but Dionysiac artists wore one made from ivy (*thallou*

Attic red-figure cup showing a bearded adult, dressed in a long shawl, kissing a young boy, also clothed, who allows the man to draw his head towards him. Briseis Painter, circa 480 BC. Kept in the Louvre (inv. G 278).

---

26 Plato, *Phaedrus*, op. cit., 255–6.

27 M. I. Finley and H. W. Pleket, *The Olympic games: the first thousand years*, The Viking Press, New York, 1976, p. 89.

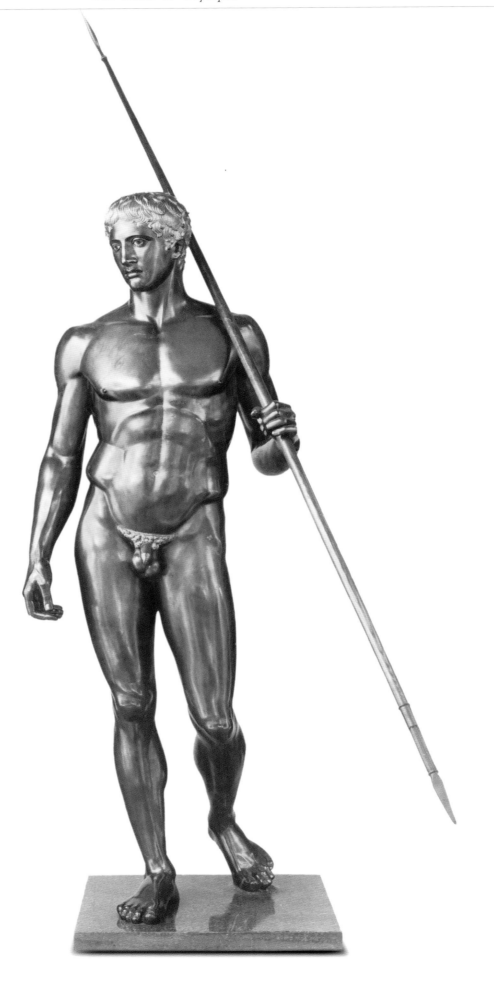

stephanos). Crowns made from oak (*dryos stephanos*) or white poplar (*leukés stephanos*) were rare and one made from myrtle (*myrtou stephanos*) would be worn in ceremonies held in honour of Aphrodite. The laurel crown (*daphnés stephanos*) was worn in honour of Apollo and was the most common.

Statues give us the best idea of the physical performance of Greek athletes. A bare athlete showed people the balanced body of someone who took part in the Games. But this did not simply invite intellectual admiration. Greek sculptors treated masculine beauty endlessly. Most statues are only known to us in the form of Roman reproductions. It is through these reproductions that we are able to enjoy this beauty: for example, the talents of one Polyclitus, a sculptor from Argos of the 5th century BC. François Chamoux[28] reminds us that this sculptor was at the height of his career at the time of the 90th Olympiad in 420-417 BC.

Polyclitus, who was a contemporary of Phidias, and like him, was ranked at the highest level by the ancients, came first in the competition in Ephese, where he competed against Phidias. His best-known masterpieces are the *Doryphorus* (lance carrier for the tyrants' guard) and the *Diadumena*, a naked man putting on his crown.[29] This statue is the copy of the original Greek one from 440-430 BC and shows a naked young man putting a victory band around his head. The balance and supple form of this representation provoked numerous copies. In carving the *Diadumena*, Polyclitus succeeded in naturalistically representing a man in motion, very different from static ancient statues such as those of Cleobis and Biton, whose figures are frozen in solemn attitudes.

In the fifth Nemean dedicated to Pytheas of Aegina,[30] the young winner in the pancratium, Pindar boasted that he was not "a sculptor and that he did not produce figures standing rigidly on their base". In fact, he hoped that the young man's Nemean victory would be made public by the first embarkation from the port of Aegina. In this way, he made a connection between local stories, legends, and their material representations. When Pindar celebrates legendary heroes, he does not forget that they too were men every bit as heroic as those who won at the Games.

Women were barred from the Games, saving them the embarassment of being confronted with naked male athletes. These athletes wore a *chlamys* or a *himation* when they were in town. If nudity was the obligatory rule of the gymnasium, in the stadium, or in the palaestra, in the street it would be seen as exhibitionism. Socrates casts a furtive glance at the young, handsome Charmides, "glimpsing in the opening of his cloak a beauty which set me alight, and I lost my mind."[31] We should not forget, though, that as Chamoux has written:[32] "The Hellenic man maintains a direct and permanent contact with nature even when it is harsh, as is sometimes the case in Greece. Among men, nudity is never far away."

The *chlamys*, a short, rectangular piece of cloth, generally attached on the right shoulder, was the favourite garment of Thessalian horsemen. It allowed freedom of movement, it could be adjusted, cast off like a shawl, or turned into a scarf,[33] thereby

28 Fr. Chamou, *La Civilisation grecque*, Arthaud, Paris, 1963, pp. 429-30.

29 Pictured in J. R. Mertens, *The Metropolitan Museum of Art: Greece and Rome*, New York, 1987, pp. 64-5.

30 Pindar, *Nemean Odes*, in *Odes, op. cit.*, V, 1.

31 Plato, *Charmides* (trans. W. R. M. Lamb), Loeb Classical Library, Heinemann, London, 1955, 155.

32 F. Chamoux, preface to G. Losfeld, *Essai sur le costume grec*, éditions De Boccard, Paris, 1991, p. 7.

33 See the diagram by G. Losfeld, *ibid.*, p. 178.

Bronze statue of the *Doryphorus* (spear carrier) by Polyclitus kept at Munich University.
© AKG London

uncovering the body. It was worn by riders and young men. In contrast, the *himation*, a long cloak covering the body, was worn by everyone. The difference between these two garments is fully illustrated by the anecdote, which, according to Hieronymus of Rhodes, was told by Athenaeus in *The Deipnosophists* (XIII.604). At 80 Sophocles dragged a young, beautiful boy out of town, who took off his own *himation* and laid it on the grass and then "once everything had been done" fled, carrying the poet's *chlamys*, the most prestigious garment with him.

The statues of athletes depict young, nude men. The theme has been treated by the greatest sculptors, allowing us to admire the perfect bodies of all those who took part in the Games.

Myron of Eleutherae, a sculptor of the 5th century, has left us the figure of a discus thrower captured in full swing. Praxiteles, an Athenian sculptor of the 4th century BC, who was considered by Pliny to be at his best in the 104th *Olympiad*, has left us a Hermes whose ambiguous grace is full of sensuality. The Hermes of Marathon, the bronze original of which was fished out of the Bay of Marathon, depicts a naked young man both slender and graceful, delighted at having found a turtle.[34] If the masterpieces of Polyclitus are the *Doryphorus* and the *Diadumenos*, superb representations of powerfully muscled young men with a disturbing appeal in repose, the Westmacott athlete in the British Museum is a superb copy in Roman marble[35] of a bronze statue made by Polyclitus. Lysippus of Sicyon, who worked from 368-318 BC, was one of the best artists working in bronze and depicting movement. We can see this in, among others, his statue of Alexander as a horseman, dated 300-250 BC, and kept at the National Museum in the Villa Giulia in Rome[36] or by his representation of a winning athlete in bronze kept at the Getty Museum in Malibu[37] or by the equestrian statue of Alexander in the Museum at Naples,[38] or again, by the young athlete in the Berlin Museum in marble and dating back to the 1st century AD.[39]

The cult of virile beauty is given expression on vases and in paintings. Unfortunately, because of their fragility they are all too rare. Let us just note a few typical examples.

A jar in the style of Fikellura (Aegean Anatolia) dating from the 3rd quarter of the 6th century and kept at the British Museum (inv. A 1311) shows us a naked runner, his efforts perfectly captured.[40] Five naked runners in full flight are painted by Euphiletos on an Panathenaic Attic amphora dating from around 530 and held in the Metropolitan Museum in New York (see p. 139).[41]

On an Attic jar dating from around 525 and kept in the Antikenmuseum in Berlin-Charlottenburg, Andocides has painted the holds of wrestlers one of whom is bearded, the other young, wrestling in front of spectators at the Games.[42] Skythes has

34 Statue housed in the national museum of Athens. Pictured in F. Chamoux, *op. cit.*, fig. 227.

35 Pictured in L. Burn, *The British Museum Book of Greek and Roman Art*, Thames and Hudson, London, 1992, p. 59.

36 Pictured in P. Moreno, *Vita e Arte di Lisippo*, Milano, 1987, pp. 65-7.

37 *Ibid.*, pp. 71-3.

38 *Ibid.*, p. 153.

39 *Ibid.*, p. 226.

40 A. Metzge, H. Metzge and J. P. Sicre, *La Beauté nue*, Phébus, Paris, 1984, illustration p.10.

41 *Ibid.*, p. 31.

42 *Ibid.*, pp. 126-7.

Red-figure vase housed in the Berlin-Charlottenburg Antikenmuseum (inv. F 2180). Three athletes, Hippomedon, Hesias and Lykon, whose names are inscribed, prepare themselves for a workout. Hippomedon is massaged by the young Tranion, Lykon, taking off his *chlamys*, is helped by a young assistant. Hippomedon and Tranion are crowned with ivy, Lykon wears an olive wreath.
© bpk. Staatliche Museen zu Berlin Preussischer Kulturbesitz.
Photo : Johannes Laurentius

painted on an Attic cup dating from around 510-500 BC a boy who is naked, slightly drunk, and carrying at the level of his thighs a lyre, renowned for its intoxicating powers (Villa Guilia inv. 20760).[43]

On a vase in the form of an Attic cup dated around 505 BC, the painter Euphronios depicted from the back, naked, the handsome Hippomedon leaning over the head of young boy. Tranion, himself also wearing a crown, can be seen massaging the foot of his master. "They are united by a tender complicity. In Athens, as elsewhere, the boundary between massage and caress is quickly crossed."[44] D. Pralon recalls an epigram by Strato (*Greek Anthology* XII, 192) that gives a good account of the atmosphere in the palaestra.

> *Neither hair nor excessive artificial curls please me*
> *that do not show the work of nature:*
> *rather the dirt and sand on a boy in the palaestra*
> *and the colour given to his limbs by his oiled flesh.*

The Greek, and in particular the Athenian painters, were pleased to paint these *ephebes* who were no longer children nor yet adults; the youngest were between 12 and 13, the oldest between 17 and 18.

The only dress the *ephebes* needed was their youthful grace as can be seen on Euphronios's vase.[45]

43   A. Metzge, H. Metzge and J. P. Sicre, *op. cit.*, pp.128-9.

44   *Ibid.*, pp. 140-1.

45   *Ibid.*, p. 45.

Detail from the vase on the left: Hippomedon is
massaged by the young Tranion.
© bpk. Staatliche Museen zu Berlin Preussischer Kulturbesitz.
Photo : Johannes Laurentius.

Towards 480, the Berlin Painter depicted the perfection of Ganymedes' naked
body as he played with a hoop. This is on a vase in the shape of an Attic bell (Louvre,
inv. G 175). Ganymedes is waving a cock offered to him by his lover, Zeus. This scene
is illustrated on the other side of the vase.[46] Pralon refers to the text by Theognis
(*Elegies*, II):

> *To love a young boy is a pleasure*
> *since, in times gone by, Ganymedes too*
> *was loved by the Cronus King of Immortals*
> *who carried him to Olympus, and made him*

---

46   A. Metzge, H. Metzge and J. P. Sicre, *op. cit.*, pp. 152-3.

Brygos Painter. Detail from a red-figure Attic cup, circa 480 BC, kept in the Ashmolean Museum (inv. 1967/304).
© Ashmolean Museum, University of Oxford

a god, with the sought after flower of youth.
So do not be surprised, Simonides, because I, too,
I have exposed myself, overcome by love
for a young and beautiful boy.

The Brygos Painter, on an Attic cup from around 480 BC depicts a scene in the palaestra that must have been common.[47] Having put down his stick, his sponge, and his strigil and having thrown off his *himation* to display his body, a bearded athlete has his hand towards the pubis of a young, naked boy who can see the state in which he is putting his cup-bearer, and who already consenting, strokes his neck as he leans toward him, grateful for the sack of tidbits that the older man has offered him.

---

47 A. Metzge, H. Metzge and J. P. Sicre, *op. cit.,* pp. 164-5.

Red-figure *pelikos* showing Zeus abducting
Ganymedes, from Phocis circa 470 BC.
© National Archaeological Museum of Athens

The hare was also a present given to boys to attract their favours. On an Attic cup from the beginning of the 5th century (British Museum, inv. E 46) Onesimos shows us a naked *ephebe* running not only after a hare but also no doubt after an adventure that has rather less to do with hunting. On an Attic cup from around 460 BC (Bibliothèque Nationale de France, inv. 820) a bearded man, having thrown off his *himation* but not yet having shown his intentions, pulls a young lute player towards him who seems unwilling but who has already lost his *chlamys* to show off his bodily perfection.[48]

It would be possible to multiply the examples of this taste for bodily perfection that inspired artists and that permeated the Games and the athletes' training. There is nothing obscene, then, in these representations which have nothing to do with the

48   A. Metzge, H. Metzge and J. P. Sicre, *op. cit.*, pp. 210-1.

erotic and pornographic scenes to be seen on the Attic cup by the Pedicus Painter that is in the Louvre.[49]

Beauty and youth expressed the hope of overcoming inevitable death. As Pindar expressed so elegantly at the end of the tenth Olympian:[50]

> I have praised the beauteous son of Archestratus, whom, on that day, beside the Olympic altar, I saw winning victory with the might of his hands, one who was fair to look upon, and was graced with that bloom which, in olden days, by the blessing of Aphrodite, warded from Ganymedes a ruthless fate.

A man offers a hare, an erotic symbol, to a boy. Red-figure *pelikos* from Atalante, Locris, circa 460 BC. The man has a cloak draped across his chest, revealing one shoulder. He leans on a stick, eyeing the boy lecherously. The fresh-faced youth is wrapped in a cloak up to his neck from which he peers innocently, gripping a lyre. Perhaps he is on his way home from a music lesson.

© National Archaeological Museum of Athens

49   P. Quignard, *Le sexe et l'effroi*, Gallimard, Paris, 1994, pp.18-9.

50   Pindar, *Olympian Odes, op. cit.*, X, 120-5.

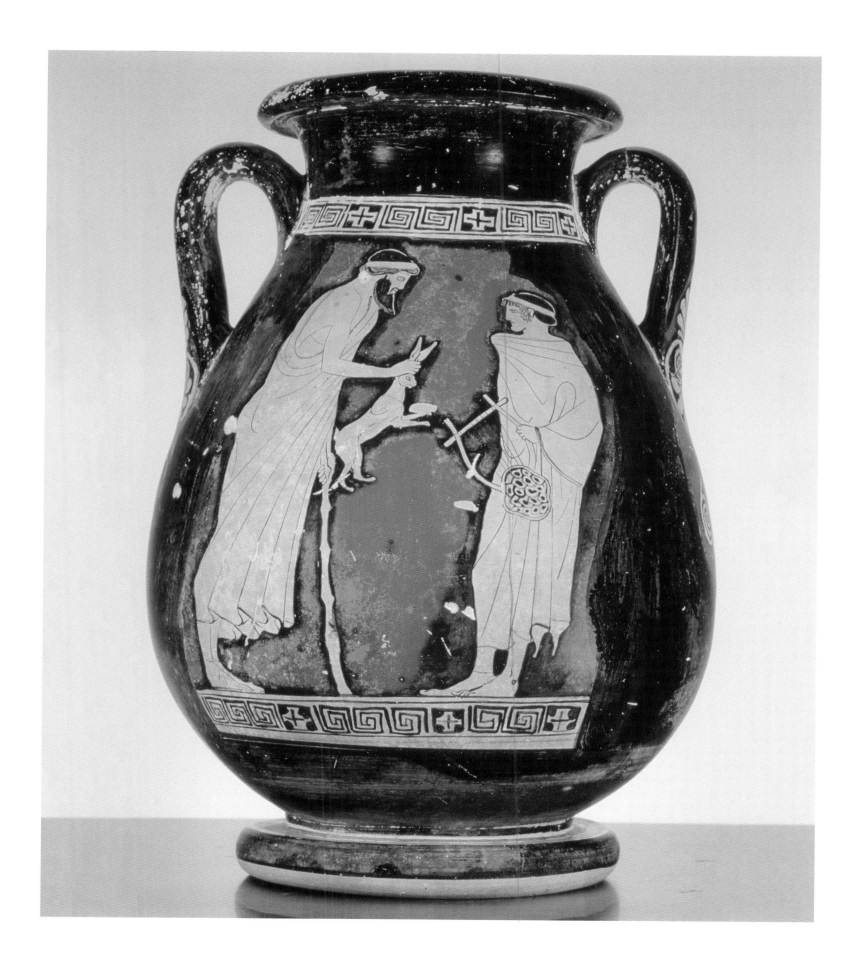

Chapter VIII
Regional games

While the major Games, that is those belonging to the "season" (Olympian, Delphian, Isthmian and Nemean Games) were the most prestigious and conferred the most fame to the victors, there were also regional games in which talent could make its mark and bode well for a panhellenic career. These games accorded honour in proportion to the importance of the city in which they took place. For all that, they remained local affairs, such as the festival of the Panathenaea at Athens.

The Panathenaea

This festival in honour of Athena comprised two types of event. The Lesser Panathenaea was an annual festival that took place in the month of Hecatombaion, the first month of the Attic calendar, corresponding to the second half of our month of July and the first half of our month of August, the hottest period of the year. The importance of this month is revealed by its very name, which signified that one hundred (*hekaton*) oxen or animals of various kinds were sacrificed (this figure should not be taken literally). The prestige of Athens was such that from 566–565 BC the Greater Panathenaea was held, which became the great civic festival of Athena. The fact that the Panathenaea was celebrated every four years, that is to say was a *pentaetéris* festival, to use the Greek term, shows that the Games, although local, achieved a measure of the glamour of the major Games.

This festival included equestrian and athletic contests, whose winners each received as a prize a Panathenaic amphora, filled with oil produced by sacred olive trees. These games lasted four full days and also included a nocturnal race with flaming torches (*lampadedromes*), which may prefigure what in the modern era became the carrying of the Olympic flame.

These festivities, in which citizens, women, young men, girls, priests, magistrates, horsemen and charioteers took part, began with a vast procession (*pompê*) that can be imagined from the sculptures of the Ionic frieze of the Parthenon. The motive for the festival was the offering to Athena Polias ("protector of the city") of a *peplos* that the women and young girls of Athens, known as *ergastinai* (workers), had woven over a period of nine months. On this sacred item of clothing were represented scenes from the Gigantomachy, the battle of the gods, in which Athena had played a key role. The goddess was depicted on the pediments of the Parthenon. The eastern one depicted the birth of Athena, armed, the incarnation of clear courage watching over the city. The western pediment portrayed the quarrel of Athena and Poseidon for the possession of Attica. The civilising and pacifying role of the goddess was underlined by the gift of the olive tree, symbol of peace and producer of the oil necessary not only for food but used also in the gymnasium.

We can imagine this procession of the Panathenaea thanks to the Ionic frieze showing the preparations for and course of the procession. These metopes have unfortunately been dispersed in various museums. The organisation of this procession began in the southwestern corner, the right-hand corner of the façade as seen from the Propylaea. Two streams of people could be seen filing past on each of the four

Panathenaic prize amphora, signed by the Nikias Painter from Attica circa 560 BC, showing the goddess Athena Polias in armour and wearing a helmet and shield. Black-figure on a red background.
The Metropolitan Museum of Art, The Bothmer Purchase Fund, 1978. (1978.11.13) Photograph © 1979 The Metropolitan Museum of Art

sides of the building, converging in the middle of the east side. On the western frieze we witness the preparations for the departure of the procession. The rounding up of the riders can be seen, with a magistrate and a priest controlling the pace of the procession. On the north side the group of riders could be viewed in procession, then chariots, people carrying olive branches (*thallophoroi*), women and old men, then people leading heifers for sacrifice, magistrates, musicians and young girls carrying baskets of offerings (*kanéphorai*). The procession became calmer as it approached the eastern side. It ended in a scene where gods and heroes, divided into two groups, welcomed the two streams of people.

There is no precise description of this ceremony in ancient texts, merely brief sketches. Thus Herodotus (490-425 BC) tells us of Hipparchus's dream the night before the Panathenaea. The son of Pisistratus and brother of the tyrant Hippias, Hipparchus was to be killed by Aristogeiton and Harmodius. The episode illustrates resignation in the face of death:[1]

> Now this was the vision which Hipparchus saw in a dream: in the night
> before the Panathenaea he thought that a tall and handsome man stood over
> him uttering these riddling verses:
> O lion, endure the unendurable with a lion's heart.
> No man on earth does wrong without paying the penalty.
> As soon as it was day, he imparted this to the interpreters of dreams, and
> presently putting the vision from his mind, he led the procession in which he
> met his death.

The decorum of bowing to fate was one of the favourite themes of Pindar and Bacchylides.

According to Andocides (468-391 BC) the ceremony of the Panathenaea gave rise to some unethical dealings:[2]

> It was therefore publicly resolved that such members of the court of the
> Thesmothetae as were initiates should be presented with the informations of
> the several claimants and decide between them. As a result the principal
> reward was voted to Andromachus, the second to Teucrus; and at the festival
> of the Panathenaea, Andromachus received ten thousand drachmae and
> Teucrus one thousand.

Thucydides (circa 460-circa 395 BC) recounts the twelfth year of the Peloponnesian War (March 420–February 419) and mentions the conclusion of the treaty of alliance between Athens and Argos, Elis and Mantinea. The date of the Greater Panathenaea is given as the *terminus ante quem* of these negotiations:[3]

Terracotta Panathenaic prize amphora with lid dating from circa 363-362 BC, attributed to the Painter of the Wedding Procession and signed by the potter Nikodemos. Decorated with an armed Athena and inscribed, "awarded as a prize in Athens".
© The J. Paul Getty Museum, inv. 93. AE. 55

1   Herodotus, *Histories* (trans. A. D. Godley), Loeb Classical Library, Harvard University Press, Cambridge, MA, 1920, V, 56.

2   Andocides, "On the Mysteries" in *Minor Attic Orators*, Vol. I, Loeb Classical Library, Harvard University Press, Cambridge, MA, 1969, 28.

3   Thucydides, *History of the Peloponnesian War*, Books 1-8 (trans. C. F. Smith), Loeb Classical Library, Heinemann, London, 1930, V, 47.

Red-figure vase in the British Museum, showing a
torch-lit religious procession. The bearded torch
bearer, one of the winning team, wears a crown.
Behind the altar stands a priest and winged Victory
approaches the torch bearer. Two beardless youths
with pointed crowns frame the scene.
© The British Museum

The oaths will be repeated by the Athenians who will travel to Elis,
Mantinea and Argos, thirty days before the Olympic Games, and by the
Argives, Mantineans and men of Elis who will travel to Athens ten days
before the Greater Panathenea. The agreement relating to the treaty, oaths and
alliance will be engraved on marble stelae set up on the Acropolis at Athens,
in the temple of Apollo at Argos, and at Mantinea in the temple of Zeus on
the agora. The cities participating in the treaty will together erect a bronze
stele at Olympia in the course of the next Olympic Games.

Lysias (440–380 BC) gives us an idea of the expense that could be incurred in
these competitions:[4]

I was certified of age in the archonship of Theopompus: appointed to
produce tragic drama, I spent thirty minae and two months later, at the
Thargelia, two thousand drachmae, when I won a victory with a male chorus;

4   Lysias, "Defence Against a Charge of Taking Bribes", in *Lysias* (trans. W. R. M. Lamb), Loeb Classical Library,
     Harvard University Press, Cambridge, MA, 1930, 1926, 1-2.

and in the archonship of Glaucippus, at the Great Panathenaea, eight hundred drachmae on Pyrrhic dancers. Besides, I won a victory with a male chorus at the Dionysia under the same archon, and spent on it, including the dedication of the tripod, five thousand drachmae; then, in the time of Diocles, three hundred on a cyclic chorus at the Little Panathenaea. In the meantime, for seven years I equipped warships, at a cost of six talents.

Isocrates (436-338 BC) mentions the date of the Greater Panathenaea to indicate that at the time he was exposed to the defamatory remarks of his opponents, at the time of the great civic festival of Athens:[5]

Nevertheless, as long as they confined themselves to abusing my discourses, reading them in the worst possible manner side by side with their own, dividing them at the wrong places, mutilating them, and in every way spoiling their effect, I paid no heed to the reports which were brought to me, but possessed myself in patience. However, a short time before the Great Panathenaia, they stirred me to great indignation.

It was in fact during these major festivals that the public readings of the great orators took place. The Panathenaea was the moment for talent, whether intellectual or athletic, to make itself known.

From Xenophon (430-355 BC) we know that horse-races took place at the Greater Panathenaea. Xenophon's *Symposium* tells us this explicitly: [6]

The occasion was a horse-race at the great Panathenaic festival. Callias, the son of Hipponicus, being a friend and lover of the boy Autolycus, had brought the lad, himself the winner of the pankration, to see the spectacle. As soon as the horse-race was over, Callias proceeded to escort Autolycus and his father, Lycon, to his house in the Piraeus, being attended also by Niceratus.

Aristophanes (circa 445-385 BC) speaks of the dances performed at the Panathenaea. Indeed, Just Reason blames Unjust Reason for making the dancers wear coats and hide their private parts with their shields. This was an insult to Athena Tritogenia, who was perfectly content for athletes to be naked:[7]

You teach the men of today to spend their lives muffled in cloaks; and so I choke with rage when they're supposed to be dancing at the Panathenaea and one of them's holding his shield in front of his haunch with no regard for Tritogeneia!

This was of course the Pyrrhic dance, where the performers carried their weapons. No doubt the shield was a more effective defence than the fig leaf used in the Christian era.

---

5   Isocrates, *Panathenaicus*, in *Isocrates* (trans. G. Norlin), Loeb Classical Library, Heinemann, London, 1980., XII, 17.

6   Xenophon, *The Symposium* (trans. H. G. Dakyns), *The Banquet*, I, 2.

7   Aristophanes, *Clouds*, (ed. and trans. Jeffrey Henderson), Loeb Classical Library, Harvard University Press, Cambridge, MA, 1998, 987-9.

In *The Frogs*[8] Aristophanes introduces us to the race with flaming torches and imagines a comic dialogue between Heracles and Dionysus. The former advises the latter to go down to the Ceramic, climb up to the so-called Timon tower (after the famous misanthrope), and when the spectators shouted "jump", hurl himself down. The race started at the Academy where the tower stood and finished six *stadia* away (1100m) at the Double Gate (*Dipylon*) separating the inner Ceramic from the outer Ceramic.

Plutarch (circa 46 BC – 120 AD) gives us a late account that attributes the origin of the Panathenaea to Theseus. According to this the hero carried out the unification of Attica by gathering together all the towns that were spread about into one city that took the name of Athens. It was then that he introduced a common sacrifice (*thusia koiné*), the Panathenaea. On the sixteenth day of the month of Hecatombaion he also founded the festival of the *metoikia*, which Thucydides (2, 15, 2) calls the Synoikia and which occurred twelve days before the beginning of the Panathenaea.[9]

Not only the games at Athens but also games celebrated in various cities are mentioned in the *Odes* of Pindar (518–446 BC) or Bacchylides (circa 507–430 BC).

Regional variations

These songs of triumph not only celebrate the winners of the major Games. Victories in local games are often mentioned in these odes, often mistakenly thought to be composed only for the winners of the Games of the "season".

Thus in the seventh *Olympian*, written for Diagoras of Rhodes, boxer and *periodonikes* (that is winner at the four major Games), Pindar does not hesitate to point out that this great champion was also honoured in local festivals. Diagoras belonged to a family of champions, descended from the Eratides, who held high rank in the town of Ialysos on Rhodes. Son of Damagetos, he was 2m tall, if *Scholion* 28a is to be believed. His eldest son, another Damagetos, won the prize for the pancratium at Olympia. Another of his sons, Dorieus, won at Olympia three times. His third son, Acousilaos, won the boxing at Olympia like his father. His grandsons, Eucles and Peisirhodos, also triumphed at Olympia and Delphi. From Pausanias (VI, 7) we learn that at Olympia statues of Diagoras and his descendants could be seen, the bases of which still exist. On the day of the victory at Olympia of Acousilaos and Damagetos, Diagoras, Olympic champion and father of two Olympic champions, was carried in triumph.

His daughter Callipateira was granted permission to attend the Games (usually out of bounds to women), because she was the mother, daughter, sister or aunt of six Olympic champions.[10] Pindar mentions the local games where the champion made a name for himself:[11]

> Twice hath Diagoras crowned himself, and at the famous Isthmus four
> times, in his good fortune; and, again and again, at Nemea and at rocky

8 Aristophanes, *Frogs*, (ed. and trans. Jeffrey Henderson), Loeb Classical Library, Harvard University Press, Cambridge, MA, 2002, 129-34.

9 Plutarch, *Theseus*, in *Lives* (trans. John Dryden), Modern Library Classics, New York, 1992, 24, 3-4.

10 Pindar, *Olympian Odes* (trans. Dianne Svarlien), Perseus Project, Yale, 1991.

11 *Ibid.*, 151-62.

Athens; while he is not unknown to the shield of bronze in Argos, and the works of art given as prizes in Arcadia and at Thebes, and to the duly ordered contests amid the Boeotians, and to Pellana, and to Aegina, where he was six times victor, while in Megara the reckoning on the tablet of stone telleth no other tale.

But do thou, O father Zeus, that rulest over the height of Atabyrium,[12] grant honour to the hymn ordained in praise of an Olympian victor.

In the ninth *Olympian* Pindar celebrates Epharmostos of Opuntia, winner at wrestling, and crowned at Olympia, Delphi, the Isthmus and Nemea (several times). But the poet does not neglect the fact that the champion had triumphed in local games:[13]

> [...] at Argos he gained glory in a contest of men, and as a boy at Athens. And, when reft from the beardless company, what a glorious contest for the prize of silver cups did he maintain at Marathon, among the men! and, having vanquished those wights by the cunning skill that swiftly shifts its balance but never falls, amid what loud applause did he pass round the ring, a victor in life's prime, noble fair, and one who had wrought most noble deeds! Then again he seemed marvellous to look upon, amid the Parrhasian people, at the festival of the Lycaean Zeus, and also on that day when, at Pellana,[14] he carried off as his prize a warm remedy against the chilly blasts; and the tomb of Iolaus beareth witness to him and the shore of Eleusis telleth of his glorious prowess.[15]

We learn from this text that a strict distinction between age groups did not exist, and the transition from the beardless to the adult group was somewhat vague. This fact is corroborated by a more explicit text by Pausanias, VI, 14,1–2:

> At the seventieth Olympiad Pherias of Aegina, whose statue stands next to that of the Athenian Ariston, was considered young and, not being allowed to wrestle, was excluded from the competition, but at the following festival he was admitted to the child category and won the wrestling. What happened to Pherias is different from, in fact the opposite of, what happened to Nikasulos of Rhodes at Olympia. Indeed, when he was eighteen and the Aeolians would not allow him to wrestle in the child category, he was admitted to the adults and won. Later he was proclaimed winner at Nemea and the Isthmus. But when he was twenty he submitted to the decrees of destiny before returning home to Rhodes.

In the thirteenth *Olympian*, an ode in honour of Xenophon of Corinth, who won at the stadium and the pancratium, Pindar recalls the family of the Oligaithides,

---

12   This mountain lies in the centre of the chain which spans the island of Rhodes.

13   Pindar, *Olympian Odes, op. cit.,* IX, 132-51.

14   Pellana was a town in Achaea, the ruins of which lie close to modern Trikala. The prizes were wool coats.

15   The Games near the tomb of Iolaos were Theban; those in Eleusis, the *Demetria,* were held in honour of Demeter.

three times Olympic champions. At the end of the ode he reminds us of the local victories which made these champions famous:[16]

> And the prizes won beneath the brow of Parnassus, six in number, and, all in Argos, and in Thebes, and all that shall be witnessed by the royal altar of the Lycaean mount that ruleth over the Arcadians, and by Pellana, and Sicyon, and Megara, and the fair-walled precinct of the sons of Aeacus, and Eleusis, and fertile Marathon, and the cities beauteous in wealth beneath the lofty crest of Etna, and Euboea – aye, even throughout all Elis, you may search and find them too many for the eye to view.

In the first *Isthmian* Pindar composes the ode for Herodotus of Thebes, winner of the chariot event at the Isthmus. He recalls the winner's victory in local games, at Orchomenus, Eleusis, Euboea and Phylake in Achaea:[17]

> For us it is right to celebrate the earth-shaking son of Cronus, returning a good deed to our beneficent neighbor, the lord of horse-racing and chariots; and to invoke your sons, Amphitryon, and the secluded valley of Minyas, and Eleusis, the famous precinct of Demeter, and Euboea, when we speak of curving race-courses. Protesilas,[18] I add besides your sacred ground in Phylace, the home of Achaean men. But the brief limits of my song prevent me from telling of all the victories that Hermes, lord of games, granted to Herodotus and his horses. Truly, often that which is hushed in silence actually brings greater pleasure.

In the fourth *Isthmian* Pindar calls to mind the famous Melissus of Thebes, winner at the pancratium. He reminds us that the Cleonymides of Thebes, ancestors of the winner and rich and well respected men, were rewarded only by wreaths gained in contests of minor importance, that is in local games:[19]

> [...] in the fertile fields of Athens, proclaimed their chariot, as victorious, and also in Sicyon at the games of Adrastus; and thus gave them from the bards of old leaves of minstrelsy that are like unto mine. Nor from the general games did they keep aloof their curved chariot, but striving with all the Hellenic hosts, they rejoiced in spending their wealth upon steeds. For those who make no trial have an inglorious obscurity; and, even when men strive indeed, fortune doth not show herself until they reach the final goal. For she giveth of this, and of that; and ere now hath the skill of weaker men overtaken and overturned a stronger than they.

This theme of the quirks of fate is dear to Pindar, who sees success as the result of merit but also as an effect of the benevolence of the gods. Failure should not discourage us, but success should not breed hubris.

---

16 Pindar, *Olympian Odes, op. cit.*, XIII, 150-63.

17 Pindar, *Isthmian Odes* (trans. D. Svarlien), Perseus Project, Yale, 1990, I, 76-89.

18 Protesilaos, the Thessalian commander, was the first Greek soldier to be killed in the Trojan war.

19 Pindar, *Isthmian Odes, op. cit.*, 42-56.

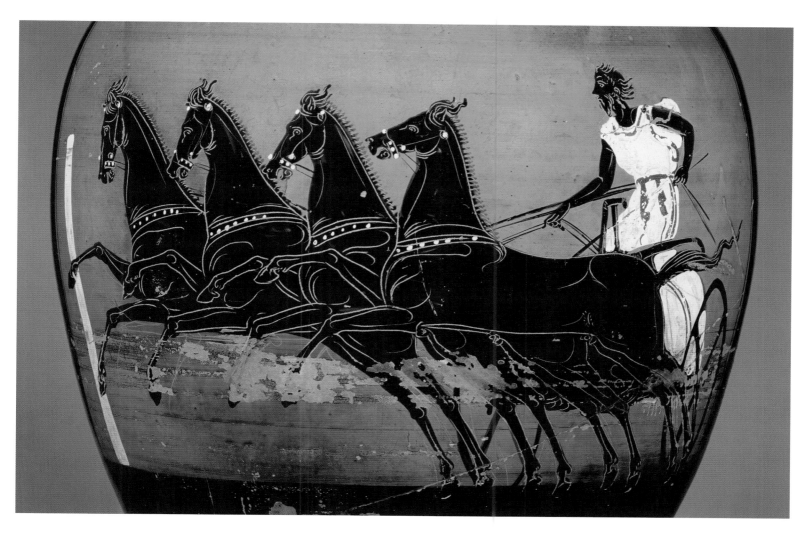

Four-horse chariot at a gallop with an elderly driver dressed in white. Black-figure Panathenaic-type Attic amphora, circa 400 BC, kept in the British Museum (inv. B606).

© The British Museum

The eighth *Isthmian* sings the exploits of Cleander of Aegina, winner of the pancratium, and recalls the champion's former victories in less illustrious games, those of Megara and Epidaurus. It also notes that his cousin, Nicocles, who had also gained the prize for the pancratium at the Isthmus, had demonstrated his talent at neighbouring games:[20]

> and therefore doth the Muses' car start forth to sound aloud the glory of the boxer, Nicocles. O praise ye him, who won the crown of wild Dorian celery in the Isthmian glade, since he too, in his day, was victorious over all that dwelt around him, smiting them with his resistless hands. He is not dishonoured by the offspring of his father's noble brother. Therefore let a bright crown of myrtle, in honour of the pancratium, be entwined for Cleandros by one of his comrades, since the contest of Alcathous, and the young men of Epidaurus gave him welcome aforetime. 'Tis fitting for the good to praise him, for he hid not the spirit of his youth in a hole unknown to fame.

20 Pindar, *Isthmian Odes, op. cit.*, VIII, 133-52.

The ninth *Nemean*, celebrating Chromios of Aetna, the lieutenant of Hieron, winner of the chariot race, reminds us that the winner had won in minor games, the Pythian games of Sicyon:[21]

> But we shall wake the pealing lyre, shall wake the flute, in honour of the most exalted of all contests with the steed – contests which Adrastus at the streams of Asopus[22] founded in honour of Phoebus; and when I make mention thereof, I shall deck with loudly-sounding words of praise the hero who, erst, when he was monarch there, exalted and glorified his city with fresh festivals and contests that prove men's strength, and with chariots of cunning work.

In the tenth *Nemean*, written for the wrestler Theaeus of Argos, we learn that before his triumph at the Olympic Games, Theaeus had won at the Panathenaea and had been rewarded in Athens by the gift of a Panathenaic amphora filled with oil and decorated with figures:[23]

> Yet, amid the sacred rites of the Athenians, twice did voices sweet exalt him in the prelude of a triumphal ode, and in earth baked by the fire came the olive oil in richly painted bases to the manly people of Hera.

The third triad of the tenth *Nemean* is devoted to Theaeus' mother's family, and in particular to two of its members, Thrasylos and Antias. It points out that they won the chariot race and lists the crowns gained by them or other members of the family at the Isthmus, at Nemea and in other contests of inferior rank, that is in local games:[24]

> And from Sicyon they returned with silver wine-goblets, and from Pellana with soft wool cloaks around their shoulders. But it is impossible to give a full reckoning of their countless prizes of bronze – for it would require long leisure to number them – which Cleitor and Tegea and the upland cities of the Achaeans and Mount Lycaeon set by the racecourse of Zeus for men to win with the strength of their feet and hands.

They received not money but silver cups. At Pellene woollen coats were offered to the winners of the games in honour of Hermes. The games of the town of Clitor took place in Arcadia and were celebrated in honour of Cora, those of Tegea in honour of Athena Alea (protector). We do not know which cities of Achaea are intended here.

The ninth *Nemean*, written for the prytane Aristagoras of Tenedos, is not a triumphal ode, but reports the modesty of this individual who, not daring to tackle the major Games, was content to win in local games:[25]

> Yet right it is that he should be praised with friendly words by his fellow

---

21 Pindare, *Nemean Odes* (trans. D. Svarlien), Perseus Project, Yale, 1991, IX, 22-9.
22 A river which flows past Sicyon and Phlius.
23 Pindare, *Nemean Odes, op. cit.,* X, 61-68.
24 *Ibid.,* 79-90.
25 *Ibid.,* XI, 22-43.

Black-figure vase showing a bearded driver seated on a chariot drawn by two mules.
© The British Museum

citizens; right it is that we should celebrate him by adorning his fame with honey-sweet strains. For, by those who dwell around him, Aristagoras and his famous clan were crowned by sixteen glorious victories in the wrestling-match and in the proud pancratium. But the halting hopes of his parents restrained his strength, as a boy, from competing for the prizes at Pytho and Olympia. Else, I solemnly aver that, in my judgement, had he entered the lists, he would have returned with greater glory than his rivals, whether they strove beside Castalia, or beside the tree-clad hill of Cronus, after celebrating the quadrennial festival ordained by Heracles, and after binding his hair with gleaming garlands. But, among mortals, one is cast down from his blessings by empty-headed conceit, whereas another, underrating his strength too far, hath been thwarted from winning the honours within his reach, by an uncourageous spirit that draggeth him back by the hand.

Pindar reflects on the usual alternation, within the same family, of talented generations with less gifted ones. But he does not criticise Aristagoras for his lack of ambition, and besides makes his parents responsible for this excessive modesty. He favours neither people who delude themselves about their capabilities nor those who underestimate themselves. Excess and lack of ambition both return us to our mortal state and our submission to the will of Zeus, who alone judges our hopes.

The triumphal odes of Bacchylides (597–430 BC) also evoke these victories, not all of which were obtained in the major Games, but rather in local games. Thus in the first *Epinician*, celebrating Argeios of Chios, youthful winner of the boxing at the Isthmian Games, the poet notes that "Chronides on his sublime seat placed other dazzling crowns in his path".

In the tenth *Epinician*, written for an Athenian who had won the race at the Isthmian Games twice, Bacchylides points out that other cities welcomed the winner:[26]

> [...] twice in Nemea, beside the sacred altar of Zeus son of Cronus.
> Glorious Thebes also welcomed him fittingly, and spacious Argos, and Sicyon,
> and those who dwell in Pellene, and in Euboea rich in grain, and on the holy
> island Aegina. Each man seeks a different path on which to walk to attain
> conspicuous glory; and the forms of knowledge among men are countless.

The eleventh *Epinician* is written for Alexidamos of Metapontum, child winner of the wrestling at the Pythian Games. As a reward for his victory processions of young people come to celebrate his example at Metapontum.[27]

The fourteenth *Epinician*, for Cleoptolemos of Thessaly, winner of the chariot race, refers to an event occurring not in one of the major Games but in the games of Thessaly, celebrated in honour of Poseidon and famous only locally:[28] "To be helpful to Cleoptolemos we must now celebrate the sanctuary of Poseidon Petrian, as well as the champion of the chariot race, the famous son of Pyrrichos."

---

26 Bacchylides, *Odes* (trad. D. Svarlien), Perseus Project, Yale, 1991, I, 2.
27 *Ibid.*, XI, 11-14.
28 *Ibid.*, XIV, 19-22.

Theatre of Dionysus on the Acropolis in Athens.
© 1990 Photo Scala, Florence

These local games resorted to details that are not always easy to understand. This is the case with the epithet "Petrian" applied to Poseidon. The editors note that the earliest mention of this epiclesis is found in Pindar (*Pyth.* IV, 138). The scholiast explains the term by the myth of the opening of the Tempe Gorge to let the Penea pass through, since the earthquake that caused the breach was in Poseidon's domain. Other, fairly unconvincing explanations have been given.

To summarise the importance of these local games, it can be said that they were both a preparation and a rehearsal for the major Games. The latter attracted crowds from every part of the Greek world, while these local games allowed a permanent interest notably in gymnastics to be established or maintained in the framework of far more modest contests in each city.

The winners of the major Games showed those who had not been able to attend those great events that they did not forget people who could not travel to them. In this way the cities' solidarity was reinforced in a democratic manner. Moreover the youth of the cities, admiring the great champions appearing in their towns, could dream of becoming Olympic champions one day and discover the feats that they would need to accomplish.

A comparative study of the games played at other times and in other periods of history would be most welcome. For example, games common in Egypt, such as can be seen on wall paintings in the tombs of Beni Hassan, show similarities with the hand-to-hand fighting, jumping and ball games practised in Greece.[29] Surviving illustrations on pottery show us how certain exercises were carried out. One example is the ostrakon (tile) in Cairo museum showing wrestlers, or the ostrakon in Turin museum portraying a female acrobatic dancer.[30] In the same way Etruscan art allows us to draw some interesting parallels. The dance scene that decorates the bronze vase of Bizentio, dating from the second half of the 8th century BC, gives us a version of the Pyrrhic dance.[31] The athletic games represented in the tomb of the Olympiads at Tarquinia, dating from the 6th century BC, prefigure what is shown on Greek vases.[32] Many more examples of this kind could be given.

More profoundly, the meaning of the Greek games is made fully clear if we look at games practised in Central America and represented in numerous Mexican and Guatemalan sites including ball games. Let us not forget that the ancient Mexicans had at their disposal rubber, unknown to the Greeks. All the Nahua (Aztec) or Mayan sites of the Yucatan, Guatemala, Honduras and Costa Rica had one or more pelota courts where the players who confronted each other were driven by an ideal very different from that of the Greek games.

In his remarkable book, *Mesoamerica: Art and Anthropology* (Flammarion, Paris, 1999, pp. 66-7), Christian Duverger studies the ball game as it was practised in Central America for thousands of years. The game finished with a sacrifice and every sacrifice was preceded by this game. The Nahuatl language, he says, possesses only one word (*ollin*) to designate rubber and the notion of movement. "It is evidently the bouncing capacity of rubber that fascinated the Mesoamericans and suggested a symbolic relationship with the movement of the cosmos, while of course the spherical form of the ball recalls the heliacal star... For the Maya, blood and rubber were one and the same thing and known by the same word: *kik*."

Just as the Greek games were practised in specific places (gymnasium, stadium, palaestra, hippodrome), similarly the pelota game or *tlachtli* took place in a space in the form of a capital "I", the play area varying in size.[33] It was flanked on either side by a sloping bank, extended at the bottom by a seat of around 1m high, which allowed the ball to bounce at waist height. The court had stone rings in the centre to act as goals. The players, divided into two teams, tried to make the rubber ball pass through the hole in the discs. The winner or winners were sacrificed at the end of the game. Their beating hearts were torn out with a sacrificial knife of volcanic glass.

"Sahagun", which as Duverger specifies, is the term for a sacrifice carried out on the teotlachco, the "divine pitch" situated at the foot of the temple of Quetzalcoatl at the heart of the ceremonial centre of Tenochtitlan, tells us that the victims were four in number. "And when they had been killed, their bodies were dragged over the whole court as if the ground was being combed with their blood."

---

29 See P. Newberry, *Beni Hassan (Part 1) Archaeological Survey of Egypt*, Egypt Exploration Fund, London, 1893, II, pl. V, VIII, XIII, XV, or J. G. Wilkinson, *Manners and Customs of the Ancient Egyptians*, Scribner & Welford, New York, 1879, II, p. 54.

30 A. Lhote, *Les chefs-d'œuvre de la peinture égyptienne*, Hachette, Paris, 1954, p. 230, fig. 10 and 11.

31 P. Parlavecchia, *Les Etrusques et l'Europe*, Réunion des musées nationaux, Paris, 1992, p. 81.

32 *Ibid.*, p. 98-9.

33 These measurements are given in C. Duverger, *La fleur létale, économie du sacrifice aztèque*, éditions du Seuil, Paris, 1979, pp. 138-42. The reader might also be interested in Duverger's *L'esprit du jeu chez les Aztèques*, éditions du Seuil, Paris, 1978.

In this civilisation the aim of sport was not the victory of one team over another, but the efficient working of the world through the perpetuation of movement. This is light years away from the Greek games which aimed at and enhanced the development of the individual, the surpassing of oneself and the desire for glory. Hermes and Heracles, the gods of the gymnasium, demanded only effort, not death.

Chapter IX
Winning prestige

Panhellenic Games

Local games were open to athletes and artists who felt able to win and were categorised by age group according to whether they ranked as children (*paides*), youths (*ageneioi,* literally "beardless"), or men (*andres*). The divisions were not always strict, allowing some to compete, with varying luck, in different categories. Local contests became much more prestigious if they were defined as sacred (*agônes hieroi*), if it was decided to award wreaths (*agônes stephanitai*) or if they were declared equal in honours to the Olympic Games (*agônes isolympioi*) or Pythian Games (*agônes isopythioi*). Local festivals would then draw competitors from every part of the Greek world. They became panhellenic.[1]

Louis Robert has clearly defined the nature of these prestigious competitions known as the Panhellenic Games. His comments deserve to be quoted here in full:

> We call contests of the same kind as the Soteria (at Delphi) "panhellenic" contests, and there is no problem with giving them this title, on one condition: that we do not forget that it is given to them by modern scholars, and not by ancient documents; indeed the latter call them *agônes hieroi, isolympioi, isopythioi.* Having dubbed them "panhellenic", we must not conclude from that that they are regulated in a way that corresponds to the content of the word "Panhellenic". W. Kolbe makes this very mistake, with serious consequences.
>
> Where did W. Kolbe get the idea that transforming a contest into a *stephanitês* contest would involve a change in the events of the contest or the origins of the competitors? These two things are completely independent of the *stephanitês* character of a contest. In a *thematitês* music contest, just as in a *stephanitês* contest, there are inevitably aulos players, cithara players, etc, divided into *andres* and *paides* for some of these categories. Artists may flock to a *thematitês* contest or a *talantiaios* contest from every corner of the Greek world; there are many examples of this…
>
> When a contest is termed "panhellenic" *stephanités*, it is, as the Soteria inscriptions tell us, *isopythios* or *isonemeos,* etc. by virtue of two things: *tais timais kai tais hélikiais: tais hélikiais* denotes that ranking in the class of *andres* or *paides* (or *ageneioi* in some athletic contests) takes place following the rules applied at Delphi and Nemea: they will have *timai isolympioi*, etc., which are different in different places (hence the class of *paides pythikoi, isthmikoi, aktiakoi,* etc.); *tais timais* denotes that both at the site of the festival and in their homeland the winners will enjoy the honours accorded to winners at Delphi or Nemea, or Olympia, etc. What is more, the lists of winners give us

---

[1] L. Robert, *Opera Minora Selecta*, Hakkert, Amsterdam, 1969-90, II, pp. 768-86. Robert explains this very clearly in his article "Recherches épigraphiques II : Smyrne et les Soteria de Delphes" which was published in *Revue des Études Anciennes*, 1929, 13-20, 225-6.

neither the rules that governed ranking according to age group, nor the honours awarded; we are told that such-and-such won at cithara playing: the mention will be the same whether a *stephanités* or a *thematikés* contest is meant.

Here we recognise a specific characteristic of the life of the Greek cities, the reluctance to standardise and generalise the rules of institutions.

The rewards granted to the winners could be the attribution of right of residence and even the right to participate in assemblies. It goes without saying that the city of origin and the city of adoption organised festivals and gave presents to the winners of these prestigious games.

A Milesian athlete

The events were the same as those of the major Games. Let us refer, for example, to the decree honouring "a Milesian athlete", published and commented on by Louis Robert,[2] who has left it up to the reader to translate the text, but has reconstructed and analysed the document, known from three fragments. He explains the way in which he proceeded:

> We now know the whole career of this Milesian runner-up until the point when these statues were erected. Inscription A (l. 1-15) gives us the beginning; C (l. 11-19), which includes as its first four lines the end of A, gives us the whole of the end of the list of victories; moreover B (l. 11) gives an incomplete version of the final lines, which I combine with C (l. 13-19) to form a complete text (or very nearly so).

The editor reconstructs part of the patronymic from an inscription at Olympia with which he establishes a connection. The text dates from the 190th Olympiad, that is 20 BC. It gives us all the victories gained by this Milesian runner at contests that increased in number during the Hellenistic and Roman periods, when cities organised games attracting all the athletes or artists of the Greek world to these festivals. I translate from the text offered by the editor:

> [Such-and-such, son of …krates, a Milesian, having won at Olympia, at the double race] at the 190th Olympiad, and at Pythia, men's category, at the stadium, double race and armed race, on the same day, and at Nemea, male class, at the stadium, double race and armed race, successively in the same year, being in first place, and at the Eleutheria instituted at Plataea by the Confederation of Hellenes, men's category, at the stadium and at the race in arms starting from the trophy, and having been proclaimed "best of the Hellenes", in first place and alone among those coming from Asia, and at the great Aktia Kaisareia, men's category, at the stadium, double race, armed race, on the same day, "in first place", and at Nemea again, at the double race and armed race, and at Sebasta Romaia instituted by the Confederation of Asia, at the armed race, "the first of the Ionians" and at Isthmia at the armed race,

---

2   L. Robert, *Hellenica*, Maisonneuve, Paris, 1949, VII, pp. 117-25.

The archaeological site at the theatre of Dionysus,
on the Acropolis in Athens.
© 1990, Photo Scala, Florence

"first of the Ionians" and at Pythia for the second time, at the stadium and the armed race, "first of the Ionians" and again at the stadium, double race, armed race and at the race in arms starting from the trophy and having been proclaimed for the second time "best of the Hellenes", in first place and alone and having been honoured by the Confederation of Hellenes, with a gold wreath, as a reward for valour, and at Isthmia, for the second time at the armed race and at the Great Dionysian instituted by the people of Athens, at the double race and armed race, and having been honoured by the people of Athens with right of residence, a statue and a wreath, on the grounds of his courage and at the contest of Sebasta Romaia instituted by the confederation of Asia, at the armed race, "first of the Ionians" and at Isthmia at the armed race "first of the Milesians", and at Pythia again, at the stadium and at the armed race, "first of the Ionians", and at the contest instituted by the *hieronikai* and *stephanitai* of all the inhabited land, at the stadium, double race, armed race, "in first place", and at the Heraia of Argos, at the stadium, "first of the Milesians" and at the armed race, and at Nemea, again at the stadium, double race, armed race, "first of the Ionians", and at the Halieia of Rhodes, at the stadium and the armed race, and at the Eleutheria of Plataea, instituted by the Confederation of the Hellenes, again at the stadium, double race, armed race and at the race in arms starting from the trophy, and having been proclaimed for the second time "best of the Hellenes", in first place and alone and having been honoured by the Confederation of the Hellenes with a gold wreath, a prize for courage, and at Isthmia for the second time at the stadium and the armed race, and at the Great Dionysian instituted by the Athenian people, at the double race and the armed race and having been honoured by the Athenian people with right of residence, a statue and a wreath of leaves on the grounds of his courage.

This text, among many others,[3] bears witness to the permanence of the Greek games, even when the kingdoms appeared in the Hellenistic and Imperial periods. We know that after the defeat of the Athenians and the Thebans, in 338 BC, at Chaeronea in Boeotia, where Philip II of Macedonia won the victory, the Greek cities certainly did not disappear, but they had to take their conquerors into account. The dream of Alexander the Great was to enrich and unify the cities in the vast conglomeration that was to be his kingdom.

By organising prestigious Games throughout the Greek world, just as much in Greece proper as in Asia or Egypt, the cities, instead of tearing each other apart as they did in the Classical period, could show that they shared a common ideal and prove that they belonged to a common civilisation.[4] It was not out of obedience to the will of the conqueror, but out of allegiance – that is, recognition of the spiritual and moral

---

3 The many articles by L. Robert on the Games – which he called "competitions ("concours") – are listed in the index of the *Bulletin épigraphique*. T. F. Scanlon, *Greek and Roman Athletics, a bibliography*, Ares Publishers, Chicago, 1984 rounds up articles from a host of learned academics from many countries who have taken part in the continuing study of the Games. See especially: p. 44, no 140; p. 67, no 519; p. 73, no 619-26; p. 76, no 682; p. 83, no 834; p. 84, no 861; p. 85, no 882; p. 103, no1172-3; p. 105, no1215; p. 114, no 1377 and 1378; pp. 117-8, no 1451-68; p. 125, no 1572.

4 See A. Bernand, *Leçon de civilisation*, Fayard, Paris, 1994, pp. 161-84.

authority of ancient Greece – that in the cities the games increased in number after the fashion of the Classical period. Under Roman domination, in the province of Asia where the official language was Greek, the vitality, or rather revitalisation of the ancient Games, shows that the same values were still respected and that there had not been a rupture with the past and its prestige.

As L. Robert notes, the eulogy of the Milesian runner shows us clearly that the cities that had instituted Games wished to respect the hierarchical order of the Major Games. The order of the victories won respects both chronology and the dignity of the victories. Firstly, victories at Olympia, Delphi (Pythia), and Nemea are mentioned. Then those won at Plataea (Eleutheria), at Nicopolis (Aktia Kaisareia), at Nemea for the second time, at the games instituted by the province of Asia (Sebasta Romaia), at the Isthmus (Isthmia), at Delphi for the second time, at the *panegyris* of the hieronikai, no doubt in the province of Asia, at Argos (Heraia), at Nemea for the second time, at Rhodes (Halieia), again at the Eleutheria of Plataea, at the Isthmia for the second time, at Athens (Eleusinia).

The winning combination

As in the major Games, the champion is celebrated for having triumphed several times, at Pythia, at Nemea and at Isthmia, with a list of his achievements in the three main track events: the *stadion*, run over approximately 192m; the double *stadion* or *diaulos*, circa 384m; and the *hoplitodromos* or "race in armour", run over the same distance as the *diaulos*. Just as for the *periodonikai* (the winners at the four major Games), the number and succession of victories is elaborated, for example, this athlete's victories in all three events at the Pythia and at the Aktia Kaisareia. His greatest claim to fame is to have won a triple victory at both the Pythia and Nemea in the same year.

It is noteworthy that the three traditional types of race have been retained. A hallmark of the hyperbolic style typical of Hellenistic and Imperial inscriptions is the use of such high-flown titles as "best of the Hellenes" (*Aristos Hellénôn*),[5] which as L. Robert has shown was awarded to the winner of the race in armour at the *Eleutheria* of Plataea. The runner from Miletus also receives flamboyant titles, such as "best of the Hellenes, in first place and alone among all those of Asia", "best of the Hellenes, in first place and alone", "first of the Ionians", "first of the Milesians".

Freedom of the city

Bestowing right of residence established between the cities relationships that linked them to a larger community. This was the happy result of the proliferation of festivals and games. Let us turn for example to an "agonistic inscription at Smyrna" published and commented on, but not translated, by L. Robert. The editor notes that the inscription is after Hadrian and dates it to 160-180 AD. This athlete had received the right of residence in many cities, explains the editor, as well as the dignity of member of the Council, in particular at Athens, Ephesus, Pergamum, Cyzicus, Sardis, Miletus and Lacedaemon. The text states:[6]

5   L. Robert, *Opera Minora Selecta, op. cit.*, II, pp. 758-67.
6   L. Robert, *Hellenica, op. cit.*, VII, pp. 105-13.

> Markos Aurelios Antonios Loukios, citizen of Smyrna and of Athens, Ephesus, Pergamum, Cyzicus, Sardis, Miletus, Lacedaemon, and other cities, and member of the Council, having won at the games mentioned below, "alone and first among men": at Smyrna at the great Hadriana Olympia, children's and men's category, three times running, at Athens at the Olympia, children's category, at the contest of Argos and at the Nemea, at Smyrna at the contest of the province of Asia, children's and men's category, having stopped his opponents after the second drawing of lots, at Ephesus at the Balbilleia, children's and beardless category, at the Aktia, at the Panellenia children's and men's category and men in succession, "alone and first", at Cyzicus beardless category, and the next day, having switched to the men, at Rome, children's and beardless and men's category…

Louis Robert's commentary elucidates these expressions, which form part of the agonistic vocabulary but are at first sight enigmatic, given their brevity, technical nature and the historical problems they pose.

Consider the difficulty that we can experience today on reading or hearing a sporting commentary. Technical expressions such as "line-out", "to score a drop goal", "to score a try", etc., as far as rugby is concerned, or for football "to clear", "to dribble", "to mark", "to play a corner", a "penalty", "to be offside", "to get a yellow or red card", "to make a pass", etc., cannot be immediately understood by the uninitiated.

It is the same with epigraphic texts, which are the major source from which we draw the technical expressions used in the Games and the information that allows us to trace the development of this institution. In the agonistic inscription at Smyrna, L. Robert takes the very name of the athlete, Markos Aurelios Antonios Loukios, as an indication of the approximate date of the text, since the career of this athlete could not have been prior to the reign of Marcus Aurelius, which situates it in around 160-180 AD. He explains the nature of the prestigious honours that these victories brought to the man in question, the ethnic designation (*Smynaios*) being followed by a mention of the right of residence that he had received in several cities and the title of Councillor (*poleités kai bouleutés*), at Athens, Ephesus, Pergamum, Cyzicus, Sardis, Miletus and Lacedaemon. This earned him the title of "alone and first among men" (*monos kai prôtos anthrôpôn*) indicating that no other athlete can produce as many victories and honours.

The reader who is not a specialist of epigraphy cannot read L. Robert's vast work, but he should at least become aware of his method and the results of this undisputed master of the discipline. Let us look for example at the honorific inscriptions of Sparta of the Imperial period, which serve to corroborate our study of the title *Aristos Hellénôn*.[7]

Champion of the Greeks

The editor transcribes two inscriptions honouring two citizens of Sparta, father and son, who lived at the end of the 2nd and the beginning of the 3rd century AD. The text for the son states:

---

7   L. Robert, "Recherches épigraphiques", *Opera Minora Selecta, op. cit.,* II, p. 758.

The city [of Sparta has honoured]
Poplios Ailios Damakratidas
son of Alkandridas, archpriest
of the Emperor and his divine
ancestors, who loves
Caesar and who loves his country,
agoraphile for life,
winner extraordinary in many
contests, and best of the Greeks.

The text for the father states:

The city [of Sparta has honoured]
Po [plios] *Ailios Alkandridas, son*
of Damocratidas, archpriest of the Emperor,
who loves Caesar and loves his country,
twice periodonikes, *best*
of the Greeks, old man,
official in charge of ephebi, *etc.*

Two new fragments of the base for Alkandridas have been discovered by M. Woodward, so that the base has today been reconstructed in Sparta museum.[8] The lay reader could not have a better example of the shrewdness of epigraphy.

It would be possible to mention many articles by L. Robert that illustrate his mastery of the documentation and interpretation, in particular, of texts from the Imperial period in Asia Minor. His commentaries generally provide a key to understanding the text. I still regret the fact that these texts have not been translated.

Let us take for example his study of the base of a statue found in the British excavation of Ephesus and giving the list of victories won by a boxer named Photion.[9] A Hellenist unfamiliar with epigraphic texts will not understand such a text straightaway. Here I give a translation of it, prompted by the author's explanations:

Photion, son of Karpion, boxer extraordinaire,
citizen of Laodicea and Ephesus, winner at the
great Epheséa, sacred and solemn contest, men's category, at boxing,
at the Didymeia at Miletus, beardless category, at boxing,
at the Deia Sebasta, open to all comers, at Laodicea, beardless category, at boxing,
at the common games of Asia, at Ephesus, beardless category, at boxing,
at the common games of Asia, at Laodicea, beardless category, at boxing,
at the Epineikia, at Ephesus, beardless category, at boxing,
at the Traïana Deiphileia, at Pergamum, men's category, at boxing,
at the great Ephesêa, at the 517th Ephesiad, men's category, at boxing,
at the Deia Sebasta, open to all comers, at Laodicea, men's category, at
boxing, at the Eusebeia, at Pozzuoli, men's category, at boxing,

8   L. Robert, *Opera Minora Selecta, op. cit.*, II, addendum pp. 766-7.
9   *Ibid.*, pp. 1138-41.

at the Sebasta of Naples, men's category, at boxing,
at the hill of Argos, men's category, at boxing,
at the Artemeisia, at Ephesus, men's category, at boxing,
and at the contests bringing in a talent and paid when Tiberius Julius
Reginus was agônotheté, *archpriest for the second time at the temples of Ephesus.*

L. Robert's commentaries allow us to appreciate that the Epheséa are the games celebrated at Ephesus, the Didymeia are the Games celebrated at Didyma, the Deia Sebasta are the Games in honour of Zeus and the emperor, the Epineikia are the Games in honour of a victory of the emperor (here, the victory of Marcus Aurelius and Lucius Verus over the Parthians), the Traïana Deiphileia are the Games celebrated in honour of Trajan and Zeus Philios, the Sebasta are the Games in honour of the emperor, that the hill of Argos is an allusion to the hill in the form of a shield that dominates the plain of Argos (L. Robert does not explain the expression), and that the Artemeisia are the Games in honour of Artemis, at Ephesus.

Chapter X

A musical festival

In order to understand the importance of the musical Games, it is useful to recall the role that the Ancient Greeks, whether poets or philosophers, attributed to music.

Entertaining the gods

According to the poets music is a privilege of the gods. Thus Homer – or the Homeric poet Hesiod, to whom the poem is also attributed – recounts how Apollo plays the *phorminx*[1] as he walks, and arrives at the site of Delphi, then Olympia, where the Immortals play the *kithara*[2] and sing in unison. The Muses, the Graces and the Hours, with Harmonia, Youth and Aphrodite dance in a ring in which Ares, Hermes and Apollo himself come to sing and dance. The moment he was born, Apollo declared to the Immortals:[3] "Give me my lyre and my curved bow: in my oracles too I will reveal the infallible plans of Zeus." In the picture that the poet paints of the assembly of the Gods, singing, music and dancing prevail:[4]

> Leto's all-glorious son goes to rocky Pytho, playing upon his hollow lyre, clad in divine, perfumed garments; and his lyre, at the touch of the golden key, sings sweet. Thence, swift as thought, he speeds from earth to Olympus, to the house of Zeus, to join the gathering of the other gods: then straightway the undying gods think only of the lyre and song, and all the Muses together, voice sweetly answering voice, hymn the unending gifts the gods enjoy and the sufferings of men, all that they endure at the hands of the deathless gods, and how they live witless and helpless and cannot find healing for death or defence against old age. Meanwhile the rich-tressed Graces and cheerful Seasons dance with Harmonia and Hebe and Aphrodite, daughter of Zeus, holding each other by the wrist. And among them sings one, not mean nor puny, but tall to look upon and enviable in mien, Artemis who delights in arrows, sister of Apollo. Among them sport Ares and the keen-eyed Slayer of Argus, while Apollo plays his lyre stepping high and featly and a radiance shines around him, the gleaming of his feet and close-woven vest. And they, even gold-tressed Leto and wise Zeus, rejoice in their great hearts as they watch their dear son playing among the undying gods.

Theognis of Megara, a poet of the 6th century BC, whose mature years would have been in around 550-540, prays to Phoebus:[5]

---

1   The *phorminx* was a small primitive harp. More infomation is given by A. Bailly, *Dictionnaire grec-français*, Hachette Éducation, 2000 and A. Bélis, *Les musiciens dans l'Antiquité*, Hachette Littératures, Paris, 1999, p. 181.

2   The *kithara* was an ancestor of the lute or lyre. See A. Bélis, *op. cit.* illustrations 1, 2, 3, 5, 6.

3   *Homeric Hymns and Homerica* (trans. H. G. Evelyn-White), Harvard University Press, Cambridge, MA, 1914, 131-2.

4   *Ibid.*, 182-202.

5   Theognis, *in Greek Elegiac Poetry* (trans. Douglas E. Gerber), Loeb Classical Library, Harvard University Press, Cambridge, MA, 1999, I, 775-9.

> May the people in jubilation come towards you at the return of spring
> with significant hecatombs, in the delight of a festival where the sound of the
> cithara will be heard, and where they will dance the paean and shout out
> around your altar.

J. Carrière wonders whether the expression "the people in jubilation" designates all the peoples gathered together, at the festival commemorating the birth of the god, around his Delian sanctuary, or whether it denotes only the population of Megara. In any case it must refer to the Thargelia, which took place on 6th and 7th May.

Education through music

Aristophanes has described male musical education as it was practised at the time and how it comprised part of the training for the warriors at Marathon.[6] Plato has also affirmed the educational role of music. For example, in *The Laws*, he puts the following in the mouth of the Athenian:[7]

> The Gods, who, as we say, have been appointed to be our companions in
> the dance, have given the pleasurable sense of harmony and rhythm; and so
> they stir us into life, and we follow them, joining hands together in dances
> and songs; and these they call choruses, which is a term naturally expressive of
> cheerfulness. Shall we begin, then, with the acknowledgment that education is
> first given through Apollo and the Muses? What do you say? [...] Choric
> movements [dance and song] are imitations of manners occurring in various
> actions, fortunes, dispositions–each particular is imitated, and those to whom
> the words, or songs, or dances are suited, either by nature or habit or both,
> cannot help feeling pleasure in them and applauding them, and calling them
> beautiful.

The sophist Protagoras, describing the education that Athenian children received, underlines that role played by music, and more precisely by rhythm and harmony, in bringing up young people to be civilised and balanced.[8]

Music for pleasure

As a disciple of Plato, Aristotle narrows down the role of music. He states[9] that depending on their age, young people were taught four subjects in succession: literature, gymnastics, music and drawing. According to him:[10]

> Also it makes much difference what object one has in view in a pursuit or
> study; if one follows it for the sake of oneself or one's friends, or on moral

Detail of a Classical Greek red-figure vase by the Cambridge Painter, showing a dance lesson.
© Archivo Iconografico, S.A. / CORBIS

6   Aristophanes, *Clouds* (ed. and trans. Jeffrey Henderson), Loeb Classical Library, Harvard University Press, Cambridge, MA, 1998, 961-72. The play was written in 423 BC.

7   Plato, *Laws* (trans. Benjamin Jowett), Prometheus Books, New York, 2000, 654.

8   Plato, *Laches, Protagoras, Meno, Euthydemus* (trans. W. R. M. Lamb), Loeb Classical Library, Heinemann, London, 1924, 325.

9   Aristotle, *Politics* (trans. Benjamin Jowett), Dover Publications, New York, 2000, VIII, 3, 1, 1337.

10 *Ibid.*, 2, 3, 1337.

grounds, it is not illiberal, but the man who follows the same pursuit because of other people would often appear to be acting in a menial and servile manner.

Indeed, if music becomes a job, it resembles a manual occupation, the musician becoming a worker, an artisan (*banausos*) and we know that the Greeks thought this class vulgar, not to say servile. Aristotle clarifies his thinking:[11]

> And therefore our fathers admitted music into education, not on the ground either of its necessity or utility, for it is not necessary, nor indeed useful in the same manner as reading and writing, which are useful in money-making, in the management of a household, in the acquisition of knowledge and in political life, nor like drawing, useful for a more correct judgment of the works of artists, nor again like gymnastics, which gives health and strength; for neither of these is to be gained from music. There remains, then, the use of music for intellectual enjoyment in leisure; which is in fact evidently the reason of its introduction, this being one of the ways in which it is thought that a freeman should pass his leisure; as Homer says, "But he who alone should be called to the pleasant feast", and afterwards he speaks of others whom he describes as inviting "The bard who would delight them all". And in another place Odysseus says there is no better way of passing life than when men's hearts are merry and the banqueters in the hall, sitting in order, hear the voice of the minstrel.

The Greeks' infatuation for music is also displayed in the Greek songs that marked out different moments of the day and in life. In *The Wasps*, Aristophanes echoes this love. Bdelycleon retorts to the servant that the old men who are his father's friends get up late because they have spent the night humming:[12] "Consider that they always pass by when it gets to the middle of the night, humming old 'Sidonian airs, as sweet as honey, from Phrynichus'. That's what they call them outside." The *coryphaeus* of old men, walking past Philocleon's house, also declares:[13]

> What's the matter with our brother juror from this house, not showing up to join the crew? He's never been tardy before. In fact he always leads us on our way with something from Phrynichus; the man's an avid singer. Well, gentlemen, I think we should pause here and sing him out of the house. Maybe when he hears my song he'll be happy to hobble outside.

In his fine book on *La chanson grecque dans l'Antiquité*, Gérard Lambin cites, among other texts,[14] Lucian's remarks on the Abderitans' craze for Euripides, during the reign of Lysimachus (306-281 BC):[15] "they all went mad with tragedy, shouting

---

11   Aristotle, *Politics*, op. cit., VIII, 2, 6, 1338.

12   Aristophanes, *Wasps* (ed. and trans. J. Henderson), Loeb Classical Library, Harvard University Press, Cambridge, MA, 1998, 218-1.

13   *Ibid.*, 266-72.

14   G. Lambin, *La chanson grecque dans l'Antiquité*, CNRS Littérature, Paris, 1992, pp. 8-9.

15   Lucian, *How to Write History*, Vol. VI (trans. K. Kilburn), Loeb Classical Library, Harvard University Press, Cambridge, MA, 1969, 1.

Marble statue of Apollo, the centrepiece of the west façade of the great temple of Zeus.
© The Archaeological Museum of Olympia

iambics and creating a din; and they mostly sang solos from Euripides' *Andromeda*, rendering Perseus' speech in song".

In another text Lucian[16] recalls the effeminate artists who acted out mimes to bawdy songs about "love-sick minxes, the most erotic of all antiquity, such as Phaedra and Parthenope and Rhodope, every bit of this, moreover, accompanied by strumming and tootling and tapping of feet". Love songs, *hymenaioi* at marriages, laments and funeral chants, *alétis* at the festival of the swings, *lityersés* at harvests, *linos* at grape-harvests or pressing, shepherd songs, rowing songs, the warriors' paeans, secular songs, songs of a religious nature, and quest songs[17] show that the Greeks knew how to put music into all the events of life.

This cultural phenomenon explains why music was introduced into competitions where Greeks vied with each other in talent, so as to conquer the glory in which their forefathers and their cities had a share. The musical Games did not exist at Olympia, except in the year 66 AD when Nero, who wished to be admired for his talent as a cithara player, organised an *agón* there for musicians. It was Delphi that emerged as a setting for the musical Games. The Pythian Games came round every four years in the third year of the Olympiad. These Games took place in the month of *Boukatios*, that is in August-September, six months after the *spondophoroi* – that is, the heralds who, during the celebration of the Games, at Olympia and elsewhere, proclaimed the sacred truce known as the "Pythian *hieromania*" – had in this way announced "the most solemn of Apollonian festivals".[18]

We might quite well ask ourselves why the Olympic Games did not include musical competitions, and why Delphi was chosen to be the place that favoured the musical Games.

The absence of musical Games at Olympia may indicate a concern to give greater importance to gymnastic exercises, intended to provide the city with good soldiers capable of defending the city against possible invaders. In this we recognise a world of conflict necessitating a military infrastructure for the defence of the homeland, in a period when wars offered a constant opportunity to demonstrate patriotism. We may also refer to that model of wrestler and saviour embodied in the figure of Heracles, an example of courage and endurance, and (with Hermes) protector of gymnasia, where the defenders of the homeland were trained.

Why was the site of Delphi chosen to celebrate the musical Games? One answer is that, while Olympia was the domain of Heracles, Delphi was that of Apollo. In his capacity as god of music and poetry, Apollo stayed on Mount Parnassus where he presided over the Games of the Muses. At Delphi, Apollo presided as archer, bard, soothsayer, doctor and shepherd. There he slayed the dragon Python (or Delphyne) which, although it was supposed to protect the old oracle of Themis, had instead taken to carrying off flocks and villagers, ravaging the plain of Crisa and terrifying the nymphs. It was in honour of this exploit against Python that Apollo founded the Pythian Games celebrated at Delphi.[19]

From that time on the domain of the god became the centre of wisdom on

A young woman, scantily clad in a panther skin, dances to the accompaniment of a flute played by a young man wearing a *chlamys*. Attic red-figure cup, in the British Museum (inv. E 38), late 6th century BC, by Epictetus, painter and potter.
© The British Museum

16   Lucian, *The Dance*, 2. This quotation is also used by G. Lambin, *op. cit.*

17   All these songs are discussed brilliantly by G. Lambin.

18   A. Bélis, *op. cit.*, goes into more detail, pp. 128-9, referring to G. Roux, *Delphes, son oracle et ses dieux*, Les Belles Lettres, Paris, 1976, p. 171.

19   See the updated section on mythology and religion in L. Séchan in A. Bailly, *op. cit.*, pp. 2205-9.

Open-air theatre in Delphi.
© Kevin Schafer / CORBIS

earth. No site was better suited to be a home for the god of the Muses. It's one of the most beautiful landscapes in Greece. The theatre, perched above the temple of Apollo, lent itself magnificently to the sacred drama celebrating the fight of Apollo against Python, and in the musical contests citharas, flutes, songs and the paeans sung in honour of the god, echoed on the slopes of the mountain. At the foot of the Phaedriades cliffs shining in the sun, the deep gorge of the Pleistos opens out on to the plain of Kirra, covered with olive trees as far as the sea. Certainly no site was better suited to the protector of the Muses.

Of course women could not compete at the Pythian Games any more than they could at the Olympic Games. The presence of women playing the flute was intended to give pleasure to the competitors. The talents of these women flautists, depicted in short skirts on antique vases, were not only musical: they were there, acting as a kind of geisha, for the enjoyment of those who took part in these artistic gatherings.

In the leading families, the sons were given a musical education.[20] However, Plutarch reminds us that Themistocles frowned on this:[21] "When someone wanted to

20 For more about this musical education see A. Bélis, *op. cit.*, pp. 207-41, with references to the principal texts.

21 Plutarch, *Themistocles*, in *Lives* (trans. John Dryden), Modern Library Classics, New York, 1992, II, 3-5.

teach him anything that served purely to reform and civilise manners, or else something that is studied for pleasure and as a decent pastime, he learnt it in a cold and cowardly way." Conversely, Pericles had been the pupil of Damon, the great music theorist,[22] which was not without its dangers:

> The master that taught him music, most authors are agreed, was Damon (whose name, they say, ought to be pronounced with the first syllable short). Though Aristotle tells us that he was thoroughly practised in all accomplishments of this kind by Pythoclides. Damon, it is not unlikely, being a sophist, out of policy sheltered himself under the profession of music to conceal from people in general his skill in other things, and under this pretence attended Pericles, the young athlete of politics, so to say, as his training-master in these exercises. Damon's lyre, however, did not prove altogether a successful blind; he was banished the country by ostracism for ten years, as a dangerous intermeddler and a favourer of arbitrary power.

Not liking music was a sign of barbarism. Plutarch[23] said of the Scythian king Anteas, who in around 340 BC asserted that he preferred his horse's neighing to the recitals of his prisoner Ismenias, who was one of the best Greek *aulos* players, that he "kept his soul in the stables".

Conversely, according to Annie Bélis, "at the time of Theban supremacy, it was considered normal for a general or a political leader to be able to sing, play an instrument and even dance perfectly".

Not every instrument was appreciated in the same way in musical contests. Annie Bélis notes that only in the Imperial period were large curved trumpets used for the musical accompaniment of the gladiators. Examples of these instruments have been found at Pompeii, as well as in Germany: long bronze pipes, coiled up into a spiral. In the procession of the *Ptolemaia* at Alexandria, rather more modest trumpets were used, carried by Silenians, individuals of low rank.

The organ likewise only featured occasionally at the musical Games. In my *Alexandrie la Grande* (1st edition, Artaud, Paris, 1966), I reproduced (p. 201, fig. 23) a Hellenistic lamp from Fayum, preserved at the Louvre and portraying a woman playing the organ, while a dwarf sitting at her side, endowed with an enormous phallus falling to the floor, blows into a long straight trumpet. A decree of Delphi[24] mentions a very rare case: in 90 BC, the archons invited to Delphi a man by the name of Antipatros of Eleutherna so that he could give recitals when the Pythian Games came round. This person did not "compete", but "gave a recital", as expressed by the verb *agônizein*, often misunderstood.

The most beautiful instrument in the world, the human voice, was cultivated in antiquity; not only children's choirs, but also choirs of adults were common. The Athenian explains this as he speaks to Clinias in *The Laws* of Plato:[25]

22 Plutarch, *Pericles*, in *Lives*, op. cit., IV.

23 Plutarch, *On the Fortune or the Virtue of Alexander*, II, 334 B. Text alluded to by A. Bélis, op. cit. p. 209.

24 Dittenberger, W., *Sylloge Inscriptionum Graecarum*, 3, 737. A. Bélis, op. cit., p. 205 and p. 282, note 70, recalls that J. Perrot, *L'Orgue de ses origines hellénistiques*, p. 72, was mistaken in his use of *agônizein*.

25 Plato, *Laws*, op. cit., II, 664.

Ath.: The next suggestion which I have to offer is, that all our three choruses shall sing to the young and tender souls of children, reciting in their strains all the noble thoughts of which we have already spoken, or are about to speak; and the sum of them shall be, that the life which is by the Gods deemed to be the happiest is also the best – we shall affirm this to be a most certain truth; and the minds of our young disciples will be more likely to receive these words of ours than any others which we might address to them.

Cle.: I assent to what you say.

Ath.: First will enter in their natural order the sacred choir composed of children, which is to sing lustily the heaven-taught lay to the whole city. Next will follow the choir of young men under the age of thirty, who will call upon the God Paean to testify to the truth of their words, and will pray him to be gracious to the youth and to turn their hearts. Thirdly, the choir of elder men, who are from thirty to sixty years of age, will also sing. There remain those who are too old to sing, and they will tell stories, illustrating the same virtues, as with the voice of an oracle.

According to Plato these choirs were directed by Apollo, by the Muses and by Dionysus. These songs involved not only voice training, but also dietary and health education, restricting but necessary. People therefore turned to the "singing teacher" who bore the name *phônaskos*,[26] a job which according to Annie Bélis[26] appeared only at the end of the Hellenistic period and most notably in the Imperial period.

Before the Hellenistic or Roman periods the use of music was a Persian practice.[27] A text by Plutarch states:

When the kings of Persia have dinner, their lawful wives sit at their sides and take part in the feast but, if they wish to give themselves over to amusement and drinking bouts, they send them away and summon female musicians and concubines; they do not thereby act wrongly, seeing that in this way they do not associate their spouses with their debauchery and drunken impropriety.

A text by Athenaeus informs us that Strato of Sidon sent for numerous *pallakai*, female singers and musicians from Ionia and the whole of Greece, who brightened up his banquets.

Heracleides wrote in his *Persika*: "Three hundred women watch over the Great King; they sleep all day so as to stay awake at night, when they sing and play the harp continuously while the lamps burn."

In his description of the royal dinner Heracleides adds: "All through the meal the royal concubines sing and play the lyre, one of them is the soloist and the others form a choir."

From Athenaeus we know that at the famous banquet of Susa, which lasted five days and where the Greek soldiers probably slept with Persian women, Alexander and his guests applauded Indian minstrels, but also rhapsodists, harpists, flautists, singers and

---

26 A. Bélis, *op. cit.*, p. 186.

27 P. Briant gives numerous examples, a few of which are borrowed here: *Histoire de l'Empire perse : de Cyrus à Alexandre*, Fayard, Paris, 1996, pp. 289-90, 294, 296, 305-6, 341, 947.

Musicians by the Nikias Painter, circa 420-400 BC.
© Archivo Iconografico S.A. / CORBIS

Greek dancers. Athenaeus also reminds us that "in ancient times music played a central role, in particular for the *Spartiatai*".

Given its association with joy, music naturally created a festive atmosphere at the musical Games, which explains its importance at these events that were both religious and cultural. In the circuit *(periodos)* which established the *periodonikés*, or winner at the four major competitions, the musical Games were an important and difficult stage. Through the procedure of *apographé* the competitor had to get himself registered for the event he had chosen. Annie Bélis refers to a text by Plutarch,[28] which notes that at the Pythian Games, his friend Callistratos, who was *epimelete* of the *amphictyons*, that is a magistrate at the sanctuary, disqualified an *aulos* player who was both his compatriot and his friend but who had not been able to arrive on time.

There is no lack of kings or generals who were passionately interested in music. The last king of Egypt, Ptolemy XII Neos Dionysos, was nicknamed "the flautist" *Aulétés*, given the passion he displayed for that instrument, as Strabo tells us:[29]

28 A. Bélis, *op. cit.*, p. 133; Plutarch, *Symposium*, VII, 5.

29 Strabo, *Geography* (trans. C. F. Smith, Horace L. Jones), Loeb Classical Library, Harvard University Press, Cambridge, MA, 1918, XVII, 1, 11.

For Ptolemy the son of Lagus succeeded Alexander; and he in turn was
succeeded by Philadelphus, and he by Euergetes, and then he by Philopator
the son of Agathocleia, and then he by Epiphanes, and then he by Philometor,
a son always succeeding a father; but Philometor was succeeded by a brother,
the second Euergetes, who is also called Physcon, and he by the Ptolemy
nicknamed Lathurus, and he by Auletes of our own time, who was the father
of Cleopatra. Now all the kings after the third Ptolemy, being corrupted by
luxurious living, have administered the affairs of government badly, but worst
of all the fourth, seventh and the last, Auletes, who, apart from his general
licentiousness, practised the accompaniment of choruses with the flute, and
upon this he prided himself so much that he would not hesitate to celebrate
contests in the royal palace, and at these contests would come forward to vie
with the opposing contestants. He, however, was banished by the
Alexandrians; and since he had three daughters, of whom one, the eldest, was
legitimate, they proclaimed her queen; but his two sons, who were infants,
were completely excluded from service at the time.

The musical Games extended to cities other than Delphi. Thus in the Roman
period at Naples, the gymnastic and musical Games instituted by Augustus in 2 BC
were according to Strabo[30] particularly noteworthy:

And very many traces of Greek culture are preserved there – *gymnasia*,
ephebeia, *phratriae*, and Greek names of things, although the people are
Romans. And at the present time a sacred contest is celebrated among them
every four years, in music as well as gymnastics; it lasts for several days, and
vies with the most famous of those celebrated in Greece.

Music could pride itself on its exotic origin, and on the role assigned to it by
philosophers. Strabo[31] recalls that Plato and the Pythagoreans before him considered
music to be essential:

And on this account Plato, and even before his time the Pythagoreians,
called philosophy music; and they say that the universe is constituted in
accordance with harmony, assuming that every form of music is the work of
the gods. And in this sense, also, the Muses are goddesses, and Apollo is leader
of the Muses, and poetry as a whole is laudatory of the gods. And by the same
course of reasoning they also attribute to music the upbuilding of morals,
believing that everything which tends to correct the mind is close to the
gods. Now most of the Greeks assigned to Dionysus, Apollo, Hecate, the
Muses, and above all to Demeter, everything of an orgiastic or Bacchic or
choral nature, as well as the mystic element in initiations; and they give the
name "Iacchus" not only to Dionysus but also to the leader-in-chief of the

An Etruscan musician in the Tomb of the Leopards,
Tarquinia.

30   *Ibid.*, V, 4, 7.
31   *Ibid.*, X, 3, 10.

mysteries, who is the genius of Demeter. And branch-bearing, choral dancing, and initiations are common elements in the worship of these gods. As for the Muses and Apollo, the Muses preside over the choruses, whereas Apollo presides both over these and the rites of divination. But all educated men, and especially the musicians, are ministers of the Muses; and both these and those who have to do with divination are ministers of Apollo.

The openness of Greece to contributions from abroad is apparent in the welcome given to foreign cultures and cults, and rituals and rhythms from elsewhere. Strabo has remarked on this:[32]

> From its melody and rhythm and instruments, all Thracian music has been considered to be Asiatic. And this is clear, first, from the places where the Muses have been worshipped, for Pieria and Olympus and Pimpla and Leibethrum were in ancient times Thracian places and mountains, though they are now held by the Macedonians; and again, Helicon was consecrated to the Muses by the Thracians who settled in Boeotia, the same who consecrated the cave of the nymphs called Leibethrides. And again, those who devoted their attention to the music of early times are called Thracians, I mean Orpheus, Musaeus, and Thamyris; and Eumolpus, too, got his name from there. And those writers who have consecrated the whole of Asia, as far as India, to Dionysus, derive the greater part of music from there. And one writer says, "striking the Asiatic cithara"; another calls flutes "Berecyntian" and "Phrygian"; and some of the instruments have been called by barbarian names, "nablas", "sambyce", "barbitos", "magadis", and several others.

We may therefore note that the rapid expansion in music was founded on the respect that surrounded this discipline, on the variety of instruments and on the capacity to adapt or adopt many different kinds of instrument. Annie Bélis has classified the musical instruments that were valued most highly in antiquity.[33] She shows that singing was linked to the musical accompaniment. The Homeric bard accompanied himself on his *phorminx*, an early form of the cithara. The *rhapsodist* recited to the accompaniment of an *aulôdos* blowing into a double flute. Athenaeus (*The Deipnosophists*, XIV, 621) informs us that, while the wreath was awarded to the singer, it was the *aulos* player who was the centre of attention. The same author (XII, 538 f) describes a musical contest where it was a choir who accompanied the rhapsodist: three *kitharistoi* (cithara players), two *kitharôdoi* (who played the cithara and sang), two *aulôdoi* (flute players) five *aulétai* players (soloists with choir), tragic and comic actors and a harpist.

According to Annie Bélis,[34] the *kitharôdoi* were the musicians who were the most admired, since they had to be excellent singers and at the same time cithara players. She writes:

> During his performance, the soloist remained standing. What was expected

---

32 Strabo, *Geography, op. cit.*, X, 3, 17.

33 A. Bélis, *op. cit.*, p. 179-206.

34 *Ibid.*, pp. 185-6 and illustration 8.

of him? Our sources tell us that he had to take care "of everything at the same time": for the singing he had to produce the sound without stumbling over a word, and for instrumental technique he needed virtuosity and the independence of his two hands, the right hand striking the string with the aid of the plectrum, the left hand with the tips of the fingers. Similarly, he had to ensure a perfect conformity between the inflections of his voice and the playing of the instrument, and everything had to be faultlessly in time, beaten with slight movements of the feet. It was also demanded that they should be very expressive, but not to the point of excess, and move their hands harmoniously, but without gesticulating.

The demand for so many talents explains why Apollo was represented playing the cithara in statuary of the 2nd century AD.

Nero will not have forgotten that Apollo was the most prestigious cithara player. Just as he was acclaimed and associated with Heracles for his gymnastic exploits, he was hailed as Apollo for his talent as a musician. A text by Dio Cassius[35] reveals Nero's pretensions in this respect, when he returned from a journey to Greece where he had accumulated victories and agonistic wreaths:

> It was necessary to award a tribute worthy of the performance accomplished: Nero himself appeared in the theatre, announced under his real name by Gallion. This Caesar stood on stage, dressed in the costume of a citharodist. The emperor declared: "Gentlemen, kindly be good enough to listen to me". And this Augustus sung on the lyre a piece called "Attis" or "The Bacchantes", while numerous soldiers stood at his side, and the people sat on the available seats listening to him, although it is said that he had a weak and indistinct voice, the kind that provoked everyone to both laughter and tears. Next to him stood Burrus and Seneca, like teachers acting as prompters, and they moved their hands and their togas at each of the noises he produced, inviting the others to do the same. The fact is that Nero kept ready a special corps of around five thousand soldiers, called the "Augustians", who launched the applause, and everyone was obliged to join in the ovation, even against their will, Thrasias being the exception since he would never help Nero in that sphere. But all the others, and most of all the important people, despite their criticism, zealously acted as a body and joined their cheering to that of the "Augustians", as if they were delighted. And they could be heard saying: "Glorious Caesar, our Apollo, our Augustus, unique Pythian, we swear on you Caesar, that no one triumphs over you." After this performance, he invited the people to a banquet on the ships, at the site of the naval battle fought by Augustus. Then at midnight he reached the Tiber via a canal.

Apollo the *kitharôdos* must have found little to boast about after such a farce, and we may well wonder whether it can be called a "music festival".

---

35   Dio Cassius, *Roman History*, Vol. VI (trans. E. Cary and H. B. Foster), Harvard University Press, Cambridge, MA, 1969, XLII, 20. The text is mentioned by L. Robert, *Études épigraphiques et philologiques*, Champion, Paris, 1938, p. 111, note 3.

This very excess helps us to understand the prestige of music and the place that it held in the musical Games. A whole range of expressions brought out the glory of the winners of musical competitions. The winner was declared *paradoxos* (unparalleled), *paradoxonikés* (astonishing winner), *heis kai monos* (the first and the only), *pleistonikés* (holder of numerous victories), *periodonikés* (winner of the "circuit"), that is at the great musical contests (Olympia, Delphi, the Isthmus, Nemea). Nowadays we award honours more readily to sportsmen than to musicians. In antiquity, it could be declared that a musical contest was *eiselastikos*, meaning that it theoretically gave a person the right to enter his city through a breach made in the wall.

In the strict sense, the "musical Games" were competitions. But according to a broader definition the term designates everything that belongs to the sphere of the Muses. These nine goddesses governed the liberal arts: Clio, history; Euterpe, music; Thalia, comedy; Melpomene, tragedy; Terpsichore, dance; Erato, elegy; Polyhymnia, lyric poetry; Urania, astronomy; and Calliope, eloquence. Not all of these fields gave rise to contests. But competitions of eloquence, recitation, declamation and reading pitted contestants against each other and the winners were rewarded, as athletes were, for their performances. The training given by the sophists encouraged these competitions in the liberal arts. The theatre provided themes for reflection and discussion. The taste for and practice of oratory were such that these intellectual confrontations contributed to the formation of citizens and allowed them to assess and to reward their talents. For the Ancient Greeks these battles of the intellect were one of the pleasures of life – and remain so in modern Greek society.

3
LIGHT AND SHADE

Image on the previous page:
Hermes carrying the child Dionysus, attributed to
Praxiteles.

Chapter XI
The meaning of valour

All agonistic inscriptions contain the formula *arétes charin*, meaning "on account of his valour", to describe the motive for the honours awarded to an athlete or artist. The translation "virtue" should be avoided, for this is not the quality that is demanded of these winners, nor the one for which they are rewarded. But what is "valour"?

The answer is not easy, for the concept of valour varies according to the author. The great merit of Valérie Visa-Ondarçuhu's thesis, *L'image de l'athlète d'Homère à la fin du Vᵉ siècle avant J.-C.*, lies in its presentation of texts that are often little known, allowing us to answer this difficult question and to mitigate the effusive praise accorded to athletes. I set forth here texts presented in translation and commented on by the author of this exemplary study.

Courage and valour

During the war that set Messenia against Sparta in around 640 BC, the Spartan poet Tyrtaeus defined valour as courage. In one of his *Elegies* he develops at length his concept of valour:[1]

> I should not consider a man worthy to be remembered, nor think highly of him, merely because he was a good runner or wrestler, even though he was as big and strong as the Cyclops, swifter than Boreus the Thracian, more handsome than Titho, richer than Midas or Cinyras, stronger than King Pelops, son of Tantalus; though his speech was softer than Adrastus' and he enjoyed every kind of fame – unless he was also valorous in arms, unless he could stand fast in battle... that is the true valor – *arété* – the highest reward that a man can obtain from his fellows.
>
> It is a good common to all, a service to the city and the people as a whole, when every man can stand firm on his two feet in the front line and rid his heart of all idea of flight, but rather putting his life and the ardour in his heart at risk, encouraging with words the person next to whom he stands. This is what it is to be courageous in war. He puts the ranks of cruel enemies to immediate flight and quickly manages to stop the fury of battle. As for him, if he falls in the first ranks and loses his life, he wins fame for his city, his people and his father, after being struck several times in the chest on his rounded shield and armour. Young and old alike mourn him, the whole city experiences a sad and bitter grief, his tomb, his children are remarkable in the eyes of the world, as are his children's children and all his descendants after them. He never loses his noble glory nor his renown, and even buried underground he lives, as he who held his own in bravery, waited with firm stance and fought for his land and his children when impetuous Ares caused his death. If on the other

---

1   Tyrtaeus, *Fragments*, 12, quoted by V. Visa-Ondarçuhu, *L'image de l'athlète d'Homère à la fin du ve siècle avant J.-C.*, Les Belles Lettres, Paris, 1999.

hand he escapes a violent death which causes much pain and, winning, gains illustrious glory in combat, everyone does him honour, young and old alike, and it is after experiencing many pleasures that he goes down to Hades: in his old age, he stands out among his citizens, and no one is disrespectful towards him nor does him harm, everyone gives him precedence, the young as much as those of his own age or the old. May we therefore make an effort to rise to this valour, and not slacken our courage in war.

Funerary epigrams provide numerous examples of cases where "valour" is a synonym for "courage". I cite only two texts of the Hellenistic period that celebrate courage. In a funerary epigram from Koptos,[2] the officer Ptolemaios explains for his part that he was a victim of his own courage, as was his son.

> Passer-by, here a tomb contains me, Ptolemaios, an officer who died in a violent fray, with my child Menodoros. A bold and intrepid warrior, when I led impetuous Ares against the enemy, with the Macedonian troops under my command. When in the first rank of fighters we slaughtered the vast host of enemies, cruel Ares took hold of both of us. We died after rendering him distinguished services. Formerly I was a *gymnasiarchos*, valorous on many occasions among the foot soldiers, and when I had to give an opinion, I received the praise that wisdom brings. Well, greetings to you from valiant Ptolemaios, who lies among the dead. Once you have spoken to my son, traveller, move on.

Having been a *gymnasiarchos*, Ptolemaios, who helped to train athletes, resorts to the vocabulary of the *agôn*. He has won the prize for courage, but on top of this comes the prize for wisdom. Adolf Wilhelm has given numerous examples of this union of two notions, *areté* and *sophia*.[3]

Another officer, Ptolemaios' son Apollonios, wished to imitate the courage of his father, who had taken part in a distant and dangerous naval expedition against Syria, and who claimed kinship with royalty. The following epigram uses the term *arété* in the sense of courage, but adds the term *eunoia*, which designates devotion (applied to a monarch it means benevolence). The union of these two terms shows the connotation that can be given to the term "valour". In these lines Apollonios addresses a passer-by:

> Come and find out my homeland, who I am and who my father is, stranger, before continuing happily on your way. Yes, I am Apollonios, son of the distinguished Ptolemaios, to whom the Euergetes awarded the honour of the garland, sacred privilege of the glory belonging to the "relatives of the king". His dedication led him to the interior of the land as far as the Ocean. This is why, as I contemplated my father's magnificent renown, the desire sharpened in me to achieve the same valour and to choose the noble expansion of my beautiful homeland, this sacred steep city of Phoebus, by

---

2   Étienne Bernand, *Inscriptions métriques de l'Égypte gréco-romaine*, Les Belles Lettres, Paris, 1969, 4-5.

3   Adolf Wilhem, *Aigyptiaka*, Akademie der Wissenschaften, Vienna, 1946, 38-46.

Bronze statue of a veteran boxer, showing the ravages of his trade. Kept in the Museo Nazionale Romano, Rome.

putting to sea with my father's friends, good foreigner, when the War of the Sceptres came to Syria. I was a dedicated man and respected sweet loyalty and by my lance and bravery I outmatched everyone. But Destiny, who spins out our days, subdued me – why should you learn of it – when I was thinking of a sweet return, without being tired of life, and before my heart had its fill of the sight of my dear children, who I left at home. You who know these details, stranger, may you say to the father who paid me his last respects: "Do not torture yourself, but remember life". As for you, I hope that you may tread a good road in happiness, alongside your affectionate children.

Mind and body

If *arété* means both courage and wisdom, why should we grant more respect to the athlete than to the intellectual, the winner of contests rather than the man of reflection, brawn rather than brains? Despite the prestige given by Olympic wreaths, some writers of the Classical period dared to question the importance and the glory given to athletes. In his play *Autolykos*, Euripides takes issue with "the likes of athletes":[4]

> *Among the countless evils in Greece,*
> *the worst is the likes of athletes.*
> *First of all they do not learn how to manage their houses well,*
> *and would be incapable of it. For how could a man*
> *who is a slave of his jaws, and conquered by his stomach,*
> *earn something with which he could increase his inheritance?*
> *Furthermore they are not capable of being poor and submitting to a reverse*
> *of fortune. They have not learnt good habits nor*
> *experienced painfully a deterioration in their standard of living.*
> *Moreover they are splendid in their youth and show themselves*
> *here and there as embellishments of the city.*
> *But when bitter old age comes upon them*
> *they pass by displaying threadbare fabric.*
> *Similarly I have criticised the custom of the Greeks*
> *who organise a gathering in favour of these men and*
> *for a banquet set store by satisfaction that is devoid of all usefulness.*
> *What indeed is a man who, because he has wrestled well, has been quick on*
> *his feet, has lifted the discus well or struck someone on the jaw,*
> *receives a wreath to satisfy the city of his forefathers?*
> *Do we fight enemies with a discus in our hands,*
> *or repel enemies of our homeland by striking shields with our arms?*
> *Thus it is wise and good men who should*
> *be crowned with wreaths, those who show the city*
> *the best way through wisdom and justice*
> *and those who dispel evil with their words,*
> *putting an end to war and sedition. For it is*
> *on this that the good of the entire city and all the Greeks depends.*

Boxer adjusting the strips of leather wound round his hands. Red-figure vase in the Kunsthistorisches Museum, Vienna.

4   See Euripides, *Aegeus to Autolycus*. Text quoted by V. Visa-Ondarçuhu, *op. cit.*, pp. 240-3.

Boxers on a Panathenaic amphora from the Archaic
period, circa 6th century BC.
© Gianni Dagli Orti / CORBIS

This condemnation of athletes went against the tide of those who flattered the exploits of which the crowds were so fond. The doctors of the Hippocratic tradition were not to be outdone, and made an inventory of everything in the competitions that could damage the health of the ordinary man. In the exordium of his *Panegyricus*[5] Isocrates developed a similar line of thought:

> I have often been surprised that the founders of solemn feasts and organisers of gymnastic contests should have judged physical merit to be worthy of such great reward, whereas they have awarded no honour to those people (in whom it would have been right and proper to be particularly interested) who have worked personally for the common interest and have elevated their souls in order to make them suitable even for serving other people. Indeed, if athletes doubled their strength, other men would gain no benefit but if a single individual thinks well, it can be of profit to everyone who wishes to share his ideas.

5   Isocrates, *Panegyricus*, 1-2. Text quoted by V. Visa-Ondarçuhu, *op. cit.* p. 238, who also draws attention to other passages from Isocrates and contrasts them to speeches by Gorgias, who praises the athletes.

198

Fists shake, heels knock, *cesti* smash into pieces and whips tear but no one will accuse the president of the *agôn* because he exposes men to violence in the stadium, bruises and blood do not count, only garlands, glory, emoluments, public privileges, civic pensions, portraits and statues; the boxer himself does not complain, for he wants this: the wreath stops the wound and the prize masks the blood.

In the *Idylls*, Theocritus describes a boxing match opposing a boxing champion of the Dioscuri, Pollux and Amykos, king of the Bebrykes, a mythical people of Bithynia. His description fits the denouement of a an actual Olympic boxing match:[6]

And so the twain braced their hands with the leathern coils and twined the long straps about their arms, and forth and entered the ring breathing slaughter each against the other.

Now was there much ado which should have the sunshine at his back; but the cunning of my Polydeuces outwent a mighty man, and those beams did fall full in Amycus his face. So goes master Amycus in high dudgeon forward with many outs and levellings o' fists. But the child of tyndareus was ready, and catched him a blow on the point o' the chin; the which did the more prick him on and make him to betumble his fighting, so that he went in head-down and full-tilt. At that the Berrycians holla'd him on, and they of the other part cried cheerly unto the stalwart Polydeuces for fear this Tityus of a man should haply overpeise him and so bear him down in that narrow room. But the son of Zeus stood up to him first on this side and then on that, and touched him left and right and left again; and for all his puissance the child of Poseidon was stayed in 's onset, insomuch that he stood all drunken with his drubbing and spit out the crimson blood. Whereat all the mighty men gave joyful tongue together by reason of the grievous bruises he had both by cheek and jowl; for his eyes were all-to-straitened with the puffing of their sockets.

I will examine in more detail in Chapter 13 the form that ancient boxing took:[7]

Even as thou seest, stranger, his stout heart in the bronze image, so Elis saw the might of Clitomachus. For when he had put off the blood-stained *cestus* from his hands, he straightway fought in the fierce pancratium. In the third event he fouled not his shoulders in the dust, but wrestling without a fall won the three contests at Isthmus. Alone among the Greeks he gained this honour, and seven-gated Thebes and his father Hermocrates were crowned.

Pausanias reports in detail the main exploits of this extraordinary athlete who demonstrated his courage in the most violent events.[8]

---

6 Theocritus, *Idylls*, in *The Greek bucolic poets* (trans. J. M. Edmonds), Loeb Classical Library, Harvard University Press, Cambridge, MA, 1969, XXII, 80-136.

7 *Greek Anthology* (trans. W. R. Paton), Loeb Classical Library, Harvard University Press, Cambridge, MA, 1918, IX, 588, p. 247.

8 Pausanias, *Description of Greece* (trans. W. H. S. Jones and H.A. Ormerod), Loeb Classical Library, Harvard University Press, Cambridge, MA, 1988, VI, 15, 1-5.

The statue of Cleitomachos of Thebes was dedicated by his father Hermocrates. At the Isthmus he won at wrestling, in the men's category, and on the same day surpassed all the competitors at boxing and at the pancratium. His three victories at Pytho were all at the pancratium. At Olympia Cleitomachos was the first after Theagenes of Thasos to be proclaimed winner both at boxing and at the pancratium. He won at the pancratium at the 141st Olympiad (216 BC). The following Olympiad saw Cleitomachos competing in the pancratium and in the boxing, and he had to confront Kapros of Elis on the same day at wrestling and at the pancratium. Polybius described in detail how Cleitomachos swayed the opinion of the crowd, who were supporting the underdog:[9]

When a humble and much inferior combatant is matched against a celebrated and seemingly invincible athlete, the sympathy of the crowd is at once given to the inferior man. They cheer him on, and back him up enthusiastically; and if he manages to touch his opponent's face, and gets in a blow that leaves any mark, there is at once again the greatest excitement among them all. They sometimes even try to make fun of the other man, not out of any dislike for him or disapproval but from a curious sort of sympathy and a natural instinct to favour the weaker. If, however, one calls their attention at the right time to their error, they very soon change their minds and correct it. This was what Cleitomachus did, as is told. He was considered to be a quite invincible boxer, and his fame had spread over the whole world, when Ptolemy, ambitious to destroy his reputation, trained with the greatest care and sent off the boxer Aristonicus, a man who seemed to have a remarkable natural gift for this sport. Upon this Aristonicus arriving in Greece and challenging Cleitomachus at Olympia, the crowd, it seems, at once took the part of the former and cheered him on, delighted to see that some one, once in a way at least, ventured to pit himself against Cleitomachus. And when, as the fight continued, he appeared to be his adversary's match and once or twice landed a telling blow, there was great clapping of hands, and the crowd became delirious with excitement, cheering on Aristonicus. At this time they say that Cleitomachus, after withdrawing for a few moments to recover his breath, turned to the crowd and asked them what they meant by cheering on Aristonicus and backing him up all they could. Did they think he himself was not fighting fairly, or were they not aware that Cleitomachus was now fighting for the glory of Greece and Aristonicus for that of King Ptolemy? Would they prefer to see an Egyptian conquer the Greeks and win the Olympian crown, or to hear a Theban and Boetian proclaimed by the herald as victor in the men's boxing-match? When Cleitomachus had spoken thus, they say there was such a change in the sentiment of the crowd that now all was reversed, and Aristonicus was beaten rather by the crowd than by Cleitomachus.

In order to be declared the winner at wrestling, a competitor had to make his opponent fall three times. A satirical epigram from Book 11 of the *Greek Anthology*[10]

9   Polybius, *Histories*, Books 1-39 (trans. by W. R. Paton), Loeb Classical Library, Harvard University Press, Cambridge, MA, 1922, XXVII, 9.

reports in this connection an incident experienced by Milon of Crotona, the famous wrestler who died in 510 BC after having won six times at the Olympic Games and six times at the Pythian Games: the seventh time he was crowned with a wreath because no opponent dared to face him. This was an *akoniti* victory, meaning that he did not sprinkle himself with dust and oil for combat. The technical terms *aptôs* or *aptôtos*, "not overcome", "unthrowable", designated this victory gained through the opponents' default.

> Milo the wrestler was once the only one who came to the sacred games, and the steward of the games called him to crown him at once. But as he was approaching he slipped and fell on his back, and the people called out: "Do not crown this man, as he got a fall when he was alone!" But he, standing up

10 *Greek Anthology, op. cit.*, XI, no 316. The text is commented on at length by Louis Robert in his essay "Les épigrammes satiriques de Lucillius" in *L'épigramme grecque*, Vandoevres, Geneva, 1968, pp. 179-291.

Marble statue showing two pancratiasts in action. Housed in the Galleria degli Uffizi, Florence.
© 1990, Photo Scala, Florence – courtesy of the Ministero Beni e Att. Culturali

in their midst, shouted back: "Are there not three falls? I fell once; now let someone give me the other two."

Children could be boxers. This is the case, for example, in an agonistic inscription of Ancyra, published by L. Robert.[11] The city of Ancyra, the "metropolis" of the province, put up a statue, erected on a column, to a victorious athlete, a boxer who won in the category of the *paides puthikoi*, or children recruited according to the same rules as at the Pythian Games. The editor tells us that this Aur(elius) Tertullus, son of Eutyches, was a native of Heraklion of Pontus, in Bithynia, and his first name Aurelius comes from the *Constitutio Antoniniana* of 212 AD. The text is as follows: "To good fortune, at the first Pythian of the great Asklepeaia Soteria Antoniniana, the metropolis (has raised) this statue to Aurelius Tertullus son of Eutyches, of Heraklion of Pontus, winner."

Aristotle[12] criticises the athletic training that the Spartans imposed on children, which in his eyes turned them into beasts:

> Now at the present time some of the states reputed to pay the greatest attention to children produce in them an athletic habit to the detriment of their bodily form and growth, while the Spartans although they have avoided this error yet make their boys animal in nature by their laborious exercises, in the belief that this is most contributory to manly courage.

Aristotle prohibits overfeeding until puberty and gives as evidence of the harmful nature of this practice the fact that overfed and overtrained children do not become victorious athletes when they reach manhood:[13]

> Until puberty, fairly easy exercises should be preferred and any fixed dietary regime or work banned, so that no obstacle impedes growth. There is very clear evidence for this conclusion: among the winners of the Olympic Games one would find only two or three who were victorious as both man and child, because training while still young leads a person to lose his strength through gymnastic exercises. When after puberty he has devoted himself to other exercises for three years, then the following period can be suitably given over to tiring work combined with a set dietary regime.

Anankophagia

The term *anankophagia* used by Aristotle designates the diet imposed by the needs of training. According to their disciplines athletes should make use of the kinds of food that are necessary for them. This does not therefore imply a single diet restricting food but an adaptation of the diet to the exercises practised. A wrestler or pancratiast needed richer food than a runner or a chariot driver.

The job of athlete therefore involved specific demands. Aristotle's teacher Plato recommends in particular to athletes the regimen followed by Ikkos of Tarentum –

11 L. Robert, *Hellenica*, Maisonneuve, Paris, 1949, XI-XII, pp. 350-1.

12 Aristotle, *Politics* (trans. Benjamin Jowett), Dover Publications, New York, 2000, VIII, 3, IV, 1, 1338.

13 *Ibid.*, VIII, 3, IV, 1, 1338-9.

an athlete who won the pentathlon in 476 BC – namely sexual abstinence:[14]

> And have we not heard of Iccus of Tarentum, who, with a view to the
> Olympic and other contests, in his zeal for his art, and also because he was of
> a manly and temperate disposition, never had any connection with a woman
> or a youth during the whole time of his training? And the same is said of
> Crison and Astylus and Diopompus and many others.

The need for an appropriate diet – *anankophagia* – is also recommended by
Epictetus (40–125 AD), which shows how long the rules of athletic training last. In a
fictitious dialogue he states:[15]

> "I wish to conquer at the Olympic games." "And I too, by the gods: for it
> is a fine thing." "But consider here what precedes and what follows; and then,
> if it is for your good, undertake the thing. You must act according to rules,
> follow strict diet, abstain from delicacies, exercise yourself by compulsion at
> fixed times, in heat, in cold; drink no cold water, nor wine, when there is
> opportunity of drinking it. In a word you must surrender yourself to the
> trainer as you do to a physician. Next in the contest, you must be covered
> with sand, sometimes dislocate a hand, sprain an ankle, swallow a quantity of
> dust, be scourged with the whip; and after undergoing all this, you must
> sometimes be conquered. After reckoning all these things, if you have still an
> inclination, go to the athletic practice. If you do not reckon them, observe
> you behave like children who at one time play as wrestlers, then as gladiators,
> then blow a trumpet, then act a tragedy, when they have seen and admired
> such things. So you also do: you are at one time a wrestler, then a gladiator,
> then a philosopher, then a rhetorician; but with your whole soul you are
> nothing: like the ape, you imitate all that you see; and always one thing after
> another pleases you, but that which becomes familiar displeases you. For you
> have never undertaken anything after consideration, nor after having explored
> the whole matter and put it to a strict examination; but you have undertaken
> it at hazard and with a cold desire."

Greek doctors insisted on the need for a diet for athletes, in order both to avoid
excess and above all to prevent food from being ill suited to different constitutions.
In the Hippocratic corpus we find a concern for dietetics that varies according to the
individual. Hence at the beginning of the second book of the *Prorrhetic* we find the
following piece of advice that in case of sickness would allow a prognosis to be
rectified:[16]

> To discover in athletes and in people that are carrying out exercises and
> exertions prescribed because of illnesses whether they have failed to eat some

---

14 Plato, *Laws* (trans. Benjamin Jowett), Prometheus Books, New York, 2000, VIII, 840.

15 Epictetus, *Moral Discourses* (trans. Elizabeth Carter, ed. WHD Rouse), Everyman's Library, New York, 1966, III, XV, 2-5.

16 Hippocrates, *Prorrhetic (Corpus hippocraticus)*, in *Works* (trans. W.H.S. Jones), Loeb Classical Library, Heinemann, London, 1923, 2, 1, IX.

of their meal, or they have eaten something of a different kind, or have taken too much to drink, or omitted part of their walk, or practised venery.

In Philostratus' treatise *On Gymnastics*, in the 3rd century AD, we find a condemnation of medicine:[17]

> which brings cooks and kitchen boys who treat the athletes to delicious meals, make them greedy and turn their stomachs into a bottomless pit; it [medicine] feeds them fish, a food that is completely contrary to the rules of gymnastics.

Porphyry (233-303 AD) modified the diet of athletes. Indeed he states:[18]

> That it is not, however, impious to slay and feed on animals, is evident from this, that Pythagoras himself, though those prior to him permitted the athletes to drink milk, and to eat cheese, irrigated with water; but others, posterior to him, rejecting this diet, fed them with dry figs; yet he, abrogating the ancient custom, allowed them to feed on flesh, and found that such a diet greatly increased their strength.

In another work Porphyry relates that Pythagoras ensured success for an athlete of small stature thanks to a diet of meat:[19]

> Pythagoras took charge of the Samian athlete Eurymenes, who thanks to his wise advice and despite his small stature triumphed at Olympia over many opponents of larger stature. Indeed, while the other athletes retained the old habit of eating cheese and figs, he followed the advice of Pythagoras and was the first to eat every day a set quantity of meat which fortified his body.

While the body was cared for, musical training, which came under the remit of the Muses, was not neglected in the Games. In this respect the Games varied, for there were never musical contests at Olympia, while at Delphi they were celebrated with particular enthusiasm. And while readings, performances and indeed mimes took place, it was music that took precedence over all the other exercises.

---

17 Philostratus, *On Gymnastics*, 44. Quoted by V. Visa-Ondarçuhu, *op. cit.* p. 275.

18 Porphyry, *On abstinence from animal food* (trans. Thomas Taylor, ed. Esme Wynne-Tyson), London, Centaur Press, 1965, I, 26.

19 Porphyry, *Life of Pythagoras*, 15. Quoted by V. Visa-Ondarçuhu, *op. cit.* p. 276.

Chapter XII

From Greek festival to Eastern splendour

In the Greece of the kingdoms, the sobriety of the Greek festival gives way to Oriental splendour. The procession organised at Alexandria by Ptolemy II Philadelphus (who reigned from 285 to 246 BC) is the best illustration of this evolution.

The Greek contests, where individual valour asserts itself, are replaced by competition in the display of power. It is no longer a matter of proving the superiority of the individual but of making manifest the riches of a kingdom. This is a move towards what, under the Roman Empire, will become the triumphal spectacle. This kind of unrestrained and unbridled carnival contrasts with the laws and regulations of the Olympic Games. Excess, immoderation and debauchery show themselves in a parade that it would be better described as an act of defiance or means of letting off steam. While the Games belong to the field of culture, this procession originates in nature, the mother of all excesses. Drunkenness, obscenity and provocation are given free reign.

Callixeinus' processions

The Dionysiac procession of Alexandria is known to us through the description written by Callixeinus and preserved for us by Athenaeus of Naucratis, a sophist of the first half of the 3rd century AD, in *The Deipnosophists*.[1]

> "Since we have described the pavilion and its contents, we will now give an account of the procession. It was held in the city stadium.
>
> "At the head marched the 'division of the Morning Star' because the procession began at the time that star appears. Then came that part of the procession which was named from the parents of the king and queen. After these came the divisions named from all the gods, having decorative symbols appropriate to the story of each divinity. The last division, as it happened, was that of the Evening Star, since the season of the year brought the time consumed by the procession down to that point. If anyone wishes to learn the details, let him take and study the records of the quadrennial games.
>
> "In the Dionysiac procession, there marched at the head Sileni who kept back the crowds; they were dressed in purple riding-cloaks, some in red.
>
> "These were closely followed by Satyrs, twenty at each end of the stadium, carrying torches ornamented with gilt ivy-leaves.
>
> "After these came Victories with gold wings. These carried censers nine feet high, ornamented with gilt ivy-sprays; the women had on

---

[1] Athenaeus, *The Deipnosophists* (trans. Charles Burton Gulick), Loeb Classical Library, Harvard University Press, Cambridge, MA, 1928, pp. 392-419.

embroidered tunics, and their persons were covered with much gold
jewelry.

"After them followed a double altar nine feet long, ornamented in
high relief with gilt ivy-foliage, and having a gold crown of grape-leaves
twined with striped white ribbons.

"Following this came one hundred and twenty boys in purple tunics,
carrying frankincense and myrrh, and, moreover, saffron upon gold
trenchers.

"After them marched forty Satyrs crowned with gold crowns in ivy
pattern; their bodies were smeared in some cases with purple, in others
with vermilion and other colours. These also wore a gold crown
wrought in grape and ivy patterns.

"After them came two Sileni[2] in purple riding-cloaks and white
shoes. One of them wore a broad-brimmed hat and held a herald's staff
of gold, the other carried a trumpet.

"Between these walked a man over six feet tall, in tragic costume and
mask, carrying a gold horn of plenty; he was called 'The Year.'

"He was followed by a very beautiful woman as tall as he, dressed in
a striking tunic and adorned with much gold, and carrying in one hand
a crown of persea, in the other a palm-branch; she was called 'Lustrum'.

"She was closely followed by the four Seasons gaily dressed and each
carrying the fruits appropriate to her. Next these were two censers, nine
feet tall, ornamented with ivy pattern in gold; also a square altar
between them, of gold. Again came Satyrs wearing gold ivy-crowns and
clad in red tunics; some carried a gold wine-pitcher, others a gold
goblet.

"After them marched the poet Philiscus, who was a priest of
Dionysus, and all the guild of the artists of Dionysus. Next were borne
Delphic Tripods, being prizes for the managers of the athletes; the one
intended for the manager of the boys' class was thirteen and a half feet
high, the other, for the manager of the adults' class, was eighteen feet.

"After these came a four-wheeled cart, twenty-one feet long and
twelve feet wide, drawn by one hundred and eighty men; in this stood a
statue of Dionysus, fifteen feet tall, pouring a libation from a gold
goblet, and wearing a purple tunic extending to the feet, over which was
a transparent saffron coat; but round his shoulders was thrown a purple
mantle spangled with gold. In front of him lay a gold Laconian mixing-
bowl holding one hundred and fifty gallons; also a gold tripod, on which
lay a gold censer and two saucers of gold full of cassia and saffron. Over
him stretched a canopy decorated with ivy, grape-vine, and the other
cultivated fruits, wands[3], tambourines, fillets, and satiric, comic, and tragic

---

2   The half-god Silenus was the progeny of Pan and a nymph and the friend and tutor of Dionysus. Following his
example the Silenians (or Silini) were lewd and outlandish worshippers of Dionysus. These bawdy entertainers
represented the elementary forces of the cosmos.

3   These "wands" were called *thyrsi* – staffs carried by Dionysus, Satyrs and others who engaged in Bacchic
festivities and rites. They were often decorated with a pine apple or fir-cone at the end, since the pine was
dedicated to Dionysus as its cones were used for making wine.

Black-figure vase kept in the British Museum. A
bearded adult restrains the younger man in a
headlock.
© The British Museum

masks. The cart (was followed) by priests and priestesses and those who had charge of the sacred vestments, sacred guilds of every description, and women carrying the winnowing fans."

What is striking about Callixeinus' description is the obsession with gold. Victory has golden wings, the women are covered in gold jewellery, the trays carrying incense, myrrh and saffron are made of gold. The altar bearing the colossal censers is made of gold. The Satyrs carry ivy wreaths made of gold. The statue of Dionysus pours libations with a golden goblet, the Laconian crater is made of gold, as are the tripod and cups. Golden cupboard, vases and altar. Even the elephant wears a golden harness and around his neck a gold ivy wreath. As for the Satyrs, an interesting detail is given which deviates from Greek usage, whereby there was only one winner and hence no silver or bronze medals.

The 120 Satyrs walking behind the little girls have golden, silver or bronze accoutrements, for which no explanation is offered. There is no need to count the wreaths, cupboards, statues and chariots made of gold. The obsession with gold is obvious, and the description concludes in a way which would have delighted La Fontaine if he read Callixeinus' description: it is not Persia, nor Babylon, nor the waters of Pactolus, that are the source of gold. There is, if we may put it this way, something worth more than gold itself, for Egypt is an inexhaustable source of food, the "treasure hidden within." Callixeinus said as much when he recalled Triptolemus, the Eleusinian hero linked to the myth of Demeter, sowing grains of corn everywhere. Well before Callixeinus, Herodotus had declared Egypt to be a "gift of the Nile".

"Next came Macedonian bacchants, the so-called 'Mimallones', and 'Bassarae' and 'Lydian women', with hair streaming down and crowned with wreaths, some of snakes, others of smilax and vine-leaves and ivy; in their hands some held daggers, others snakes.

"After these women came a four-wheeled cart twelve feet wide and drawn by sixty men, in which was seated an image of Nysa, twelve feet high; she had on a yellow tunic with gold spangles, and was wrapped in a Laconian shawl. Moreover, this image could rise up automatically without anyone putting his hands to it, and after pouring a libation of milk from a gold saucer it would sit down again. It held in the left hand a Bacchic wand bound with fillets. Moreover, Nysa wore a crown of gold ivy-leaf and very rich grape-clusters of jewels. She also had a canopy, and at the corners of the cart were fastened four torches with gold bands.

"Next there followed another four-wheeler, thirty feet long, twenty-four feet wide, drawn by three hundred men; in this was set up a wine-press thirty-six feet long, twenty-two and a half feet wide, full of grapes. And sixty Satyrs trod them while they sang a vintage song to the accompaniment of pipes, and a Silenus superintended them. The new wine streamed through the whole line of march. Next came a four-wheeled cart thirty-seven and a half feet long, twenty-one feet wide, and drawn by six hundred men; in it was a wine skin holding thirty thousand gallons, stitched together from leopard pelts; this also trickled over the whole line of march as the wine was slowly let out. Following the skin came a hundred and twenty crowned Satyrs and Sileni, some carrying wine-pitchers, other shallow cups, still others large deep cups – everything of gold.

"Immediately next to them passed a silver mixing-bowl holding six thousand gallons, in a cart drawn by six hundred men. It bore, beneath the brim and handles and under the base, figures of beaten metal, and round the middle ran a gold band, like a wreath, studded with jewels.

"Next were carried two silver stands for drinking-cups, eighteen feet long and nine feet in height; these had end-ornaments on top, and on the swelling sides all round as well as on the legs were carved figures, many in number, two and three feet high.

"And there were ten large basins and sixteen mixing-bowls, the larger of which held three hundred gallons, while the smallest held fifty. Then there were twenty-four cauldrons ornamented with an acorn boss, all of them on stands; and two silver wine-presses, on which were twenty-four jars, a table of solid silver eighteen feet long, and thirty more tables nine feet long. Added to these were twenty-four feet, plated throughout with silver, while the other three, which were smaller, were studded with jewels in the centre. After these were borne along Delphic tripods of silver, eighty in number, but smaller than those just mentioned; at their corners (were figures in beaten metal), and the tripods had a capacity of forty gallons. There were twenty-six water-jars, sixteen Panathenaic amphoras, one hundred and sixty wine-coolers; of these the largest contained sixty gallons, the smallest twenty. All these vessels were of silver.

"Next to these in the procession came those who carried the gold utensils, four Laconian mixing-bowls with bands of vine-leaves... others with a capacity of forty gallons; and two of Corinthian workmanship, on stands; these had on the brim seated figures in beaten metal, very striking; and on the neck and round the bowl were figures in relief, carefully fashioned; the capacity of each was eighty gallons. There was also a press containing ten wine-jars, two basins, each holding fifty gallons, two drinking-cups holding twenty gallons, twenty-two wine-coolers; of these the largest held three hundred gallons, the smallest ten. Four large gold tripods were carried in the procession; and there was a gold chest for gold vessels, studded with jewels and having a height of fifteen feet, with six shelves, on which stood a great number of figures carefully fashioned, four spans high; there were also two stands for cups, and two glass vessels studded with jewels; two gold stands six feet high, beside three smaller ones, ten water-jars, an altar four and a half feet high, and twenty-five bread-plates."

If we add up the litres of wine held in the various containers, we arrive at a staggering total, and understand how "all the people in the stadium gorged themselves". Not counting the *oinochai* and various jugs and jars, let us note only the wine skin of 3,000 *metrétai* (166,640 litres), the silver crater of 600 *metrétai* (23,328 litres), the crater of five *metrétai*, the 16 craters of which the biggest

contained five *metrétai* (195 litres) and the smallest three (116 litres). These fountains of wine must have been well stocked if they were to flow all day.

"After all this there marched one thousand six hundred boys who had on white tunics and wore crowns, some of ivy, others of pine; two hundred and fifty of them carried gold pitchers, four hundred, silver pitchers; while another band of three hundred and twenty bore gold or silver wine-coolers. After them other boys carried jars intended to be used for sweetmeats; twenty of these were of gold, fifty of silver, and three hundred were adorned with encaustic paintings in all sorts of colours. And since the mixtures had already been made in the water-jars and casks, all persons in the stadium were duly showered with sweetness."

Parade of the exotic

"Next to these in his catalogue were six-foot tables on which were borne remarkable scenes lavishly presented. Among these was included the bridal chamber of Semele, in which certain characters wear tunics of gold bejewelled with the costliest gems.

"And it would not be right to omit the following mention of the four-wheeled cart, in length thirty-three feet, in width twenty-one, drawn by five hundred men; in it was a deep cavern profusely shaded with ivy and yew. From this pigeons, ring-doves, and turtle-doves flew forth along the whole route, with nooses tied to their feet so that they could be easily caught by the spectators. And from it also gushed forth two fountains, one of milk, the other of wine. And all the nymphs standing round him wore crowns of gold, and Hermes had a staff of gold, and all in rich garments.

"In another cart, which contained 'the return of Dionysus from India', there was a Dionysus measuring eighteen feet who reclined upon an elephant's back, clad in a purple coat and wearing a gold crown, of ivy and vine pattern; he held in his hands a gold wand-lance, and his feet were shod with shoes fastened by gold straps. Seated in front of him on the elephant's neck was a Satyr measuring seven and a half feet, crowned with a gold pine-wreath, his right hand holding a goat-horn of gold, as though he were signalling with it. The elephant had trappings of gold and round its neck an ivy-crown in gold.

"This cart was followed by five hundred young girls dressed in purple tunics with gold girdles. Those who were in the lead, numbering one hundred and twenty, wore gold pine-crowns; following them came one hundred Satyrs, some in gold, some in silver, and some in bronze panoply.

"After them marched five troops of asses on which were mounted Sileni and Satyrs wearing crowns. Some of the asses had frontlets and harnesses of gold, others of silver. After them were sent forth twenty-four elephant chariots, sixty teams of he-goats, twelve of short-horns, seven of gazelles, fifteen of hartbeestes, eight teams of ostriches, seven of gazelles, fifteen of antelopes, four teams of wild asses, and four four–

Greek statue, in bronze with copper inlays, of a victorious youth by an unknown sculptor, dating from 300-100 BC. The young man stands naked, resting on his right leg. He crowns himself with a wreath, probably of olive. An olive wreath was the first prize at the Olympic games.
© The J. Paul Getty Museum (inv. 77. AB. 30)

horse chariots. On all of these were mounted little boys wearing the tunics and wide-brimmed hats of charioteers, and beside them stood little girls equipped with small crescent shields and wand-lances, dressed in robes and decked with gold coins.

"The lads driving the chariots wore pine crowns, the girls wore ivy. Next after them came six teams of camels, three on either side. These were immediately followed by carts drawn by mules. These contained barbaric tents, under which sat Indian and other women dressed as captives.

"Then came camels, some of which carried three hundred pounds of frankincense, three hundred of myrrh, and two hundred of saffron, cassia, cinnamon, orris, and all other spices. Next to these were negro tribute-bearers, some of whom brought six hundred tusks, others two thousand ebony logs, others sixty mixing-bowls full of gold and silver coins and gold dust.

"After these in the procession, marched two hunters carrying gilded hunting-spears. Dogs were also led along, numbering two thousand four hundred, some Indian, the others Hyrcanian or Molossian or of other breeds. Next came one hundred and fifty men carrying trees on which were suspended all sorts of animals and birds. Then were brought in cages, parrots, peacocks, guinea-fowls, and birds from the Phasis and others from Aethiopia, in great quantities."

After he has spoken of very many other things, and enumerated many droves of animals he adds:

"One hundred and thirty Aethiopian sheep, three hundred Arabian, twenty Euboean; also twenty-six Indian oxen entirely white, eight Aethiopian, one large white she-bear, fourteen leopards, sixteen panthers, four lynxes, three panther-cubs, one giraffe, one Aethiopian rhinoceros.

"Next in a four-wheeled cart was Dionysus at the altar of Rhea, having found refuge there while being pursued by Hera; he had on a gold crown, and Priapus stood at his side, with a gold ivy-crown. The statue of Hera had a gold diadem. Then there were statues of Alexander and Ptolemy, crowned with ivy-crowns made of gold. The city of Corinth, standing beside Ptolemy, was crowned with a gold band.

"Beside all these figures were placed a stand for cups, full of gold vessels, and a gold mixing-bowl of fifty gallons capacity. Following this cart were women who wore very rich robes and ornaments; they bore the names of cities, some from Ionia, while all the rest were the Greek cities which occupied Asia and the islands and had been under the rule of Persians; they all wore gold crowns. In other carts, also, were carried a Bacchic wand of gold, one hundred and thirty-five feet long; in another was a gold phallus one hundred and eighty feet long, painted in various colours and bound with fillets of gold; it had at the extremity a gold star, the perimeter of which was nine feet."

Many and varied though the things are which have been mentioned as belonging to these processions, yet I have selected for mention only those things which contained gold and silver. For there were numerous

articles worth mentioning, and quantities of wild beasts and horses, and twenty-four huge lions.

"There were other carts besides, which carried images of kings and of gods as well, many of them. After them marched a choral band of six hundred men; among them three hundred harp-players performed together, carrying harps gilded all over, and wearing gold crowns.

"After them two thousand steers, all of the same colour and with gilded horns, came by, having gold stars on their foreheads, wreaths between the horns, and necklaces and aegises on their breasts; all these were of gold.

"And after this came marching in the carnival a division in honour of Zeus and one of other gods in great number, and following all one devoted to Alexander, whose effigy in gold was borne, Victory and Athena on either side, in a chariot drawn by elephants."

To the prestige of gold, the Dionysiac procession adds the curiosity aroused by exoticism. The evocation of perfumes and spices leads us into a world that is almost unknown. Young boys carry on their trays incense, myrrh and saffron. Camels transport huge loads of incense, myrrh, saffron, cassia, cinnamon, iris and other spices. The fragrances of India, Egypt and Arabia drift over this Alexandrian procession.

Strange animals accompany the asses, billy goats, she-goats, sheep, gazelles, oxen, bulls, horses and mules: elephants, buffalo, ostriches, Ethiopian or Arabian sheep, white oxen of the Indies, Indian dogs, Hyrcanians or big ferocious dogs, a white she-bear, 14 leopards, 16 panthers, four lynx, a giraffe, an Ethiopian rhinoceros, 24 enormous lions and birds from far-away places: eagles, parrots, peacocks, guinea-fowl, pheasants and tropical birds. Precious woods accompanied the familiar palms, vines and pine trees, including 2,000 trunks of precious ebony wood.

Automata were a speciality of Alexandrine engineers. The procession is not lacking in them: the statue of Dionysus poured a libation of wine, the statue of Nysa stood up, poured a libation of milk and then sat down again. The highlight was no doubt the 55m long phallus with a 3m circumference. It probably had articulated joints, which would have offered a lively sight.

Various tableaux called to mind those distant countries that Alexander and his successors dreamed of annexing. The camel caravans, the barbarian tents, the hunters with their gilt hunting-spears, all these tableaux broadened the horizons of the onlookers and inspired them to dream of other possible conquests.

The colourful, shimmering clothing, sparkling with precious stones, of the people taking part in the procession contrasted with the customary sobriety of the Classical Greeks. The Silenians, playing the role of *rhabdophoroi*, a kind of police agent, wore purple or scarlet *chlamys*. The women had embroidered tunics and were covered in jewels. The young boys wore purple tunics. The Satyrs following them were not clothed but painted in purple or vermilion. The statue of Nysa was dressed in a yellow dress embroidered with gold and draped in a shawl. Diamonds of all kinds represented grapes. In contrast to all this luxury was the unkempt appearance of the Macedonian bacchantes, their hair hanging down and encircled with snakes, and the white tunics of the children. The 500 small girls were dressed in purple tunics and wore gold belts. Even the asses were decked out in ornamental plaques and gold or silver harnesses. The 2,000 bulls had gilded horns, golden plaques, wreaths on their heads and chains round their necks. The elephant carrying the statue of Dionysus, more than 5m high, and led by a Satyr, had a gold harness and around its neck an ivy wreath made of gold.

It is noteworthy music played such an important role in the procession. Thus after a chariot carrying effigies of kings or gods, came a troupe of 300 cithara players. The *chorégoi* of the solo flautists and children's choirs were rewarded by tripods, the children's ones being 4m–5m high. The 60 Silenians who were crushing grapes sang a Bacchic song, accompanied by flutes. The Silenian at the start of the procession had only a trumpet at his disposal.

The procession was enlivened by entertainments. One of the most amusing was without doubt the flight of pigeons, doves and turtledoves flying out of a cave covered in ivy and yew. The ribbons attached to their feet allowed the onlookers to catch them. The trees populated with animals and birds must have been very successful. The Africans carrying 600 elephant tusks and 2,000 trunks of ebony also presented a startlingly exotic spectacle.

"In the procession also were many thrones constructed of ivory and gold; on one of these lay a gold diadem, on another a gilded horn, on still another a gold crown, and on another a horn of solid gold. Upon the throne of Ptolemy Soter lay a crown made of ten thousand gold coins.

"In the procession also were three hundred and fifty gold censers, and gilded altars wreathed with gold crowns; on one of these, four gold torches fifteen feet long were affixed. And two gilded braziers were also carried in the procession, of which one was eighteen feet in circumference and sixty in height, the other measured twenty-two and a half feet. There were also nine Delphic tripods of gold of six feet each, more of nine feet, another of forty-five feet; on this were figures in gold seven and a half feet high, and a vine-wreath of gold encircled it. There went by also seven gilded palm-trees twelve feet high and a gilded herald's staff sixty-seven and a half feet long, a gilded thunderbolt sixty feet long, also a gilded temple measuring sixty feet all round; there was a double horn in addition, twelve feet high. A very large number of gilded figures were in the procession, the most of which were eighteen feet high; and there were figures of wild beasts of extraordinary size, and eagles thirty feet high.

"Three thousand two hundred gold crowns were shown in the procession, and there was another mystic crown of gold one hundred and twenty feet in circumference, adorned with precious stones; this was hung round the portal of Berenice's shrine; there was similarly a gold aegis. And there were also very many gold diadems in the procession, carried by girls richly dressed; one diadem was three feet high, and it had a perimeter of twenty-four feet.

"There was paraded also a gold breastplate eighteen feet in length, and another of silver, twenty-seven feet, with two gold thunderbolts on it fifteen feet long, and an oak crown of gold studded with jewels.

"Dionysus crossing the Sea": red Attic *kylix*, or drinking cup, by the Exekias potter, circa 540 BC, illustrating the lines from the Homeric *Hymn to Dionysus* below.

© Staatliche Antikensammlungen und Glyptothek München (inv. 8729) / Photo: R. Kuehling

[...] and the wind filled the sail and the crew hauled taut the sheets on either side. But soon strange things were seen among them. First of all sweet, fragrant wine ran streaming throughout all the black ship and a heavenly smell arose, so that all the seamen were seized with amazement when they saw it. And all at once a vine spread out both ways along the top of the sail with many clusters hanging down from it, and a dark ivy-plant twined about the mast, blossoming with flowers, and with rich berries growing on it; and all the thole-pins were covered with garlands [...] and when the sailors saw it they leapt out overboard one and all into the bright sea, escaping from a miserable fate, and were changed into dolphins.

Hymn to Dionysus, in *Homeric Hymns and Homerica* (trans. Hugh G. Evelyn-White), Loeb Classical Library, Harvard University Press, Cambridge, MA, 1914, VII, 33-41

Twenty gold shields, sixty-four suits of armour in gold, two pairs of gold
greaves four and a half feet long, twelve gold hods, saucer-shaped cups in
very great number, thirty wine-pitchers, ten large ointment-holders,
twelve water-jars, fifty bread-platters, various tables, five stands of gold
vessels, a horn of solid gold forty-five feet long. And these articles of
gold were exclusive of those carried by in the division of Dionysus.
Further, there were four hundred cartloads of silver vessels, twenty of
gold vessels, and eight hundred of spices.

"After all these marched the cavalry and infantry forces, all
wonderfully armed cap-à-pie. The infantry numbered about 57,600, the
cavalry 23,200. All of these marched dressed in the garments proper to
each, and in their appropriate panoply. But beside the panoplies worn by
all these troops, there were very many others stored in chests, of which
it is not easy to set down even the number." Yet Callixeinus gave the list.

"And in the games twenty persons were crowned with gold crowns;
Ptolemy was first, then Berenice, who were honoured with three
portrait-statues in gold chariots, and with precincts at Dodona. The total
expense, in currency, amounted to two thousand, two hundred and
thirty-nine talents and fifty minas; and all this sum was paid in to the
managing officials before the exhibition was over, through the
enthusiastic zeal of those who gave the crowns. And their son, Ptolemy
Philadelphus, was awarded two gold portrait-statues, in gold chariots,
mounted on columns, one of nine feet, five of seven and a half feet, and
six of six feet."

"What monarchy, fellow-banqueters, has ever been so rich in gold?
Surely not any that appropriated the wealth of Persia or Babylon, or that
had mines to work, or that owned the Pactolus river, washing down
gold-dust. No; for it is only the Nile, the river truly called 'gold-
flowing', that with its boundless crops of food actually washes down
unadulterated gold which is harvested with no risk, so that it can supply
all men sufficiently; being, like Triptolemus, sent forth into every land.
For this reason the Byzantian poet by the name of Parmenon says 'Thou
Nile, Egypt's Zeus!'"

Dreams of conquest

We should not take literally the descriptions of processions, chariots, objects or
persons presented. They have above all a symbolic value, giving concrete
expression to the aspirations of the Hellenistic kingdom, which will be taken up
by the Roman Empire. We should look upon this procession, which is at one and
the same time a kind of carnival, a musical revue and a military review, as also an
imaginative hyperbole. But we should not forget that this show of riches expresses
an economic, political and cultural ideal of which Alexandria was the expression.

This dream of riches and power proceeds from the reality of Pharaonic
Egypt which, in this description, is mingled with details from Greek life. The fact
that this event takes place in the stadium and that this festival is celebrated every
four years can be attributed to the Greek model. The statue "Quinquennial
festival" in the leading group reminds us of this chronology.

But right at the beginning of the description, we learn that the procession

Statue of Hermes carrying the child Dionysus,
attributed to Praxiteles.
© Sonia Halliday Photographs

only lasts one day, from morning till evening, while the Greek contests lasted several days. A feature unknown to the Greek contests is the dating according to "the relatives of the sovereigns", and not according to the Olympiad. In the description, the gods come after the sovereigns. This means that the religious aspect is preceded by the evocation of symbols of power and riches. Out of the four elements of the Greek games, comprising prayer, procession, sacrifice and competition, the Alexandrians have retained only the *pompé*.

Alexander and the Ptolemies feature in the procession. The statue of Alexander is made of gold and transported on a chariot dragged by elephants. The king is in good company: Zeus, Victory, Athena. Ptolemy I Soter is the first to be crowned with a wreath and Queen Berenice is eligible for three statues. Earlier it is mentioned that the throne of Ptolemy Soter bore a crown assembled from 10,000 pieces of gold. Beforehand Callixeinus notes that Alexander and Ptolemy Soter were honoured with statues bearing ivy wreaths made of gold. On the chariot transporting them, they were accompanied by gods: Dionysus, Priapus, Hera, Valour. Ptolemy II Philadelphus is honoured with two statues mounted on columns 2m high.

The enumeration of the participants is not without a certain sense of humour. Fifty Satyrs cavorted behind the young boys, and another 120 Satyrs followed the young girls, placing these children in situations that, given the morals of the pursuers, could be dangerous. All the more so given the free flow of wine. The example was set by the monumental statue of Dionysus who, under his arbour, poured libations, a crater of 580 litres before him. The Satyrs, responsible for crushing the grapes, quenched their thirst on sweet wine. The wine skin of 116,640 litres was followed by the ever-thirsty Satyrs.

The god serving as a model for athletes, Heracles, does not feature in the procession. It is Dionysus who sets the tone, for this festival is in his honour. He is surrounded by Nymphs and escorted by Hermes. One chariot represents "The Return of Dionysus from India".

It is difficult to enumerate the chariots and to make a distinction between objects carried by hand or on vehicles. The procession shows us that numerous chariots were reserved for Dionysus. The text makes clear that they are four-wheeled chariots, vehicles capable of bearing heavy weights. One hundred and eighty men were needed to pull a chariot over 6m wide and 3.55m long, on which a 6m high statue of Dionysus was raised, a crater of 3 litres at its feet. A smaller chariot, 3.5m wide, that of Nysa, was pulled by 60 men. The chariot of the Satyrs crushing grapes was nearly 9m long and over 6m wide: it was pulled by 300 men. The next chariot, 11m long and over 6m wide, carried an enormous wine skin of more than 100,000 litres, flowing continuously in a thin stream.

Since it was followed by 120 Satyrs or Silenians, it must have been emptied as they progressed, serving as their refreshment. Six hundred men were needed to pull the chariot transporting craters, dressers, cupboards, wine presses, cauldrons, earthenware jars, *hydrides* and tripods. The next chariot, bearing the objects made of gold, was also loaded with craters, wine presses, bowls, crockery and trays. The chariot carrying the birds, nearly 10m long and over 6m wide, needed 500 men to transport its cavern, fountains of milk and wine and bird-cages.

The chariot containing the "Return of Dionysus from India" bore a statue nearly 5.5m high, perched on an elephant. We are not told how many men were pulling it. Callixeinus notes that the chariots were generally followed by various processions. Dionysus was also entitled to a chariot showing him in company with the statues of Priapus, Hera, Alexander, Ptolemy Soter and an "allegory of Corinth".

A special chariot was reserved for Zeus, accompanied by numerous gods but also by gold statues of Alexander, Victory and Athena. The chariots following these transported a whole variety of precious furnishings.

It is hard to assess the military forces taking part, perhaps 57,600 foot soldiers and 23,200 cavalrymen. These numbers are relatively modest, if we compare them to the figures of the great battles of antiquity.[4] But since they come from a single town, they denote a huge procession and are a sign of the importance of the greatest city in the kingdom.

In a highly stimulating chapter of his fine book, *Histoire de l'Empire perse*,[5] Pierre Briant recalls the procession organised by Artaxerxes III Ochos (358–337 BC), which is prior to that dreamed up by Ptolemy II Philadelphus (285–246 BC). In both of these festivals, the king showed both his riches and his power. The historian draws an apposite parallel with the text of Theopompus of Chios (F. Gr. H. 115 F 263 a), which he suggests may be set in 343 BC, at the time of the expedition led by Artaxerxes III Ochos to reconquer Egypt, and which he translates *in extenso*:

> What city or people of Asia did not send an embassy to the king? What product of the earth or beautiful and precious product of their craft industry did they not bring as a present (*dôron*) to set down before the king? Many magnificent blankets, fine blankets, some dyed purple, others of every colour, others white, many tents and costly and magnificent beds and also chased silver and gold worked to perfection, goblets and craters, some inlaid with precious stones, others appearing to be worked with both economy and sumptuousness. Over and above all that, countless myriads of weapons, Greek or barbarian, and an improbable number of harnesses and fat animals for sacrifices, as well as numerous *medimnes* of seasoning, many leather bags, purses and a large amount of paper made from papyrus, and among all the other things everything that is necessary for subsistence, including meat from sacrificial victims preserved in salt in such a quantity that, coming from far off, people approaching thought that they saw mountains and hills arising in front of them.

While these sumptuous demonstrations had as their origin Achaemenid practices, we must admit that at the *Ptolemaia* of Alexandria the Egyptians have gone further in exuberance and extravagance, creating the greatest possible splendour. Callixeinus' description becomes not only fantastic but even fantastical. It expresses a dream more than it describes a reality. It thus gains in magnificence what it loses in verisimilitude.

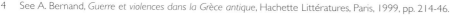

4   See A. Bernand, *Guerre et violences dans la Grèce antique*, Hachette Littératures, Paris, 1999, pp. 214-46.
5   P. Briant, *Histoire de l'Empire perse*, Fayard, Paris, 1996, pp. 178-216, particularly pp. 204-5 and 212-3.

In the Pharaonic period, the pylons and walls of Egyptian temples develop scenes where the Pharaoh shows his strength, holding clusters of prisoners by the hair, but also his riches, welcoming processions bringing him offerings. In the Achaemenid kingdom, Pierre Briant reminds us that, on the façades of their tombs, on the walls of their palaces or on stelae, Darius and his successors represented the people carrying the royal throne or bringing animals and various objects to the Great King. Iconography therefore supports information from texts to celebrate the strength, riches and extent of royal power.

Chapter XIII
Distractions

A very fine essay by Maurice Genevoix, (in the eleventh volume of his *Complete Works* published in Geneva) which is never cited by "professional" Hellenists, gives us a picture of the life of the gymnasium that illustrates the distractions alluded to in the heading. This essay reveals not only the author's talent for description, but great scholarship combined with a gift for evocation. This hero of the last two wars, at first categorised as a "war historian" and then as a "regionalist writer", shows himself to be outstandingly learned.

Maurice Genevoix conjures up first of all the palaestra of Taurosthenes at Sicyon,[1] a city in the north of the Peloponnese a short distance from the coast of the Gulf of Corinth. Strabo (writing at the time of Augustus) mentions it often in Book 8 of his *Geography*. In particular he tells us:[2]

> In earlier times Sicyon was called Mecone, and in still earlier times Aegiali, but Demetrius rebuilt it upon a hill strongly fortified by nature about twenty stadia (others say twelve) from the sea; and the old settlement, which has a harbor, is a naval station. The River Nemea forms the boundary between Sicyonia and Corinthia. Sicyon was ruled by tyrants most of the time, but its tyrants were always reasonable men, among whom the most illustrious was Aratus, who not only set the city free, but also ruled over the Achaeans, who voluntarily gave him the authority, and he increased the league by adding to it both his native Sicyon and the other cities near it.

Sicyon's port was not far from the city, occupying the site of the modern town of Kiato, near the mouth of the Helisson. In the 2nd century AD, Pausanias in his *Description of Greece* speaks at length about the history and site of Sicyon.[3] Pausanias often digresses to relate myths with a connection to the region and its sanctuaries.

Pausanias lists a series of monuments: at the entrance to the territory of Sicyon, coming from Corinth, the tomb of Lycos the Messenian on the opposite bank of the Asopos, an *Olympieion* and more tombs. He notes that the acropolis of his day contained a sanctuary of the "Fortune of the Mountain", then a sanctuary of the Dioscuri, whose statues were made of wood. The theatre was built at the foot of the acropolis. Past the theatre there was a temple of Dionysus. Pausanias adds that once the Sicyonians carried in procession, from the *Kosmétérion* to the *Dionysion*, by the light of torches and to the sound of local hymns, statues that were kept secret: a statue called

1 See the excellent book by G. Roux, *Pausanias en Corinthie*, Les Belles Lettres, Paris, 1958, II, 1-15, which gives an archaeological and topographical commentary on the passage. The photographs of the site and a few ruins are mediocre, but the book includes an excellent map at the back.

2 Strabo, *Geography* (trans. C. F. Smith, Horace L. Jones), Loeb Classical Library, Harvard University Press, Cambridge, MA, 1918, VIII, 6, 25.

3 Pausanias, *Description of Greece* (trans. W.H.S. Jones and H.A. Ormerod), Loeb Classical Library, Harvard University Press, Cambridge, MA, 1988, V, 2, 12; 51.

Baccheios, another *Lysios*. There was also a temple of "Artemis of the Marsh". At the entrance to the agora was a "sanctuary of Persuasion". After the *heroon* of Aratos could be seen an altar of "Poseidon of the Isthmus", then a *Zeus Meilichios* and an *Aphrodite Patroa*. In the gymnasium, next to the agora, a Heracles in marble, the work of Scopas. From the gymnasium a path led to the sanctuary of Asclepius. Other sanctuaries existed: one dedicated to Aphrodite, another to Artemis, another to Apollo, another sacred to Hera.

Secrets of the training ground

Genevoix's art lies not simply in description, but also in evoking and bringing to life scenes peopled with invented characters. His description of the palaestra, for example, is striking:

> The palaestra was merely a large sandy courtyard, enclosed by a high wall, full of sunshine. A single tree, in the middle of the bright arena, a beautiful plane tree with a slender trunk, spread at its feet an oasis of slight shadow splashed by golden *ocelli*. Surrounding the tree stood a stone bench where a few men of mature years sat conversing, and watching the athletes train.
>
> There were not yet many of these. But they could be seen, one by one, leaving the small changing-room, dazzling under its cool limewater, which flanked the postern at the entrance. Entirely naked, some hopping on the spot, others spreading over their arms and thighs the oil that they had just

Black-figure Attic *skyphos* dating from the 5th century BC. Two seated men watch four naked youths. The adults, dressed in white tunics with red and black sleeves show interest in the boys. In the centre a naked bearded youth looks another boy in the eye, while his left hand touches the young man's thigh. The cock painted across the boy's body is an erotic symbol. Two sphinxes, one male on the left, the other female on the right, turn their backs on the scene.

© National Archaeological Museum of Athens (inv. 366).

poured on them, they reached the jumping pits and tracks, chose a javelin, *cesti* strips, dumb-bells for jumping.

In a very reserved manner, Genevoix evokes the special friendships that often developed between these young people who cultivated physical beauty and, proud of athletic nudity, were able to compare the strength and grace of their young bodies. We know through statuary how much male beauty was valued by the Greeks. The *kouroi* remind us of this tendency in Greek society.

We know, in particular through Plato, how adults came to watch these gymnastic exercises in order to discover the loved one. Inscriptions between *erastes* and *eromenos* leave no room for doubt. Let us not forget that homosexuality was not condemned in Ancient Greece, insofar as it respected certain prohibitions: not to resort to force, not to use money to bribe the partner, not to take advantage of young slaves, not to choose an adult of one's own age, for between the loved one and the lover there had to be a difference in age. The appearance of the beard and hair had to mark the end of a homosexual relationship. There was deviation or deviancy only if these rules were not observed.

Genevoix relates how a certain Hermon engraved on the bark of a tree: "How desirable is Sostratos, the son of Aithon". Hermon was quite willing to recognise this: "Of course it's me, said Hermon calmly. Wherever you go here, his name jumps out at you. Each of these four walls vies with each other in singing of his charm and beauty". For all that, among Genevoix's young people, a fair number do not hide their

Attic red-figure *skyphos*-cup from Camiros, Rhodes by the Amasis Painter, circa 540 BC showing flirtation between men and *ephebes* and men and women. Kept in the Department of Greek, Etruscan and Roman antiquities, the Louvre (inv. A 479).

© Photo RMN – Chuzeville, Louvre

heterosexual relationships. Like Aristophanes, some of them make fun of ostentatious homosexuals.

One beautiful passage compares a statue of the athlete to the athlete himself. An old man, Menestheus, calls to mind Olympic glory in the presence of Sostratos, and admires both the statue of an *Olympionikés* and the stature of the young man:

> The athlete of bronze, one leg moved slightly forward, let his left hand dangle, its fingers half-open; his right hand was stretched out in a gesture of offering and he smiled, like the young mortal, with that mysterious smile one sees on ancient statues. His thighs, from the knees, opened out in long ascending lines and, onto his smooth stomach, onto the double plane of his muscular chest, the light streamed as onto flesh endowed with life. A thin veneer of copper reddened the tips of his nipples, his lips of swollen pulp, and he watched Menestheus with his strangely fixed eyes, eyeballs of white enamel in which were embedded pupils of green quartz.
>
> But the other, the living man, what beauty was his! He had the same long legs, slowly opening out from the two knees. On his slim sides, strapped up with smooth muscles, rested the strength of his torso. At first one would have thought him to be motionless, but the sun caused warm shadows to move in the hollows of his young flesh, seeming to put life into his whole body. At intervals, his eyelids blinked over his blue eyes, his breath, imperceptibly, shifted the lines of his chest and, under the bulge of his left breast, against the skin, the beating of his heart could be guessed at.

That fascination, not erotic but aesthetic, that the physical perfection of the male body exerted on the ancient Greeks could not be better expressed. We understand that by frequenting the Olympic Games, old Menestheus was well able to appreciate young male beauty. He criticises admirers of Sostratos for being importune, and inveighs against women, especially the beautiful Megallis, with whom Sostratos is in love. He recalls beautiful Euthymos, son of the rich Astyches and Melantho. This athlete came from Epizephyrian Locris, a city near Crotona and Sybaris in southern Italy.[4]

This boy was attracted to girls, especially to a certain Pasithea. But he was desired by a lover of boys, Herodoros, a sophist and palaestra prowler, who could not bear Pasithea:

> [He] drew closer to the boy, his eyes lit up with lust. Your cicada, Euthymos, is I. Love me, your whole being escapes me. Oh how far will I not be able to rise! She [meaning Pasithea] is debauchery, don't you understand? What is her tongue? What is her stomach? Shame on your disgusting caresses… As kindled wax melts in the flame of the torches, I want to melt with the beloved in the contemplation of the beautiful.

As we see, the palaestra was not a restful place. Nor was the education that

Two male couples kiss and cuddle. Red-figure Attic cup by Peithinos, circa 510 BC. Berlin-Charlottenburg, Antikenmuseum (inv. F. 2279).
© bpk. Antikenmuseum Staatliche Museen zu Berlin Preussischer Kulturbesitz. Photo : Johannes Laurentius

---

4   For more on Epizephyrian Locris see the wonderful book by G. P. Carratelli, *The Western Greeks, Classical Civilisation in the Western Mediterranean*, Thames and Hudson, London, 1996, pp. 243, 338, 356.

prepared a future athlete a holiday. Genevoix imagines that Euthymos was brought up by an old Sarmatian, a barbarian by nature both harsh and severe, called Artimmes:

> Grumbling constantly, in a voice more hollow than the drum of a
> Corybant, a bundle of sticks at his belt, watchful, merciless, no peccadillo
> escaped his surveillance, and no prank was allowed: "Don't cross your legs,
> Euthymos: it's bad manners… Is that how you help yourself, your whole hand
> in the meat dish? Two fingers only, I've already told you."

Excesses committed by tutors were common in the upbringing of children. In well-off families, such as that of Euthymos, whose father ran a munitions factory, made perfume and manufactured fabric, trustworthy men of humble origin were given the task of bringing up the children. Mothers were confined to the house and domestic arrangements. In a time of high infant mortality, there was often little respite between successive pregnancies.

Genevoix evokes the sights of the streets that delighted the child and the memories of the old Sarmatian recounting to the child the forays of his compatriots to capture wild horses or unhorse enemies with lassoes.

In counterpoint, scenes from a Greek banquet are described, where young people played *kottabos* (cottabus), a game of Sicilian origin, which involved throwing the remains of a goblet of wine into a metal bowl, invoking the name of a prospective lover. If the throw produced a resonant sound it was the sign of a shared love. Euthymos and his friends played a variation, throwing the remains of the wine on to the mosaic floor and according to the shape of the stain, assessed their chances of success in love.

It was the sculptor Eucherios, whom Pasithea introduced as her lover, who lured Euthymos into his studio and wanted to make a statue of him. He had guessed that this beautiful young man would one day win at Olympia and he admired the boy's perfect body, predicting many glorious victories for him.

> Watching Euthymos naked, he had him walk in the studio, lift a block of
> marble, lie down on the ground and jump up again. He drew nearer, without
> taking his eyes off him, watched closely the play of the muscles under his
> skin, sometimes felt his body with the tips of his fingers or, moving away into
> a corner, he enveloped him completely with a wide and motionless gaze, lost
> in his contemplation and holding his breath.
>
> But at last a deep sigh stirred in his chest, and he seemed to awaken: "The
> gods be praised", he cried. "For I have seen you, Euthymos. I will resume this
> rough and hurried shape, which for you is still indecipherable. And perhaps
> tomorrow, you will encounter before your eyes a Euthymos of marble or
> bronze, not the young mortal we see here, the Locrian son of Astycles, but the
> perfectly beautiful athlete who resembles you like your divine double.
>
> Conjuring up in this way in the eyes of the ardent boy this ideal image of
> himself, he brought him once again to the desire that he had inspired in him,
> the surpassing of oneself, that difficult victory that would perhaps lead him,
> with the help of the gods, to the glorious triumphs of the stadium.
>
> So at last he spoke to him of Elis, of Olympia, of the oleanders of the
> Alpheus, of the Altis with its beautiful plane trees, of the banks of grass where

A Greek athlete lifting weights.
© Archivo Iconografico, S.A. / CORBIS

the crowd of Hellenes jostles, of the clamour echoing far off that greets the
winning athlete.

Before attaining this ideal one needed to make a huge effort. Genevoix imagines
the training that the *aleiptés* made Euthymos undergo (literally "one who anoints",
referring to the oil with which the body of the athlete was rubbed). The *aleiptés* was
the athlete's trainer or manager. He was often a man of humble origins, in the prime
of life, as demanding of himself as of his pupil.

Ancient texts more often evoke the athlete's triumph than they do his
exhausting preparation. But running on steep slopes, clearing at one bound bushes or
streams, throwing boulders, boxing against tree trunks, making attacks on the *aleiptés*,
knocking out a wolf with a blow of the fist, these were the ordeals that it was
necessary to endure before aspiring to the winner's prize. In this way Milon of
Crotona achieved his glory.

Old Menestheus tells beautiful Sostratos about the solemn occasion of the
Olympic Games. He reminds him that the *helladonikai*, that is the judges of the

contest, clothed in red tunics, had to plan for each day the order of the exercises, match the competitors, arbitrate differences of opinion, and attend to the processions, prayers, libations and sacrifices in honour of the gods. He describes the enclosures where the Games took place:[5]

> Three enclosures, I told you: the most immense is the Xystus where the runners, jumpers and pentathletes practise. There is not one of them who does not think of the gigantic shadow of Heracles wandering among these very plane trees. He jumped on the sandy arena, made the javelin fly here, ran on the round track or, walking at a slow pace upon the still brambly ground, he tore out the wild thorn bushes and brambles with his powerful hands. The Xystus is followed by the Tetragon: this is the enclosure where Euthymos and his boxing rivals train. After that, in the sandy and tiresome Malko, the adolescents confront one another. Everywhere stand altars, statues of heroes and gods: Pelops the Lydian, the first among all heroes, Heracles of Ida, Theseus conqueror of the Minotaur. The marble and bronze light up and gleam through the flow of sunlight, the trembling shadows of the foliage.

A great landscape painter, Genevoix imagines the progress of the Olympic procession from Elis to the site of Olympia and vividly evokes the charm that radiated from that soothing landscape, so different from the other regions of Greece:

> They admired fertile Elis, the happy land, blessed by the gods. Euthymos saw again the arid Locrian hills, the mounds of sand and pallid clay, the cracked swamps where sedge and horsetail abound. The Athenian thought of his stony homeland, of the bare lines of the horizon under the blazing sun, the Greek of the islands thought of marble cliffs rising from the sombre sea, and the Greek of the mountains thought of gorges where torrents rumble, the harshness of the ridges where painful winds whirl. But everyone felt the coolness of the holy valley flow in them, and admired, on the other side, the soft hills with their beautiful trees, the summits of Menalo and Mount Pholoe towering above them in the distance, sylphlike and blue in the azure air.
>
> [...] The first, the sea route rejoined the Sacred Way. Brought together side by side for a moment, the two human streams mingled. In this way the two triphylian routes converged by turns, then the route of Herakleia and at each new route a new human flood, with the noise of footsteps and the hum of voices, the procession swelling and foundering in its hugeness. The chariot wheels grated, the mules resolutely shook their bells, the horses became incensed, crushed by the bustle that stirred up the crowd of pedestrians, and the asses jogged along, very small, the sandals of their riders skimming the earth of the path.

---

5   The reader unable to access the writings of the learned archaeologists who have been carrying out excavations at Olympia since 1875 might like to refer to the notes and summary provided by F. Chamoux, *La Civilisation grecque*, Arthaud, Paris, 1963, p. 416-7. Much more evocative is the excellent book by P. de Carbonnières, *Olympie, La victoire pour les dieux* ("Patrimoine de la Méditerranée" collection), CNRS éditions, Paris, 1995, which includes a map of Olympia at the time of Pausanias (2nd century AD), drawn by J.-C. Golvin, black & white and colour photographs, and many illustrations.

Black-figure hydria, housed in Rome, depicting the women's race, by the Micali Painter .
© 1990, Photo Scala, Florence.
Vaticano, Museo Gregoriano Etrusco

The description of the monuments of the sanctuary and the mention of the events and sacrifices make us relive with startling precision the enthusiasm of the participants in these Games, the joy of the winners, the pride of their fathers and their cities.

In the modern Olympic Games, the practice of selecting the site after (sometimes dubious) negotiations between competing cities, repudiates the ancient tradition of alternating the events between only four sanctuaries. These days we build venues from scratch, with facilities specially designed to meet the very particular demands of the events. The unique character of sites such as Olympia, Delphi, the Isthmus and Nemea conferred on the ancient Games a natural specificity. It was nature, and not business, that determined the choice of these sacred sites.

The consequences of the modern organisation of the Games are serious, since they reduce a national and religious celebration to the status of an enterprise. Olympic villages and indeed towns are built, whereas in antiquity it was the rustic context that gave the festivals their charm. There was no need to build hotels or shops. The participants, actors or spectators camped and picnicked in the wilds, under sun or stars. Just as Pindar sings in the first Olympian: "Do you wish to sing of the Games, oh my soul? Do not seek, in the deserted sky when the day is bright, a star that blazes more than the Sun, and do not hope to celebrate more glorious lists than Olympia."

An athlete receives a massage under the watchful eye of a trainer, who leans on a stick. Red-figure vase housed in the Villa Giulia in Rome.
© 1990, Photo Scala, Florence – courtesy of the Ministero Beni e Att. Culturali

Religious overtones

We should not forget that the setting for the major Games was not a city, but a sacred site. At Olympia the trees offered natural shelter, rivers such as the Kladeos or the Alpheius allowed pilgrims to refresh themselves and to wash, and the mildness of the climate encouraged people to sleep out-of-doors. Mount Kronion was a favourite camp site, as its wooded summit provided a cool place to sleep as well as shelter

It is difficult to imagine the joyful crush of those crowds to whom the Olympic truce gave the leisure, rare at the time, to forget war and to celebrate joy. This sense of rural community would have resembled the jostling that can be experienced in modern Greece, which occurs regularly around any minor public event, such as the arrival of a boat in a harbour. We have to imagine a joyful, noisy and motley festival, where animals intended for sacrifice mingled with souvenir sellers and campers on the banks of the Alpheius or the Kladeos.

The clamour of sheep, bulls or oxen sacrificed to the gods, the smoke from the pyres, the blaring of trumpets or flutes, set the scene in which all traditional religious festivals took place: procession, prayer, libations and sacrifices. Priests, pilgrims, whip carriers formed a crowd in which enthusiasm overrode discipline. Calm only descended at the moment when the athletes entered the lists.

Attic red-figure amphora, showing two pairs of wrestlers, by the Andokides Painter, circa 525 BC. Each couple is made up of a bearded adult and a boy. Kept in the Berlin Charlottenburg, Antikenmuseum (inv. F. 2159).

© bpk. Staatliche Museen zu Berlin. Photo: Ingrid Geske

The events

Not all events aroused the same interest[6] – track events reigned supreme: the *stadion*, a race over the length of a stadium, generally around 192m; the double *stadion* or *diaulos*, over a distance of around 384m; the long-distance event, *dolichos*, which could vary from between 1,500 and 5,000m; and the *hoplitodromos*, or "race in armour", for which runners wore helmets, armour and carried heavy shields over a double *stadion*.

The pentathlon, as its name indicates, comprised five events: the *stadion*, long jump, discus, javelin and wrestling. Figures depicted on monuments show us that the positions of the athletes were very different from those of today. For example, runners started the race upright, their feet together, legs slightly bent and arms stretched forwards. The starting line or *gramme* was a furrow dug in the ground allowing a better foothold. The signal was given by a trumpet blast.

For the long jump, consisting of five successive jumps without a break, the athletes held a dumb bell in each hand, which allowed a greater distance to be covered. The discus thrower lifted the discus in both hands above his head, then bending down with his legs apart and bent, throwing the arm carrying the discus backwards, he performed a swinging motion, and then stood up again while whirling round.

For the javelin throw, the athlete used a strap wound round the javelin's centre of gravity and ending in a loop in which he inserted one or two fingers. Statues or paintings on vases give us a good understanding of these postures.

Philippe de Carbonnières, from whom I take this analysis, cites a text from Philostratus' treatise *On Gymnastics*, which indicates the esteem in which athletes in the pentathlon were held:

> He who wishes to practise the pentathlon should be heavy rather than
> light, and more light than heavy, of slender stature, solidly built, not greatly
> weighed down with muscle and free in his movements. He should have legs
> that are longer than average, supple and agile loins, because of the sudden
> turning back on himself necessary for the disciplines of the javelin or discus,
> as well as for jumping.

In order to become this all-round athlete it was necessary to practise fighting sports as well: wrestling (*palê*), boxing (*pygmê*) and the pancratium (*pankration*). These fights, being exceptionally violent, were highly appreciated by the spectators. Victory conferred great glory, for it was inspired by Heracles.

The *pale* was practised in the place to which it gave its name: the palaestra. This wrestling, in which one had to make the back or shoulders touch the ground, was like the judo of today. The opponents were naked and smeared in oil which made it difficult to get a grip. To overcome this disadvantage the fighters covered themselves with dust. The opponents rushed headlong at each other and practised the holds of our judoka: arm wrench, lift, throw to the ground, toppling, knee press on the stomach, neck locks.

The fight continued without a break until the moment when one of the opponents raised a finger or put a knee on the ground. To be declared the winner it

---

6   P. de Carbonnières, *op. cit.*, describes these trials in great detail, using well chosen source material.

The head of a boxer, in the National Archaeological
Museum of Athens.
©1990, Photo Scala, Florence

was necessary to throw the opponent to the ground three times. Bouts took place on loose ground, making it easier to skid and slide.

Pygmé was a kind of boxing that involved extreme brutality, combining blows of the fist and kicks. We can gauge the savagery of it if we note that only two moves were forbidden: biting and eye-gouging. The boxers' faces bore the imprint of previous fights: scarred foreheads, broken noses and cauliflower ears. Their equipment was not designed to cushion blows. The boxers' hands were wrapped in strips of hardened leather that allowed the fist to close and which were sometimes reinforced with metal.

From paintings on vases, we can see that blows were aimed above all at the head, as boxers are shown with their guard up. It was the direct blow to the head, not to the stomach, that was the principal blow. The swing, the hook and the uppercut seem not to have been used, nor any fancy footwork. In a sense it was static boxing, between fighters more concerned with getting in their punches than protecting themselves.

Fighting conditions were harsh: no ring, no rounds, no victory on points and no stoppage. The fight ended when one of the opponents collapsed or acknowledged defeat by raising a finger.

The pancratium was the toughest of the fighting events. The athletes fought with

Two naked and bearded pancratiasts wrestle under the supervision of the trainer, clothed in a long shawl and holding a flexible cane. One lifts his adversary's leg in an attempt to flip him over. Black-figure Panathenaic amphora attributed to the Kleaphrades Painter and housed in the Metropolitan Museum of Art, New York; Rogers Fund, 1916.
© 2001 The Metropolitan Museum of Art (inv. 16.71)

bare fists and were allowed to kick. They wrestled upright, but unlike the wrestlers could fight on the ground, in the dust. Referees would not stop the fight for injuries. Compared to modern wrestling, this form of combat resembles a combination of wrestling and Thai boxing. Another epigram shows the violence of ancient boxing matches:[7]

> Your head, Apollophanes, has become a sieve, or the lower edge of a worm-eaten book, all exactly like ant-holes, crooked and straight, or Lydian and Phrygian musical notes. But go on boxing without fear; for even if you are struck on the head you will have the marks you have – you can't have more.

In another epigram[8] Lucilius declares that twenty years of war did not stop Ulysses from being recognised by his dog Argos, but that four hours of wrestling were enough for neither dog nor friend to be able to identify him and for him not to be able to recognise himself in a mirror. The theme of the disfigurement of boxers

Fighting dirty: a wrestler tries to push his thumb into his opponent's eye and bite the arm wrapped around him. The trainer, armed with a cane, attempts to separate them.
© The British Museum

7   *Greek Anthology* (trans. W. R. Paton), Loeb Classical Library, Harvard University Press, Cambridge, MA, 1918, XI, 78.

8   *Greek Anthology, op. cit.*, XI, 77.

provided Lucilius with many variations, such as this one:[9]

> This Olympicus who is now such as you see him, Augustus, once had a nose, a chin, a forehead, ears and eyelids. Then becoming a professional boxer he lost all, not even getting his share of his father's inheritance; for his brother presented a likeness of him he had and he was pronounced to be a stranger, as he bore no resemblance to it.

Another epigram by Lucilius states:[10]

> The thick bull neck, the iron shoulders like Atlas, the hair and reverend beard like Heracles, and the lion-eyes of the Milesian giant not even Olympian Zeus saw without trembling, when Nicophon won the men's boxing contest in the Olympian games.

Boxers are sometimes presented as wild beasts. This is the case in an epigram by Antipater of Thessalonica, evoking the appearance of Nicophon and his victory in the Olympic Games in 11–12 AD, under Augustus:[11]

> Having such a mug, Olympicus, go not to a fountain nor look into any transparent water, for you, like Narcissus, seeing your face clearly, will die, hating yourself to the death.

All of these texts bear witness to the ferocity of ancient boxing and the pancratium. Still more examples could be found.

Another highly valued competition was the horse-race. The hippodromes could be on the site itself, which was the case at Olympia where the hippodrome was situated between the stadium and the Alpheius. But at Delphi the races took place in the plain of Amphissa at the foot of the mountain. These races could be dangerous and occasion foul play, especially the chariot race where, rounding the boundary marker, a driver could cause his rival to have an accident by following too closely.

We have to make a distinction between horse-races and chariot races. Let us not forget that riders had neither a saddle nor stirrups nor spurs. They rode bareback and had only a whip at their disposal. A particular kind of trotting race, the *kalpé*, demanded that the rider get down from his mount before arriving and run at its side holding the reins.

The chariot races were the most prestigious. They were *biga* races, chariots with two horses, or *quadriga* races, with four horses. The *tethrippon* (four-horse chariot) reigned supreme. Some aristocrats may have driven their own chariots, but most of the time the driver was a professional and all the glory of the victory went to the owner of the team. The *auriga* (charioteer) held two reins per horse, so eight reins for the *tethrippon*. The chariot was a frail box mounted on two wheels and it was a feat to keep one's balance in it. The competitors covered around 14km, since they had to

---

9 *Greek Anthology, op. cit.* 75.

10 *Ibid.,* 76.

11 *Ibid.,* VI, 256.

Red-figure vase showing the end of a boxing match – the defeated fighter raises his index finger to concede defeat.

© National Archaeological Museum of Athens

round the boundary markers 12 times. Accidents were not uncommon, so great was the daring of the *aurigae*.

In the *biga* races pulled by two mules (a race termed *apéné*) the distance was around 7km. The driver was in a sitting position. This type of race took place above all in Sicily, since mules were forbidden to stay in Elis, by virtue of an ancient religious decree.

Such were the events of the Games. It may be noted that, while there were some variations, these competitions were canonical, if we can put it that way. The events did not grow in number, as they do in the modern Games, where new competitions are constantly expanding the catalogue of contests.

These ancient Games demanded from athletes extraordinary courage and steadfastness. We have seen that they could be marred by excessive violence. But there was worse: fraud, cheating and endemic corruption.

The Thessalian plain near Amphissa.
© André Bernand

Chapter XIV
Corruption

Rigged refereeing

It would be naïve to think that the compatriots of Ulysses of the Thousand Tricks would not have tried to transgress the rules made for the different events of the Games. Greek ingenuity could find a thousand stratagems for defrauding, making trouble, cheating, deceiving and corrupting.

Refereeing might be unfair either through the judge's personal interest, or under pressure from the family or city anxious to participate in the Olympic glory of their champion. This is why Herodotus[1] recounts the following episode to prove the impartiality of King Psammetichos:

> While this Psammis was king of Egypt, he was visited by ambassadors
> from Elis, the Eleans boasting that they had arranged the Olympic games with
> all the justice and fairness in the world, and claiming that even the Egyptians,
> although the wisest of all men, could not do better. When the Eleans came to
> Egypt and announced why they had come, Psammis assembled the Egyptians
> reputed to be wisest. These assembled and learned all that the Eleans were to
> do regarding the games; after explaining this, the Eleans said that they had
> come to learn whether the Egyptians could discover any juster way. The
> Egyptians deliberated, and then asked the Eleans if their own citizens took
> part in the contests. The Eleans answered that they did: all Greeks from Elis or
> elsewhere might contend. Then the Egyptians said that in establishing this rule
> they fell short of complete fairness: "For there is no way that you will not
> favor your own townsfolk in the contest and wrong the stranger; if you wish
> in fact to make just rules and have come to Egypt for that reason, you should
> admit only strangers to the contest, and not Eleans." Such was the counsel of
> the Egyptians to the Eleans.

The same warning against a possible bias in the referees is attributed by Diodorus to the reign of Amasis.[2]

According to Aristotle[3] everything in the Games had to be in "good order", as in the behaviour of women, the application of the law and the education of children. This ideal of *eukosmia* had to reign in the gymnasia and in the events:

> Peculiar to the states that have more leisure and prosperity, and also pay
> attention to public decorum, are the offices of Superintendent of Women,

---

1 Herodotus, *Histories* (trans. A. D. Godley), Loeb Classical Library, Harvard University Press, Cambridge, MA, 1920, II, 160.

2 Diodorus Siculus, *Library of History* (trans. C. H. Oldfather), Loeb Classical Library, Heinemann, London, 1935, I, 95.

3 Aristotle, *Politics* (trans. B. Jowett), Dover Publications, New York, 2000, VI, 8, 22.

Guardian of the Laws, Superintendent of Children, Controller of Physical
Training, and in addition to these the superintendence of athletic and
Dionysiac contests and of any similar displays that happen to be held.

Besides bias in refereeing many other irregularities were committed. The most
frequent was bribery. In other words victory could be "bought" by greasing the palm
not only of the judges but also of the competitors.

Bribery

Describing the sanctuary of Olympia, Pausanias[4] notes that,

As you go to the stadium along the road from the Metroum, there is on
the left at the bottom of Mount Cronius a platform of stone, right by the
very mountain, with steps through it. By the platform have been set up
bronze images of Zeus. These have been made from the fines inflicted on
athletes who have wantonly broken the rules of the contests, and they are
called *Zanes* [figures of Zeus] by the natives.

Pausanias lists a certain number of acts of corruption for which fines were
imposed, leading to the establishment of this terrace of shame. Thus the Thessalian
Eupolos bribed the competitors in the boxing contest: the Arcadian Agetor, *prytanis* of
Cyzicus and furthermore Phormion of Halicarnassus who had won a victory at the
previous Olympiad. A fine was imposed on Eupolos and his competitors by the Eleans.

This condemnation was made public. Indeed on the aforementioned statues
elegiac poems were engraved. Anne Jacquemin points out that these epigrams were not
engraved on the base of the statues but on bronze stelae of around 20cm wide, of
which the mortises can be seen. The fact that Pausanias summarises these texts instead
of citing them in full is doubtless explained by the fact that he considered this poetry
fairly mediocre. One of these poems affirmed that it was not with money, but thanks
to the speed of his legs that a person won a race. Another said that the statue had been
erected in honour of the divinity, but also as a warning to cheating athletes. On
another statue the epigram recalled the fine inflicted on boxers who cheated. An
epigram also acted as a reminder that these statues were lessons intended for all the
Greeks, so that no one should pay money in order to obtain an Olympic victory.

After Eupolos there was the Athenian Callipolos, a competitor in the pentathlon
who bribed his opponents, which earned both him and them a fine imposed by the
Eleans. The Athenians dispatched Hyperides to argue against this punishment, but the
Eleans did not allow themselves to be won over. Hyperides was an Athenian orator
of the 4th century BC, a relentless opponent of the Macedonians, who had him put
to death in 322 BC.

The Athenian competitors were excluded from the Olympic contests when one
of them was caught cheating. They refused to pay the fine, and the god of Delphi was
obliged to intervene, announcing that he would deliver no more oracles until the fine
was paid to the Eleans. Six statues were then erected, bearing warnings against fraud.

---

4   Pausanias, *Description of Greece* (trans. W. H. S. Jones, H.A. Ormerod), Loeb Classical Library, Harvard University
Press, Cambridge, MA, 1988, V, 21, 1-9.

Statue bases of the Zanes in ancient Olympia, where there once stood bronze statues of Zeus. These were erected with money collected in fines as a warning to athletes not to cheat at the Games.
© Archaeological Receipts Fund

On the first it was stated that the statues had been consecrated in accordance with the oracle of Delphi who had given his assent to the decisions of the Eleans relating to the competitors in the pentathlon. The second and third statues sang the praises of the Eleans who had imposed the fine. The poem on the fourth statue announced that the contest at Olympia was a test of valour, not a matter of money. The fifth statue explained the reasons for the statues' consecration, the sixth recalled the oracle's pronouncement to the Athenians.

Pausanias also cites inscriptions fastened to two statues: one said that the Rhodians had paid money to Olympian Zeus, because of the irregularity committed by a wrestler; the second stated that the statue had been made using money paid by wrestlers who had allowed themselves to be bribed.

Wrestling was a speciality of the Egyptians. Thus Strato of Alexandria won a victory on the same day at the pancratium and at wrestling. This Strato, a son of Korrhagos of Alexandria, as Anne Jacquemin notes, is called Stratoicos by Eusebius.[5] He had taken up sport on medical advice and then earned renown in the ring. After his double victory at wrestling and at the pancratium in 68 BC, which made him the fourth successor of Heracles, he gained another victory at the following Olympic

5   Eusebius, *Ecclesiastical History* (trans. J. E. L. Oulton), Loeb Classical Library, Harvard University Press, Cambridge, MA, 1969.

Games, won four prizes on the same day at Nemea and many other successes there and at Delphi. Being extremely rich, he had a palaestra built at Aigion for his personal use.

Aelian, a writer of the first half of the 3rd century AD, relates Strato's career in the following manner:[6]

> Strato the son of Corrhagus seems to have suffered illness for a purpose. Despite coming from a rich and noble family he did not take physical exercise. But he suffered an illness of the spleen and needed treatment through gymnastic exercise. At first he took as much as was required to regain health, but he made progress in this art and began to take it seriously. At Olympia he won the wrestling competition and the pancration on the same day, and repeated his success at the next Olympiad, and at the Nemean, Pythian, and Isthmian games.

Egypt did not have a monopoly on success in the pancratium and at wrestling, as demonstrated by Caprus from Elis, Aristomenes of Rhodes and Protophanes of Magnesia. An Alexandrian boxer, named Apollonius, with the surname of Rhantes, was the first Egyptian to have a fine imposed on him for irregularity by the Eleans. Pausanias expounds this special case as follows:[7]

> It was not for giving or taking a bribe that he was condemned, but for the following outrageous conduct in connection with the games. He did not arrive by the prescribed time, and the Eleans, if they followed their rule, had no option but to exclude him from the games. For his excuse, that he had been kept back among the Cyclades islands by contrary winds, was proved to be an untruth by Heracleides, himself an Alexandrian by birth. He showed that Apollonius was late because he had been picking up some money at the Ionian games. In these circumstances the Eleans shut out from the games Apollonius with any other boxer who came after the prescribed time, and let the crown go to Heracleides without a contest. Whereupon Apollonius put on his gloves for a fight, rushed at Heracleides, and began to pummel him, though he had already put the wild-olive on his head and had taken refuge with the umpires. For this light-headed folly he was to pay dearly.

Dealings between competitors

Victory could be bought if the price was right and your opponent avaricious. Two boxers who were fighting in the final were accused and proved guilty of having come to an agreement for money. A fine was imposed on them and two statues were consecrated to Zeus, one on the right as one enters the stadium, the other on the left. The boxer who had paid the money was called Deidas, the one who had received it was called Sarapammon. Both of them were from the Arsinoite district.

A pancratiast from Alexandria, called Sarapion, became famous in another way: he was seized by such fright in the face of his opponents that the day before the

---

6   Aelian, *Historical Miscellany (Varia Historia)* (trans. Nigel G. Wilson), Loeb Classical Library, Harvard University Press, Cambridge, MA, 1997, IV, 15.

7   Pausanias, *op. cit.*, V, 21, 13.

competitors were called to the pancratium, he took flight. Pausanias notes that "he is the only athlete to be condemned for cowardice, whether in Egypt or in the whole world".

It was not only the Egyptians who made shameful dealings. An Elean, called Damonicos who, so that his son Polyctor could seize the victory wreath from Sosandros, a native of Smyrna, paid money to the latter's father. In this case, the *hellanodikai* gave the fathers a fine. This fine was used to pay for two statues: one stood in the gymnasium of Elis, the other in front of the Altis.

On the phenomenon of corruption in Olympic contests, Anne Jacquemin refers to a study, in German, by I. Weiler, "Korruption in der olympischen Agonistik und die diplomatische Mission des Hypereides in Elis", in *Achaia und Elis*, the proceedings of the conference that took place in Athens from 19 to 21 May 1989.

Substance abuse

Although of a very different nature from performance-enhancing drugs used today, abuses also existed in the ancient Games. Some athletes gorged themselves on meat. Athenaeus, an author of the first half of the 3rd century AD, gives some striking examples:[8]

> Theagenes, the athlete from Thasos, devoured a bull all alone, as Poseidippus says in his Epigrams: "And on a wager I once ate a Maeonian ox; for my own country Thasos could not have furnished a meal to Theagenes; whatever I ate, I kept asking for more. For this reason I stand in bronze, holding forth my hand." Milon of Croton, as Theodorus of Hierapolis says in his work *On Athletic Contests*, used to eat twenty pounds of meat and as many of bread, and he drank three pitchers of wine. And at Olympia he put a four-year-old bull on his shoulders and carried it round the stadium; after which he cut it up and ate it all alone in a single day.

Again, in the 4th century BC, as Valérie Visa-Ondarçuhu indicates,[9] Theophilus, an author of comedies, in his play *The Pancratiast* underlines the gluttony of the athletes, in a dialogue between the pancratiast and an interlocutor:

> The pancratiast: Three mines (1.296 kg) of boiled meat.
> B: Next?
> The pancratiast: Muzzle, ham, four pork trotters.
> B: By Heracles!
> The pancratiast: Three beef trotters, a fowl!
> B: By Apollo. And then?
> The pancratiast: Two bags of figs.
> B: And what have you drunk?
> The pancratiast: Twelve glasses of undiluted wine.

8   Athenaeus, *The Deipnosophists* (trans. C. Burton Gulick), Loeb Classical Library, Harvard University Press, Cambridge, MA, 1928.

9   Theophilus, *The Pancratiast*. Texte cité par V. Visa-Ondarçuhu, *op. cit.*, p. 243, note 3.

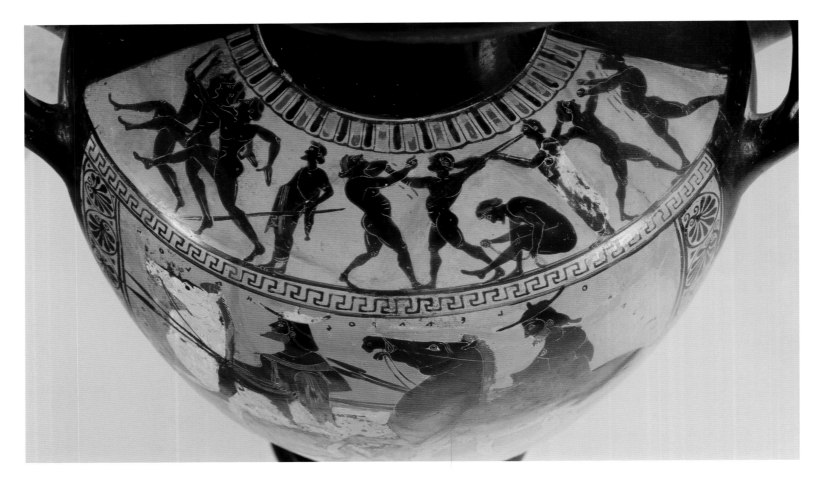

Attic black-figure hydria showing scenes from the palaestra.
© 1990, Photo Scala, Florence. Vaticano, Museo Gregoriano Etrusco

These dietary feats must have appeared all the more surprising because the Ancient Greeks ate hardly any beef, consuming mostly mutton. Beef cattle only existed in certain regions such as Thrace, Thessaly, Pieria.

Aristotle uses the term *anankophagia*, meaning "fixed dietary regime" to designate the food imposed on athletes. But he makes clear that a distinction should be made between the diets imposed on athletes according to the sporting speciality that they practised. For example, a pancratiast or a wrestler needed richer food than a runner or a chariot driver.

We therefore witness the development of what could be called a therapy of sport, going beyond the problem of food.

As far as sex was concerned, the athletes adopted absolute continence, as Philippe de Carbonnières tells us.[10] To make this asceticism easier, they resorted to frequent cold baths and if necessary the infibulation of the penis.

In the treatise *On Gymnastics* by Philostratus, medicine that does not put athletes on their guard against a bad diet is condemned. This medicine, he says,[11]

> brings cooks and kitchen boys who treat the athletes to delicious meals, makes them greedy and turns their stomachs into a bottomless pit; it

10 P. de Carbonnières, *Olympie, La victoire pour les dieux*, CNRS éditions, Paris, 1995, p. 48.

11 Philostratus, *On Gymnastics* (trans. T. Woody), Cactus editions, Athens, 1991, 44.

[medicine] gives them bread to eat, seasoned with poppy and difficult to digest; it feeds them fish, a food that is completely contrary to the rules of gymnastics.

This type of diet may, thus, sometimes have resulted in real doping.

Chicanery

Some athletes, to hide the shame of being beaten and after receiving wounds, in principle forbidden by the rules, could get themselves carried away from the site of the fight. Their feeling of sickness could be real, but they could also simulate death. Thus in an epigram by Lucilius, one Androleos, after losing an ear at Olympia and an eyelid at Plataea, and losing consciousness, is carried off, "dead or crippled", by orders of his father Demoteles:[12]

> I, Androleos, took part in every boxing contest that the Greeks preside
> over, every single one. At Pisa I saved one ear, and in Plataea one eyelid, but at
> Delphi I was carried out insensible. Demoteles, my father and my fellow-
> townsmen had been summoned by herald to bear me out of the *stadion* either
> dead or mutilated.

A false start in the foot race was considered to be an attempt at fraud and offenders were strongly reprimanded, sometimes beaten with blows of a stick. It must be said that the arrangements for the start could make fraud easier. The preliminary signal was given by a trumpet blast, but it was the herald's shout "*Apite!*" ("Go!") that actually started the race and this order could be lost in the hubbub. Moreover the posts marking out the positions of the competitors on the starting line were less efficient than the lanes of a modern race. Philippe de Carbonnières describes the start as follows:

> At first people tried to get round this difficulty by stretching a rope in
> front of the athletes. The device was not entirely satisfactory, and another one
> was perfected, the *hyspléx*. This invention probably appeared in the first half of
> the 5th century at the Isthmian Games. Each post was fitted with a thin fence
> held by a rope. A few metres behind the runners, a referee kept the ropes taut,
> thus jamming the fences. On the starting signal, he let go of all the ropes
> simultaneously, which had the immediate effect of letting the fences fall.

There is no doubt that thanks to this complicated protocol, some runners were able to take advantage of the vagueness of the operation to win some precious seconds.

Aelian describes another subterfuge:[13]

> The wrestler Democrates also suffered an illness which affected his feet.
> He went to the competitions, stood in the stadium and drew a circle around

---

12 *Greek Anthology* (trans. W. R. Paton), Loeb Classical Library, Harvard University Press, Cambridge, MA, 1918, XI, 81.

13 Aelian, *op. cit.*, IV, 15.

himself. Then he challenged his rivals to pull him over the line. They could not do so and were defeated, and he left with the victor's crown as he had maintained his firm stance unshaken.

This victory by attrition was not as glorious as that won following a fight, but it bore witness to the athlete's perseverance. The wrestler put to shrewd use the law stipulating that, if the victory remained undecided or if no participant had thrown his opponent to the floor three times by the end of the final, the wreath was offered to Zeus.

In the longer track events, which included a return (as in the chariot race), rounding the boundary marker could give rise to jostling, or violence which might pass unnoticed. An unscrupulous competitor could take advantage of the confusion, in defiance of Olympic law.

The *hellanodikai* (literally, the "judges of the Greeks") whose red tunics showed their importance, saw the number of infringements grow with the years. These stewards or referees of the Games were recruited from prestigious families, which put them beyond suspicion of corrupt practice. They were there to ensure that the Olympic rules were observed and, if necessary, to settle differences. The severity of their judgements, which could be accompanied by corporal punishment demonstrated the seriousness with which breaches were viewed.

The *hellanodikai* were both organisers, judges and priests. As organisers they had to avoid any cheating in the lists of competitors. Elected 10 months before the opening of the Games they made sure that no barbarian, slave or ex-prisoner was able to compete. They took the Olympic oath and ensured that married women did not attend the Games. They were housed at Olympia, either in the *Leonidaion*, or in the *proedria* south of the Altis, or in other buildings whose location has been lost.

They did not treat the rules regarding women lightly. Only the priestess of Demeter Chamyne could attend the Games. Spouses caught "beyond the Alpheus" were to be thrown down from a rock on Mount Typaion.

There was only one exception to this law: the case of Callipateira of Rhodes. She had cross-dressed as a *paidotribés* so as to come and encourage her son in the boxing. Since she was the daughter, sister and mother of Olympic winners, she was spared. From that moment on *paidotribai* and trainers had to appear naked.

Chapter XV
Glory and dishonour

A modern perspective

The creation and development of the modern Olympic Games, and the way in which they have evolved, allow us to to put in perspective the shortcomings of the ancient Games. The complications, excesses and tensions bound up with the modern events were not absent from the ancient Games, but the scale is altogether different.

Baron Pierre de Coubertin, the creator of the modern Olympic Games, has himself denounced the dangers that threaten the games. He wrote:[1]

> No institution whatever lasts a thousand years without changing and becoming distorted. Nothing is more instructive than to study the turns taken by the sport of antiquity. Along with success can be seen the development of complication and specialisation which lead to professionalism and corruption. The sporting spirit, that *aidôs* of which Pindar writes that its worst enemy is the desire for profit, finds itself imperilled. The grandiose period of the wars against the Persians brings about a sudden burst of energy and – if we can put it this way – of purification in sport, but soon the effect dies down and evil takes hold again. Then there are exaggerations in training. There is a mercenary attitude. There is officialdom.[1]

According to Pierre de Coubertin, a process of moral purification should be initiated. He explains:[2]

> There is a lot of cheating and lying. This is the repercussion, in the field of sport, of a decline in moral standards. Sports developed within a society that the passion for money threatens to make rotten to the core. It is now up to sports societies to give a good example of a return to the cult of honour and sincerity by driving from their precincts lying and hypocrisy.

Charles Hébert wrote:[3]

> We have brought opponents together, have sought to outdo each other, to do better, to reach a specific goal. But through money and show business sport has departed from its initial aim. Real sport should be educational: it should be dominated by usefulness which prevents it from departing from its initial aim through money and show business, or from veering towards extravagance, artificiality or a vain feat of strength, and protected from excess

---

1   P. de Coubertin, *Pédagogie sportive*, pp. 22-3. Quoted by V. Vanoyeke, *La naissance des Jeux olympiques et le sport dans l'Antiquité*, Les Belles Lettres, Paris, 1992, p. 164.

2   V. Vanoyeke, *ibid.*, pp. 164-5.

3   V. Vanoyeke, *ibid.*, p. 166.

by moderation. The three essential aspects that would harm the sporting spirit would therefore be: sport as show business, sport as a source of profit which leads to doping, and sport as prestige, putting a sporting elite at the forefront, not to mention professionalism and over-training.

These principles bore the stamp of commonsense and morality. But when we see the developments in the modern Olympic Games, we begin to think that the ancient Games were protected from certain excesses by barriers that today have collapsed.

The ancient Games were not a worldwide phenomenon and the places chosen for their celebration did not put into competition cities that try to outdo each other in ambition and lavish building programmes, behind which are concealed property speculators thirsting for profit. The cities lending themselves to the course of the games did not pay a tithe so as to have the advantage of organising these events: Olympia, Delphi, the Isthmus and Nemea were fixed venues, organised into a hierarchy. As for cities that did not form part of this traditional cycle, they organised their competitions in those cities of the Greek world where a calendar and a tradition were well established. The Games were integrated into traditional local festivals.

The course of the ancient Games did not require new and ever more expensive constructions. The palaestra, the stadium, the gymnasium and the hippodrome were places that were ready to welcome the competitions. Spectators were accommodated in stands and on banks, and the athletes competed in places that were naturally suited for the different types of event. The track for the foot race was a simple stretch of level ground, the ring for the wrestlers was loose earth, and neither the discus nor the javelin throw required costly facilities. This very simplicity sometimes led to tragedy; an accident mentioned fairly frequently in texts – in particular in epigrams – was the death of a spectator killed by a discus or by a javelin.

In the modern period the multiplication of events and their extreme variety has been and is still a reason for more and more expensive developments. A glance back at the first Olympic Games of the modern era, those organised in Athens in 1896, then at the Paris Games held in 1900, in Paris, allows us to gauge the decline of the ancient Olympic ideal and the transformation of an ideal into a sordid race for profit. On 17 June 1894, a congress opened at the Sorbonne in Paris organised by the Union of French Societies of Athletic Sports (USFSA), which marked the re-establishment of the Olympic Games. The official programme of 1900 gives a staggering list of the events that were organised.[4]

The programme of events

In Section 1 – athletic games and track events appear, recognisable from antiquity, but also a whole series of team and ball sports unknown in Ancient Greece, such as football, rugby, hockey, cricket, lawn tennis, croquet, bowls, baseball, lacrosse, real tennis, golf and pelota.

In Section 2 – gymnastics events performed in groups and with accessories (pom-poms, clubs, sticks, iron bars, etc.).

Official poster from the Paris Olympic Games, on display in the Olympic museum in Lausanne, Switzerland.

4   A. Drevon, *Les Jeux olympiques oubliés*, CNRS éditions, Paris, 2000.

Jeux Olympiques

PARIS 1900

In Section 3 – fencing and foil events, which did not exist in antiquity.

In Section 4 – shooting; naturally target-shooting and clay pigeon shooting are modern, the ancient equivalent would be archery.

In Section 5 – equestrian events; a survivor from antiquity.

In Sections 6 – bicycle-racing and 7 – motor-racing. Details such as contests between hackney cabs and light- and heavy-goods vehicles raise a smile.

Ancient water sports were not as diverse as they are today. Other innovations included speedboat races, angling contests, fire-engine manoeuvring and pigeon-racing. The beginning of the 20th century was marked by a proliferation of events, as if any form of competition, no matter how mechanised, would allow individuals to measure their valour against that of others.

Numerous sites were planned for the events, but for the most part these were concentrated around Paris and its suburbs: at Argenteuil, the île Seguin, Asnières and Courbevoie, and Maisons-Laffitte. The Hague was chosen for sailing.

A huge amount of administrative paperwork increased the number of rules and checks. Moreover, tension emerged between Baron Pierre de Coubertin, who organised the first Olympic Games of the modern era at Athens in 1896 and Alfred Picard who organised the 1900 Games in Paris. Picard was an engineer who had risen

Black-figure hydria showing a women's race.
© 1990, Photo Scala, Florence. Vaticano, Museo Gregoriano Etrusco

to become chief inspector of the Department of Civil Engineering and president of a department of the Council of State.

Baron de Coubertin was born in 1860 into a wealthy aristocratic family who owned an estate at Mireville in the Calvados, known for his conservative opinions, he was a convinced anglophile, who had studied law and published historical papers. Alfred Picard was a dyed-in-the-wool republican. Picard wanted the World Fair of 1900, in which he was involved in the capacity of steward, to be the grandiose celebration of a new century's dawn, one which would witness the triumph of industry. Hence the abundance of events paying tribute to technology. De Coubertin and Picard adhered to the same fundamental principle: a concern for the physical renaissance of French youth, which had demonstrated its unfitness at the time of their country's ignominious defeat in 1870. They deemed it imperative to train the young and give them a taste for physical exercise.

The nobility of this principle lay in striving to fulfil an ideal that was at once ethical and political, but which today appears outdated. The Games were not intended as the commercial spectacle they have become, and the modern media did not yet exist to reinforce this mercenary tendency. As André Drevon writes in *Les Jeux olympiques oubliés, Paris 1900* (CNRS editions, 2000):

The American Marion Jones wins the 100m semi-finals at Olympic Park during the Sydney Olympics in Australia, 23 September, 2000.

© 2000 Getty Images, Bill Stickland

259

The event on a scale "without precedent in the history of exhibitions", which Alfred Picard decides to organise according to a "rational philosophical plan" will find in sport and its "rivals from every corner of the globe" an unparalleled means of stirring up interest in the practice of physical education at school and that of physical exercise in the country. Sport is to become in 1900, for the space of a summer, an affair of state.[5]

Olympic revival

Alfred Picard linked the sporting festival to the World Fair of 1900 and in a note intended for Jules Sansboeuf and preserved in the National Archives, he wrote:

> The World Fair of 1900 should be the philosophy and synthesis of the century, it should possess both grandeur, grace and beauty, it should reflect the clear genius of France, it should show us to be in the vanguard of progress, just as in the past, it should honour the country and the Republic and in it we should appear as the worthy sons of the men of 1789.

These republican sentiments have not disappeared from official statements and are not without political effects and consequences.

Faced with the threat of state control, Pierre de Coubertin's plan to organise the Games with only the help of private sponsorship seemed very difficult to achieve. The USFSA decided to withdraw support from the Olympic committee's bid and the fantastic draft of modern events was drawn up without the advice of Coubertin.

Pierre de Coubertin regained the upper hand by decreeing that the Olympic Games would take place every four years, as in Ancient Greece, whereas Alfred Picard had wanted to associate the Games with the inauguration of the Eiffel Tower and the exhibition of 1900. The sheer length of this sporting festival, which began on 1st May with the first bout of fencing and finished on 28 October with the final of the rugby tournament, must have tired the public and disrupted everyday life. "Out of five and a half months, more than one hundred and thirty days in total will have been dedicated to sport", explains André Drevon, "the busiest period being June and July with the athletics in the height of summer". Some spectators today judge the length of the Olympic Games to be excessive, although they do not last nearly as long, nor do the events take place over such a wide area.

Education through sport

The originality of these Games of 1900, now forgotten, depended on the one hand on the concern for education that inspired them and on the other hand on the desire to project a unified image of France to the world. The government did not want the sporting festival to be a commercial enterprise and the aid of private sporting associations was sought, so as not to seem to squander public resources.

The role of national education was very important. The chairmanship of the Higher Commission on Competitions had been entrusted to the deputy education officer for Paris, the academic Octave Gréard, who was responsible for physical education and youth at the Ministry of Education. This member of the French

---

5   A. Drevon, *op. cit.*

Academy and of the Academy of Moral and Political Sciences inspired confidence, although his academic background might occasion doubts as to his sporting credentials. The government was anxious that the Olympic Games of 1900 be seen as the culmination of educational progress brought about by the Third Republic.

Reality has not always done justice to the noble sentiments of politicians' speeches. A century later, second-rate sporting facilities in schools and universities are testimony to the failure to live up to these high intentions. The French believe themselves to be fond of sport because they follow football, rugby, tennis or the twists and turns of the Tour de France from the depths of their armchairs. But France is far behind countries such as Denmark or Sweden, which make facilities available to amateur sportspeople free of charge.

A certain demagogy had inspired the inclusion of angling among the "sporting" disciplines. The government wished to associate the worker with the festival, physical activity being perceived as a generator of social integration. Not everyone had the means to fit themselves out for golf, sailing or horse-races. But most workers could afford a fishing rod, a tool that could improve everyday fare, even if the banks of the île des Cygnes in Paris, where the "events" took place, were not very rich in fish. The exhilaration of modernity that had taken hold of the government, the elite and the people sat uneasily with the choice of this passive pastime.

André Drevon, in *Les Jeux olympiques oubliés,* cites some hilarious accounts and draws a humorous picture of this "sport" that the competitors usually practised while sitting on a folding stool. He cites the enthusiasm of the magazine *Le Gymnaste* which declared, full of good republican intentions:

> Most certainly, angling should be considered to be a sport which has the huge advantage of being accessible to all classes of society and to all individuals.

Drevon[6] describes, from the full-page photo on the cover of the magazine *La Vie au grand air,* this ludicrous sight:

> An official in dark tail coat, top hat, white tie, with pencil and notebook in his hand, records the detailed account of the scanty row of fish that an angler has just caught, wearing a white shirt, a flannel belt like gymnasts wear, his trousers rolled to his calves, one bare foot still in the water, while the other competitors remain with their gaze fixed imperturbably on their floats.
>
> We are in the île des Cygnes. In the heart of Paris the place was well chosen, a long shady promontory, a natural stand towering above the banks of the Seine with Bartholdi's Statue of Liberty as a figurehead: success from day one – a Sunday – with 9,000 spectators. The official report estimates a total of 20,000 visitors (free entry) over the four days, and a turnout, judged to be "huge", of 600 competitors. Naturally people fished for the largest, then for the highest number of fish captured. The site was reputedly full of fish since the Seine had been given a facelift, but unfortunately the sewers had also done their work.

6   A. Drevon, *op. cit.*

But Waldeck-Rousseau, elected in 1899, on a programme for the defence of the Republic, passed himself off as "a moderate republican, but not a republican in moderation", and affirmed the educational nature of these Games.

Not just a man's game

In Ancient Greece, with the exception of Sparta, where they created an outcry by appearing in short skirts, women did not take part in the gymnastics contests. In the first modern Olympic Games there were few events reserved for women.

In the early 20th century women were expected to stay at home and raise a family. They were slowly, even furtively, allowed to participate in sports deemed to be suitable for their constitutions: tennis, golf, sailing, rowing, ballooning, gymnastics, fishing, life-saving, horse-riding, croquet. André Drevon notes that this discreet presence did not provoke controversy, and recalls that this was the period when suffragettes were making their voices heard in France, demanding the vote. They had to wait a long time; it was General De Gaulle who finally granted French women the vote. This slow development shows that the Republic was only gradually moving towards notions that today appear completely natural, such as co-educational schools.

The road of excess

The fact that participants now come from all over the world has bred nationalistic behaviour that has sometimes brought about unfortunate excesses. A question mark hangs over the wisdom of playing national anthems at the beginning of the contest and at the prize giving. Quite recently the Marseillaise was booed by some audiences,

Diskobolus (The Discus Thrower): Marble statue by 5th century BC sculptor, Myron, in the Museo Nazionale Romano (Palazzo Massimo alle Terme), Rome.
© 1990, Photo Scala, Florence – courtesy of the Ministero Beni e Att. Culturali

Robert Garrett of the USA wins the discus gold medal at the 1896 Olympic Games in Athens.
© Getty Images

Dan O'Brien during discus trials (16 March, 1992).
© Tony Duffy/Allsport/Getty Images

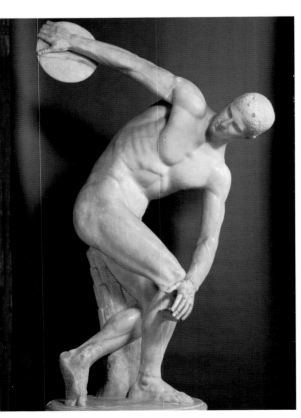

without it being clear whether this gesture was directed at France or at her President. In antiquity, people contented themselves with announcing the Olympic victory by declaring "winner such-and-such, son of such-and-such, from such-and-such a city".

The presence of mobs of supporters cheering on the game would have been inconceivable in Ancient Greece. No alcoholic drinks were imbibed and winners had to show by their demeanour that they were worthy of the tribute rendered to them.

We have seen that the rewards (wreaths, double portion of meat for the sacrifices, food for the *prytanis*) did not involve financial gain. Admittedly, a victory in local games could be rewarded with presents, but these bear no comparison with the financial incentives received by some modern athletes. The ancient Games were free of the auctioneering that reigns today in the stadium: the fees involved in athletes' transfers involve negotiations that turn modern sport into business on a worldwide scale.

As long as the Games only involved competition between the cities of the Mediterranean world, they could be controlled. But the colonisation of North and South America has meant that it is no longer cities that confront one another, but continents. On this global scale, the Games have lost their soul. The collective Games have supplanted the Games of the individual.

The original gymnastic events in which, as the name indicates, participants competed naked, could not result in the sale of their shirts. The fervour with which the hearts of ancient competitors and spectators beat has given way to the apathy and solitude of the spectator sitting in front of his television. Competitors coming from the four corners of the globe are no longer perceived as compatriots, but as intruders. Moral standards have changed and certain practices imported from America have not

Long distance javelin throw. Bronze disc with engraved image.

© bpk. Staatliche Museen zu Berlin Preussischer Kulturbesitz (Photo: Johannes Laurentius)

The American Mildred Babe Didrikson throws the javelin to win the gold medal during the women's competition at the Olympics in Los Angeles, California, 1932.

© 1932 Getty Images

Briton Steve Backley throwing the javelin at the world championships in the Olympic stadium in Athens. Backley won the silver medal (5 August, 1997).

© Gary M Prior/Allsport/Getty Images

Vilho Ritola leads Paavo Nurmi during the
5000m at the Olympic Games in Amsterdam.
© 1928 Getty Images

raised these standards. We have reached the point of putting money on a player or on a team in the same way as people bet on horses.

The Games of 1900 witnessed the triumph of American athletes whose performances, training methods, techniques and, above all, successes profoundly altered the style of the events. A newspaper cited by André Drevon exclaims: "Oh those weeks in July, where each day we came to admire the whole host of fine athletes nurtured by transatlantic universities. We watched, stunned, as feat gave way to feat and all the records – those poor records of France – fell like dead leaves."

The American athletes brought innovation, for example, Richard Sheldon in the shotput, "had allied the dynamics of momentum, efficiency and harmony, creating a kind of working drawing of the throw in profile, that will be practised by throwers for decades".

The high jump was transformed by Irving Baxter, who used an unheard-of inner twist technique which was combined with an oblique run-up to the bar, rather then the traditional "scissors", while the American Alvin Kraenzlein introduced a new technique for the hurdles that was more efficient than that used by his European competitors.

Panathenaic black-figure amphora showing three sprinters, one of whom is looking over his shoulder, by the Kleophrades Painter, circa 500 BC.
© Photo RMN – Hervé Lewandowski, Louvre

American trainers recognised the importance of athletes' warming up, and one had recourse to the good offices of a masseur (an echo of Ancient Greece), the only black member of the American team. These comparisons between the modern and ancient Games are interesting, because they demonstrate the evolution undergone by the various events. It is important to recall that the Games of Classical Greece were preceded by a variety of competitions which subsequently died out. In Minoan Crete, for example, a type of ancient sport existed, which is represented on a gold seal preserved in the Ashmolean Museum in Oxford. The athlete is depicted executing a somersault on the back of a charging bull. A fresco from Cnossos, preserved in the archaeological museum in Heraklion, represents three bull jumpers at different stages of the exercise. Boxing was also practised in the islands of the Aegean. It is represented on a fresco dating from the 2nd millennium, found on Thera and preserved in the archaeological museum in Athens.

From the Geometric period, the famous François vase preserved in the archaeological museum in Florence shows the *quadriga* race, an event organised in honour of the death of Patroclus.

At Dresden in the Staatliche Kunstsammlungen we see a boxing scene framed by two lancers on a black figure cantharus, or two-handled cup, from the Geometric period. All of these artefacts, of which this is by no means an exhaustive list, allow us to trace the development of the different events.

Olympic feats demanded that physical effort should also be aesthetic. This supposed – let us not be afraid of using plain language – an exhibition where the body appeared in all its radiance. The Greeks had understood this when they considered as obscene the use of the loincloth to hide the *médea phôtos*, that is, the genitals. In natural surroundings and in the natural state, the Greek athletes shining with oil under the blue sky, appeared clothed only in their beauty.

Pierre de Coubertin's athletes did not have this simplicity and sincerity. The vests worn in his time complemented the two-piece bathing trunks and, restricted by ridiculous clothes, shot-putters or javelin throwers, jumpers, runners and riders, exerted themselves as if to free themselves of these impediments.

The Olympic Games of the modern period do not always correspond to the conditions demanded for these exercises in Antiquity. But their great merit is that they give free rein to harmony, splendour and effort. In antiquity, it was the *stadion*, the

Gold seal, showing an athlete jumping over a bull, a Creto-Minoan sport.
© Ashmolean Museum, University of Oxford

sprint down the length of the stadium that reigned supreme. Without doubt it is in the 100m runners of today that we find a spectacle closest to the ancient event. Similarly, when Richard Sheldon put the shot with the efficiency and sobriety of the ancient athlete, the public quite naturally called him "Apollo", such was his elegant movement, his refined profile and his slender body.

In the modern world, attending athletic competitions is a way of celebrating bodies in effort and splendour. "*Honi soit qui mal y pense*"!

Poseidon's anger, at Cape Sounion, Attica.

Appendix

A sorry business

Nothing has been more harmful to the development of studies of the ancient world than the refusal to make epigraphic texts accessible by translating them systematically. This bad example has been set by what is called the *Berlin Corpus*, also known as the *Inscriptiones Graecae*. Nothing could be more daunting than the untranslated presentation of administrative, religious and political texts that use constructions hardly ever seen in literary texts. Moreover, the development of the discipline of epigraphy has provoked countless corrections, additions and modifications of these texts. The *Bulletin épigraphique* of the *Revue des Études Grecques* and numerous foreign reviews allow us to follow these developments, but the inadequacy of university libraries has made the updating of these collections more and more difficult. On top of these difficulties comes the esoterism common amongst editors of some reviews who wish to appear as the keepers of historical truth.

With my brother Étienne, I took on the establishment of a corpus of Greek inscriptions from Egypt. Having published around 20 volumes of these, we decided that it was imperative to make more texts available by translating them systematically, possibly with explanatory notes. All our volumes have been published either by the Centre National de la Recherche Scientifique (National Centre for Scientific Research), the publishing house Les Belles Lettres, the French Institute for Oriental Archaeology in Cairo, or by editors such as E. J. Brill in Leiden. Since information technology was not as well developed as it is now, we worked in the "old way", that is with index cards filling shoeboxes. According to Louis Robert this was the best method.

When I taught at the University of Lille, from 1967 to 1992, some kind souls suggested that I should make the publication of epigraphic texts more informal. I was not opposed to this idea, but asked to be given the means to organise a team of 10 people for a period of 10 years. Things went no further.

The absence of a dictionary of epigraphic terminology is one of the biggest hurdles to understanding these texts. Today we can refer to the *Index du Bulletin épigraphique* for Greek words, publications and French words. But with the death of Louis Robert in 1985 we have lost a source of encyclopaedic knowledge. An index of Louis Robert's monumental work would have been invaluable. I had applied myself to compiling just such an index until 1956, when I was expelled from Egypt following the war waged by France on that country. Along with all my possessions, the index was stolen from me by my neighbour who probably put it in the dustbin. Perhaps it was believed that they were coded cards containing military information. I have had neither the courage nor the time to redo this work.

In actual fact such a file existed, but in the sole possession of Louis Robert. When Father André Pelletier alluded one day to this inaccessible file, Louis Robert could not hide his irritation. He was well aware that he had committed himself to producing the corpus of inscriptions of Asia Minor and the dictionary of epigraphic language. However, in 40 years at the Collège de France, he produced neither, although he kept himself busy in other ways. The *Bulletin* of the *Revue des Études grecques* indulged his pastime of savaging authors of articles on epigraphy, especially those who ventured on to his private terrain, in particular Asia Minor and the Games in Greece. These were among the many topics he reserved for himself. He also took a sudden dislike to the British, for example, that excellent man A. G. Woodhead, lecturer at Cambridge, whom he kindly called "blockhead".

It is not wrong to shed some light on the shadowy world of academia. Obituary notices tell the public little about the conduct of some scholars. It is agreed that once a person is dead he becomes a saint. For the enlightenment of readers, it may be of some use to put history straight.

No ancient historian, especially of Late Antiquity and more precisely of the Imperial period, can ignore the impetus that Louis Robert has given to these studies. Before him scholars such as Theodor Mommsen, A. J. Letronne and many others have made progress in the study of history, and in particular the authors of corpora of inscriptions that provide a source for historians. What is less well known is that the person who at his classes told his audience "corpus, corpus, corpus" not only did not produce a corpus, but tried to prevent any from being produced in France.

For around 20 years we followed the classes given by Louis Robert at the Collège de France or at the 4th section of the École pratique des Hautes Études. After noting over the years the regular presence of the "faithful Bernands", he suddenly became aware that having published around 20 volumes of inscriptions, we might one day complete that corpus of Greek inscriptions from Egypt. We did not immediately understand that, for him, a bit of epigraphy was good, but a lot of epigraphy was too much. It is with great sadness that I recall this about-turn in a master who taught me everything I know about epigraphy. There is no need to mention in detail the snubs that we received. For my part, I could not publish anything in the collections of the CNRS for seven years.

After the death of Roger Rémondon in 1971, I suggested to Louis Robert that the teaching of Egyptian epigraphy should be established at the 4th section of the Hautes Études, which could not offend him because he only very rarely had occasion to deal with inscriptions from Egypt, a country that he did not know. Henri Seyrig had encouraged me along this path and in connection with it even came to Paris from his home in Switzerland. Louis Robert sent me a card beginning with the words: "Don't let your imagination run away with you". I replied with a card whose final words were: "*to sophon ou sophia*" (knowledge is not wisdom). From this moment on the rupture was sealed, and this is why, in the preface to *Pan du désert*, which appeared in the Netherlands, through Brill, in 1977, I violently denounced this behaviour as unworthy of a great scholar. That is the only time in his whole career that someone dared to tell him some home truths.

Today, thanks to Reinhold Merkelbach, the Greek inscriptions of Asia Minor as well as many welcome articles by scholars are beginning to appear. The co-author of the failed corpus of Asia Minor would doubtless not be greatly thrilled at this.

Louis Robert never set foot in Egypt, where it was not easy to stay, given a latent state of war in the area around the Suez canal. One day while we were still speaking to one another, I asked him why he didn't want to come to Egypt, and he replied: "I don't like kicks in the backside". Was he suggesting that it was all right for me to put up with them? A Bulgarian scholar, Georges Mihailov, who single-handedly produced a corpus of Greek inscriptions from Bulgaria, did not altogether appreciate the terms of my preface to *Pan du désert*, but he said to me: "You must have endured plenty of snubs to write that". He died in 1991, while reading my book *Sorciers grecs* in bed.

When Louis Robert reached retirement age, Étienne Bernand applied to be his successor at the Hautes Études. Although he had not adopted my method of protest, he too was eliminated. It was Roland Martin, lecturer at the Faculty of Dijon and director of studies in the 4th section, who was responsible for the base deed. He made use of an odious stratagem, using as a pretext a highly laudatory article that Father A. J. Festugière had devoted to our two volumes on Philae (Festugière did not usually write reviews) and where only a single reservation was made. He covered himself with this great name in order to eliminate the candidate, which some time later earned him a seat at the Académie des Inscriptions et Belles Lettres.

On the death of Louis Robert and against all academic tradition, a British lecturer had the courage to write an article of which the summary could have been "when the beast is dead, the poison is dead". Gentlemen to the core, despite the attacks with which they had been treated to in the *Bulletin épigraphique*, British scholars took their revenge by electing their detractor to the Royal Academy.

By a surprising paradox, the master of epigraphic studies endeavoured to foil the Egyptian corpus. He did not succeed, since all of our volumes have been published. He merely succeeded in obliging us to produce the remaining four or five volumes ourselves.

A fine example has been set by Jean-Yves Carrez-Maratray, lecturer in ancient history at the University of Angers. His monumental book on *Péluse*, published in 1999 in the study collection of the French Institute for Oriental Archaeology in Cairo, is an integral part of our corpus.

It is not customary to introduce readers of goodwill to the arcane mysteries of academia. But it is not always a bad idea to shed some light on certain practices. We can leave it to decent people to appreciate the final, or rather posthumous revenge of Louis Robert. After receiving complimentary copies for years of all books and articles sent to the *Revue des Études Grecques*, he arranged a new home for this invaluable collection after his death. If in future we need to go to the Institute for Advanced Study at Princeton to consult this collection, it will be an opportunity to pay tribute to American scholars.

Glossary

ageneios: beardless – the category between 'child' and 'man' in the Games.

aglaia: brilliance.

agôn: contest but also assembly or gathering.

agônes isolympioi: games equal in honour to the Olympic Games.

agônes isopythioi: games equal in honour to the Pythian Games.

agônes stephanitoi: games where wreaths were awarded.

agônistés: participant in the Games.

agônizein: to give a recital.

agora: public square.

aidôs: sporting spirit, sentiment of honour.

Akadémia: garden of the Akademos, a school of Platonic philosophy.

akamptos: straight course of a racehorse.

akôn: javelin.

Aktia Kaisaréa: festival at Nicopolis.

alsos: sacred wood.

Altis: sacred wood of the sanctuary at Olympia.

amphictyons: delegates of the Greek states gathered into political and religious confederations.

anankophagia: dietary regime imposed by training.

andres: mature men.

apéné: *biga* race, pulled by two mules rather than horses.

apite: "Go!" – cry of the herald starting the race.

apodytérion: changing-room.

apographé: enrolment in an event.

aporraxis: ball game against a wall (pelota with bare hands).

arété: courage but also benevolence.

arétés charin: on account of his valour.

aristos Hellénôn: the best of the Greeks, the winner.

Artemisia: games in honour of Artemis at Ephesus.

Asklepieia: festival in honour of Asclepius at Eleusis.

asylon: right to not be plundered.

ateleia: exemption from taxes or charges.

aulétés: solo flautist with choir.

aulétés pythikoi: musician playing in Pythian mode.

aulodés: player of the double flute.

aulos: flute.

Boukatios: month of August/September.

Chairô: to rejoice.

charis: grace.

chlamys: fairly short piece of rectangular fabric, attached to the right shoulder, originally worn by Thessalian cavalrymen.

choreia: dance and song.

chrématizein: to reward with money; to take care of money matters.

daphnés stephanos: laurel wreath.

Deia Sebasta: games in honour of Zeus.

Delia: festival of Delos.

diadymenos: "one who crowns himself". Statue, made by Phidias, of an athlete crowning himself with a wreath.

diaulodromon: two-length horse race.

diaulos: middle-distance race of about 400m.

didaskalos: school master.

Didymeia: games celebrated at Didyma.

diolkos: a paved road used for the transport of boats by land.

Dipylon: double gate that separated the two Ceramics, inner and outer.

diskobolos: discus thrower.

diskos: discus.

dolichos: long distance race of about 4,500m.

doryphorus: lance-bearer. Statue by Polyclitus.

dromos: hippodrome.

dryos stephanos: wreath of oak-leaves.

eiselastikos: games where the winner had the right to enter the city through a breach made in the wall, triumphal entry.

ek pantôn: Olympic games open to everyone.

ek tôn hippéôn: horse-race reserved for cavalrymen.

ek tôn phylarchôn: horse-race reserved for cavalry officers.

ekthesis gês kai oikias: right to acquire land and housing.

elaias stephanos: wreath of olive-leaves.

elaiothéion: oil store.

Eleutheria: festival at Plataea.

embatérion: a marching song.

emporion: a trading place or ad hoc market.

Epheseia: games celebrated at Ephesus.

epideixis: performance.

epinikion: poems celebrating a victory.

erastés: lover.

ergastinai: Athenian female workers who wove the peplos that was offered to Athena Poleas, "protector of the city".

eromenos: loved.

eukosmia: orderliness in gyms and contests.

eunoia: benevolence, devotion.

euergetés: interpreter, ambassador.

Greater Panathenaea: great civic festival of Athena celebrated every four years.

gymnasiarchos: supervisor of the gymnasium.

gymnoi: naked.

gynaikonom: inspector of women.

Halieia: festival at Rhodes.

harpaston: type of rugby.

heis kai monos: the first and the only.

hellanodikai: judges in charge of Olympic discipline.

Heraia: festival at Argos.

Black-figure vase depicting two javelin throwers on horseback aiming at a target while galloping.
© The British Museum

Heraion: temple of Hera.

hieromnémon: keeper of the sacred archives.

hieros limén: sacred port.

himation: long coat that wraps round the wearer.

himeros: erotic desire.

hippos polemistés: warhorse.

hippos: racehorse.

hoplitodromos: race in arms.

Horkios: name used for Zeus as god of the Oath.

hyspléx: system of posts and ropes that fell to mark the start of the race.

Isthmia: sanctuary and its festival on the Isthmus.

kalokagathia: being beautiful and good.

kalpé: race where the rider got down from his mount before finishing and ran beside his horse, pulling it by the reins.

kata ethnos: by nations.

kata poleis: by cities.

kission stephanos: ivy wreath.

kithara: early lute or lyre.

kitharistés: kithara player.

komé: village.

konistérion: bucket for sand.

kôrukeion: boxing hall.

kunodesmos: double meaning of dog lead and string attached to the foreskin.

lampadédromia: race with flaming torches.

Lesser Panathenaea: annual festival that took place in the month of *Hekatombaiôn* (mid-July/mid-August).

leukés stephanos: wreath of poplar leaves.

loutrion: bathroom.

Lyceum: school in the northeast of Athens where Aristotle taught.

meirakion: adolescent of 14-17 years.

Metageitniôn: Attic month (August/September).

metoikia: festival, also called Synoikia by Thucydides, which occurred 12 days before the beginning of the Panathenaea.

mikkixomenos: small boy.

monos kai prôtos anthrôpôn: alone and first among men.

Mouségétes: a suffix to the name Apollo, meaning "leader of the Muses".

nomophylakes: guardians of the law.

omphalos: navel.

ourania: ball thrown up into the sky.

paideia: culture, education.

paides pythikoi: children recruited according to the same rules as those of the Pythia at Delphi.

paidiai: toys.

paidion: small child, baby.

paidogôgos: supervisor taking a child to school.

paidonome: magistrate who kept an eye on the decency of the behaviour of children and young people.

paidotribos: gymnastics teacher.

pais: child of 7-14 years.

palaestra: ground for wrestling.

palé: wrestling with bare hands.

Panathenaic amphora: prize given to the winners of the Greater Panathenaea.

panegyric: speech inviting people to assemble.

panegyris: gathering of all the people on the occasion of a solemn festival.

pankration: a competition involving boxing and wrestling.

paradoxonikés: extraordinary winner.

paradoxos: without equal.

pentaetéris: (festival) celebrated after four years had passed.

pentathlon: combination of five contests.

periodonikés: winner in all four games.

periodos: sequence of the four Games (Olympia, Delphi, Isthmia, Nemea).

Petrean: suffix to name of Zeus meaning he who had pierced the rock to let the Penea pass through.

phoémenix: small early form of harp with three, four or seven strings.

phônaskos: teacher of *spondophoroi*, heralds who proclaimed the sacred truce at Olympia.

phyllobolia: the act of crowning with floral wreaths.

pleistonikés: winner of numerous victories.

polités kai bouleutés: citizen and member of the council.

prodikia: priority in a dispute or lawsuit.

proedréa: right of precedence, right to sit in the front rows.

promanteia: right to consult the oracle at Delphi.

prôté hélikia: infancy.

proxenia: duty of the *proxenios*.

proxenios: public host, citizen who dealt with the interests or nationals of another city in his homeland.

prytanis: supreme magistrate in Greek cities.

Ptolemaia: festival in honour of Ptolemy of Alexandria.

pygmachia/pygmé: boxing.

pyrrhic: dance in which the dancers were armed and carried a shield.

Pythaiad: festival in honour of Pythian Apollo.

Pytharestis: participant at the Pythaiad.

Pythia: festival at Delphi in honour of Pythian Apollo.

rhapsodist: singer who went from city to city reciting his poems.

Sebasta Rômaia: festival in the province of Asia.

skénikoi: theatrical games.

sôphronistai: censors ensuring the good behaviour of young people.

Sôtéria: games in honour of Zeus the saviour.

sphaira: ball.

splankna: entrails.

spondophoroi: heralds who proclaimed the sacred truce at Olympia.

stadion: single race, stadium.

tethrippon: chariot pulled by four horses.

thallou stephanos: wreath of foliage.

thematikoi: games for which the prize had material value.

theôroi: official envoys responsible for announcing the opening of the Olympic Games, who also had a role as spectators.

theôrodokai: official ambassadors receiving the theôroi.

thumelé: altar around which the choir moved.

thumelikoi: musical games held around the *thumelé*.

thusiai: sacrifices.

tomia: pieces of sacrificial meat.

Traïana Deiphileia: games in honour of Trajan and Zeus Philios.

tribein: to rub.

triéraulés: flautist on a trireme whose playing helped the rowers keep time.

xenia: hospitality, protection of foreigners.

Bibliography

Almost all of the Greek texts quoted in translation are from the Loeb Classical Library, produced by the Harvard University Press. For a small number of Classical writers, we have chosen other editions.

Selective bibliography

Aristotle, *Politics*, Trans. Benjamin Jowett, Dover Publications, New York, 2000.

Bacchylides, *Odes*, Trans. Diane Arnson Svarlien, Perseus Project, Yale, 1991.

Euripides, *Hippolytus*, Trans. E. P. Coleridge, Players Press, London, 1998.

Euripides, *Andromache*, Trans. E. P. Coleridge and William–Alan Landes, Players Press, London, 1999.

Homer, *Iliad*, Trans. Samuel Butler, Barnes & Noble Books, New York, 1995.

Homer, *Odyssey*, Trans. Samuel Butler, Jonathan Cape, London, (2nd edition) 1922.

Philostratus, *On Gymnastics*, Kaktos Editions, Athens, 1998.

Pindar, *Odes*, Trans. Diane Arnson Svarlien, Perseus Project, Yale, 1991.

Plato, *Laws*, Trans. Benjamin Jowett, Prometheus Books, New York, 2000.

Plato, *The Republic*, Trans. Benjamin Jowett, Prometheus Books, New York, 1986.

Plutarch, *Lives*, Trans. John Dryden, Modern Library Classics, New York, 1992.

Porphyry, *On Abstinence from Animal Food*, Trans. Thomas Taylor, Ed. Esme Wynne-Tyson, London, Centaur Press, 1965.

Tyrtaeus, "Fragments", in M. L. West, *Greek Lyric Poetry*, Oxford World's Classics, 1999.

Xenophon, *The works of Xenophon*, Trans. H. G. Dakyns, Macmillan and Co, London/New York, 1890-7.

Principal contributions

Baladié, R., *Le Péloponnèse de Strabon: essai de géographie historique*, Collection d'études anciennes, Les Belles Lettres, Paris, 1980.

Bélis, A., *Les musiciens dans l'Antiquité*, Hachette Littératures, Paris, 1999.

Briant, P., *Histoire de l'empire perse de Cyrus à Alexandre*, Fayard, Paris, 1996.

Carbonnières (de), P., *Olympie: la victoire pour les dieux*, Éditions du CNRS, Paris, 1995.

Marrou, H. I., *A History of Education in Antiquity*, Trans. George Lamb, The University of Wisconsin Press, Madison, WI, 1982.

Préaux, C., Byl, S., Nachtergae, G., *Le paysage grec*, Éditions de l'Université, Bruxelles, 1979.

Robert, L., *Hellenica*, Maisonneuve, Paris, 1949.

Robert, L., *Opera Minora Selecta*, II, I–VII, Hakkert, Amsterdam, 1969.

General bibliography

Achaia und Elis in der Antike (Akten für das internationale Symposium Athen, 19-21 mai, 1981), Ed. A. D. Rizakis, Athens, 1991.

Acts of the Eighth International Congress of Greek and Latin Epigraphy, Athens, 3-9 Octobre, 1982, Athens, 1984.

Aelian, *Historical Miscellany (Varia Historia)*, Trans. Nigel G. Wilson, Loeb Classical Library, Harvard University Press, Cambridge, MA, 1997.

Aeschines, "Against Ctesiphon" and "On the Unfaithful Embassy" in *The Speeches of Aeschines*, Trans. Charles Darwin Adams, Loeb Classical Library, Harvard University Press, Cambridge, MA, 1989.

Antiphon and Andocides, *Minor Attic Orators*, Vol. I, Loeb Classical Library, Harvard University Press, Cambridge, MA, 1969.

Aristophanes, *Clouds, Wasps, Peace*, Ed. and Trans. Jeffrey Henderson, Loeb Classical Library, Harvard University Press, Cambridge, MA, 1998.

Aristotle, *Athenian Constitution,* Trans. H. Rackham, Loeb Classical Library, Harvard University Press, Cambridge, MA, 1969.

Aristotle, *The Art of Rhetoric*, Trans. J. H. Freese, Loeb Classical Library, Harvard University Press, Cambridge, MA, 1959.

Athenaeus, *The Deipnosophists*, Trans. Charles Burton Gulick, Loeb Classical Library, Harvard University Press, Cambridge, MA, 1928.

Bailly, A., *Dictionnaire grec-français*, Hachette Education, Paris, 2000.

Baslez, M.-F., *Saint Paul,* Fayard, Paris, 1991.

Burn, L., *The British Museum Book of Greek and Roman Art*, Thames and Hudson, London, 1992.

Cambiano, G., "Devenir homme" in *L'Homme grec*, Éditions du Seuil, Paris, 1993.

Canciani, F., "Aurai" in *Lexicon Iconographicum Mythologiae Classicae,* (LIMC), Vol. 1, Artemis Verlag, Zurich, 1981.

Carratelli, G. P., *The Western Greeks: Classical Civilisation in the Western Mediterranean*, Thames and Hudson, London, 1996.

Chamoux, F., *La Civilisation grecque*, Arthaud, Paris, 1963.

Charnaux, P., "Liste argienne des théarodoques", in *Bulletin de Correspondance Hellénique*, 90 (1966): 156-239; 710-4.

Cipriani, M., and Avagliano, G., *Art et histoire de paestum : les fouilles et le musée archéologique* (French edition), Casa editrice Bonechi, Florence, 1999.

Colin, G., *Le culte d'Apollon Pythien à Athènes*, BEFAR, Paris, 1905.

Coubertin (de), P., and Samaranch, J. A., *Esprit olympique*, in *L'Esprit du Temps*, Bordeaux, 1992.

Delorme, J., *Gymnasion : études sur les monuments consacrés à l'éducation en Grèce*, De Boccard, Paris, 1960.

Demosthenes, *Against Aristocrates*, Trans. J. H. Vince, Loeb Classical Library, Harvard University Press, Cambridge, MA, 1969.

Demosthenes, *De Corona*, Trans. J. H. Vince, C. A. Vince, Loeb Classical Library, Harvard University Press, Cambridge, MA, 1969.

Dio Cassius, *Roman History*, Vol. VI, Trans. E. Cary and H. B. Foster, Harvard University Press, Cambridge, MA, 1969.

Diodorus Siculus, *Library of History*, Trans. C. H. Oldfather, Loeb Classical Library, Heinemann, London, 1935.

Dittenberger, W., *Sylloge Inscriptionum Graecarum*, (third edition), Leipzig, 1915-24.

Drevon, A., *Les Jeux olympiques oubliés*, Éditions du CNRS, Paris, 2000.

Duverger, C., *La Fleur létale : économie du sacrifice aztèque*, Éditions du Seuil, Paris, 1979.

Duverger, C., *L'esprit du jeu chez les Aztèques*, Éditions du Seuil, Paris, 1978.

Euripides, *Ion*, Ed. and Trans. David Kovacs, Loeb Classical Library, Harvard University Press, Cambridge, MA, 1999.

Eusebius, *Ecclesiastical History*, Trans. J. E. L. Oulton, Loeb Classical Library, Harvard University Press, Cambridge, MA, 1969.

Finley, M. I., and Pleket, H. W., *The Olympic games: the first thousand years,* The Viking Press, New York, 1976.

Gardiner, N. E., *Athletics of the Ancient World*, Clarendon Press, Oxford, 1930.

Gauthier, P., *Les cités grecques et leurs bienfaiteurs*, École française d'Athènes, Athens, 1985.

Gauthier, P., "Symbola : les étrangers et la justice dans les cités grecques", in *Annales de l'Est* (II, 42), Université de Nancy. Nancy, 1972.

Gentili, B. and Prato, C., *Poetae Elegiaci: Testimonia et Fragmenta*, Teubner, Leipzig, 1985.

Greek Anthology, Trans. W. R. Paton, Loeb Classical Library, Harvard University Press, Cambridge, MA, 1918.

Herodotus, *Histories*, Trans. A. D. Godley, Loeb Classical Library, Harvard University Press, Cambridge, MA, 1920.

Hippocrates, *Works*, Trans. W. H. S. Jones, Loeb Classical Library, Heinemann, London,1923.

Homeric Hymns and Homerica, Trans. Hugh G. Evelyn-White, Loeb Classical Library, Harvard University Press, Cambridge, MA, 1914.

Humbert, J., and Berguin, H., *Histoire illustrée de la littérature grecque*, Éditions Didier, Paris, 1947.

Inscriptiones Graecae (IG), Berlin, Berlin-Brandenburgische Akademie der Wissenschaften, 1906-

Isocrates, *On the Peace, Antidosis, Panathenaicus*, Vol. II, Trans. G. Norlin, Harvard University Press, Cambridge, MA, 1969.

Isocrates, *To Demonicus, Panegyricus,* Vol. I., Trans. G. Norlin, Harvard University Press, Cambridge, MA, 1969.

Isocrates, *Letters*, Vol. III, Trans. La Rue Van Hook, Harvard University Press,

Cambridge, MA, 1969.

Jacquemin, A., "Commentaire" in Pausanias, *Description de la Grèce*, (Vol. 5, book V), Collection des universités de France, Les Belles Lettres, Paris, 1999.

Jost, M., *Aspects de la vie religieuse en Grèce, début du Vᵉ siècle à la fin du IIIᵉ siècle av. J.-C.*, SEDES, Paris, 1992.

Jouanna, J., *Hippocrate,* Fayard, Paris, 1992.

Juvenal, "Satires", in *Juvenal and Persius*, Trans. G. G. Ramsay, Harvard University Press, Cambridge, MA, 1969.

Knab, R., *Die Periodoniken: ein Beitrag zur Geschichte der gymnischen Agone an den 4 griechischen Hauptfesten* (thèse), Giessen, 1934.

Lambin, G., *La chanson grecque dans l'Antiquité,* CNRS Littérature, Paris, 1992.

Lhote, A., *Les chefs-d'œuvre de la peinture égyptienne*, Hachette, Paris, 1954.

Losfeld, G., *Essai sur le costume grec*, préface de F. Chamoux, De Boccard, Paris, 1991.

Lucian, *Anacharsis or Athletics*, Vol. IV, Trans. A. M. Harmon, Loeb Classical Library, Harvard University Press, Cambridge, MA, 1925.

Lucian, *How to Write History*, Vol. VI, Trans. K. Kilburn, Loeb Classical Library, Harvard University Press, Cambridge, MA, 1969.

Lucian, *The Dance*, Vol. V, Trans. A. M. Harmon, Loeb Classical Library, Harvard University Press, Cambridge, MA, 1969.

Lysias, Trans. W. R. M. Lamb, Loeb Classical Library, Harvard University Press, Cambridge, MA, 1930.

Mertens, J. R., *Metropolitan Museum of Art: Greece and Rome*, Metropolitan Museum of Art, New York, 1987.

Metzger, A., Metzger, H., Sicre, J., *La Beauté nue, quinze siècles de peinture grecque*, Phébus, Paris, 1984.

Moreno, P., *Vita e Arte di Lisippo*, Milano, 1987.

Newberry, P., *Beni Hassan (Part 1),* Archaeological Survey of Egypt: memoir, Egypt Exploration Fund, London, 1893.

Parlavecchia, P., *Les Étrusques et l'Europe*, Réunion des musées nationaux, Paris, 1992.

Pausanias, *Description of Greece*, Trans. W. H. S. Jones, H. A. Ormerod, Loeb Classical Library, Harvard University Press, Cambridge, MA, 1988.

Picard, C., *Manuel d'archéologie grecque*, A. Picard and J. Picard, Paris, 1973.

Plato, *Charmides*, Trans. W. R. M. Lamb, Loeb Classical Library, Harvard University Press, Cambridge, MA, 1955.

Plato, *Lesser Hippias,* Trans. H. N. Fowler, Loeb Classical Library, Harvard University Press, Cambridge, MA, 1969.

Plato, *Phaedrus*, Trans. H. N. Fowler, Loeb Classical Library, Harvard University Press, Cambridge, MA, 1980.

Plato, *Laches, Protagoras, Meno, Euthydemus*, Trans. W. R. M. Lamb, Loeb Classical Library, Harvard University Press, Cambridge, MA, 1924.

Plotinus, *Enneads*, Trans. A. H. Armstrong, Loeb Classical Library, Harvard University Press, Cambridge, MA, 1969-1988.

Polybius, *Histories*, Books 1-39, Trans. W. R. Paton, Loeb Classical Library, Harvard University Press, Cambridge, MA, 1922.

Pouilloux, J., *Choix d'inscriptions grecques*, Les Belles Lettres, Paris, 1960.

Pouilloux, J., "Les inscriptions de la terrasse du temple et de la région. La terrasse du temple et la zone nord du sanctuaire", *Fouilles de Delphes*, t. 3, Epigraphie, fasc. IV, Paris, 1930-70.

Pouilloux, J., *Recherches sur l'histoire et les cultes de Thasos*, De Boccard, Paris, 1954.

Quignard, P., *Le sexe et l'effroi*, Gallimard, Paris, 1994.

Robert, J., and Robert, L., *Bulletin épigraphique*, Revue des études grecques, 1938-84.

Robert, L., *Études épigraphiques et philologiques*, Champion, Paris, 1938.

Roux, G., *Delphes, son oracle et ses dieux*, Les Belles Lettres, Paris, 1976.

Roux, G., *Pausanias en Corinthie*, Les Belles Lettres, Paris, 1958.

Scanlon, T. F., *Greek and Roman Athletics: a bibliography,* Ares Publishers, Chicago, 1984.

Sophocles, *Ajax, Electra, Oedipus Tyrannus*, Vol. I, Trans. Hugh Lloyd-Jones, Loeb Classical Library, Harvard University Press, Cambridge, MA, 1994.

Sophocles, *Antigone, The Women of Trachis, Philoctetes, Oedipus at Colonus*, Vol. I, Trans. Hugh Lloyd-Jones, Loeb Classical Library, Harvard University Press, Cambridge, MA, 1994.

Strabo, *Geography*, Trans. C. F. Smith, Horace L. Jones, Loeb Classical Library, Harvard University Press, Cambridge, MA, 1918.

Theocritus, in *The Greek Bucolic Poets*, Trans. J. M. Edmonds, Loeb Classical Library, Harvard University Press, Cambridge, MA, 1969.

Theognis, Mimnermus, Solon, Tyrtaeus, *Greek Elegiac Poetry*, Trans. Douglas E. Gerber, Loeb Classical Library, Harvard University Press, Cambridge, MA, 1999.

Thucydides, *History of the Peloponnesian War*, Books 1–8, Trans. C. F. Smith, Loeb Classical Library, Harvard University Press, Cambridge, MA, 1930.

Vanoyeke, V., *La naissance des jeux olympiques et le sport dans l'Antiquité*, Les Belles Lettres, Paris, 1992.

Visa-Ondarçuhu, V., *L'image de l'athlète d'Homère à la fin du Ve siècle avant J.-C.*, Les Belles Lettres, Paris, 1999.

Vitruvius, *On Architecture*, Trans. Frank Granger, Loeb Classical Library, Harvard University Press, Cambridge, MA, 1969.

Wilhelm, A., *Aigyptiaka*, Akademie der Wissenschaften, Vienne, 1946.

Wilkinson, J., G., *The Manners and Customs of the Ancient Egyptians*, Scribner and Welford, New York, 1879.

Xenophon, *Anabasis*, Vol. III, Trans. C. L. Brownson, Loeb Classical Library, Harvard University Press, Cambridge, MA, 1985.

Xenophon, *Hellenica*, Vol. I and II, Trans. C. L. Brownson, Loeb Classical Library, Harvard University Press, Cambridge, MA, 1985.

Xenophon, *Memorabilia*, Trans. E. C. Marchant and O. J. Todd, Loeb Classical Library, Harvard University Press, Cambridge, MA, 1923.

Xenophon, *Memorabilia and Oeconomicus, Symposium and Apologia*, Vol. IV, Trans. C. L. Brownson, Loeb Classical Library, Harvard University Press, Cambridge, MA, 1969.

Zaidman, L. B., and Schmitt, P., *La religion grecque dans les cités à l'époque classique*, Cursus Collection, Armand Colin, Paris, 1989.

Index of Classical texts

By the same author

Les Inscriptions grecques et latines du colosse de Memnon, in collaboration with Étienne Bernand, vol. 31, "Bibliothèque d'Etude" collection, Institut français d'archéologie orientale, Cairo, 1960.

Les Inscriptions grecques de Philae, Vol. 1: *Époque ptolémaïque*, Éditions du CNRS, Paris, 1969.

Les confins libyques (vol. 1, *Le Delta égyptien d'après les textes grecs* in three volumes with sequential pagination), *Mémoires publiés par les membres de l'Institut français d'archéologie orientale*, 91, Cairo, 1970.

Atlas du delta occidental, Imprimerie nationale, Paris, 1970.

De Koptos à Kosseir, Brill, Leyde, 1972.

Le Paneion d'El-Kanaïs : les inscriptions grecques, Brill, Leyde, 1972.

Pan du désert, Brill, Leyde, 1977.

Les portes du désert : Recueil des inscriptions grecques d'Antinoopolis, Tentyris, Koptos, Apollonopolis Parva et Apollonopolis Magna, Éditions du CNRS, Paris, 1984.

La Carte du tragique : La géographie dans la tragédie grecque, Éditions du CNRS, Paris, 1985.

De Thèbes à Syrène, Éditions du CNRS, Paris, 1989.

Leçon de civilisation, Fayard, Paris, 1994.

La prose sur pierre dans l'Égypte hellénistique et romaine, vol. 1: *Textes et traductions*, vol. 2: *Commentaires*, Fayard, Paris, 1994.

Sorciers grecs, Paris, Fayard, 1991; reprinted Paris, Hachette Littératures, "Pluriel" collection, 1995. Translated into modern Greek, *Bibliopoleion tês « Estias »*, I. D. Kollarou and Sias, Athens, 1997.

Alexandrie des Ptolomées, Éditions du CNRS, Paris, 1995. Translated into modern Greek, *ibid*.

Alexandrie la Grande, final revised edition, Hachette Littératures, Paris, 1998 (Many of André Bernand's articles are included in this book).

« *Testimonia selecta de Portu Magno et Palatiis Alexandriæ ad Ægyptum e scriptoribus antiquis excerpta»* (Selected accounts of the Great Port and the palaces in Alexandria near Egypt), in the collected work, *Alexandrie : les Quartiers royaux submergés* (F. Goddio in collaboration with A. Bernand, É. Bernand, I. Darwish, F. Dunand, A. de Graauw, Z. Kiss, J. Yoyotte and edited by D. Juncqua-Naveau and L. Harrow), Periplus Publishing London, London, 1998, pp. 59-140.

Guerre et violence dans la Grèce antique, Hachette Littératures, Paris, 1999.

Carte du delta égyptien, in *Barrington Atlas of the Greek and Roman World*, edited by J.-A. Talbert, Princeton University Press, University of North Carolina, Chapel Hill, USA, 2000.

L'Égypte engloutie : Alexandrie, in collaboration with Franck Goddio, Arcperiplus, London, 2002.